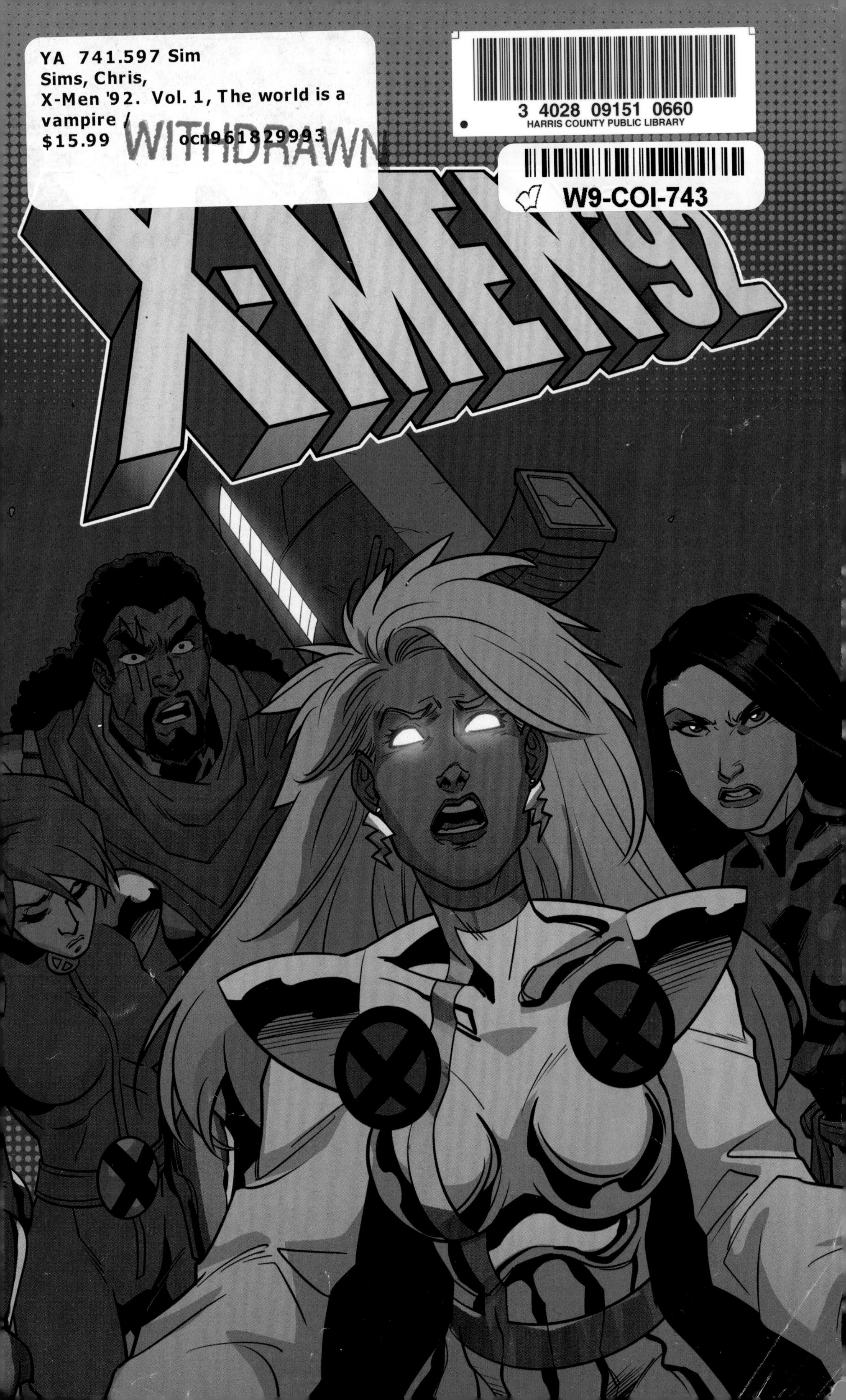
X-MEN 92

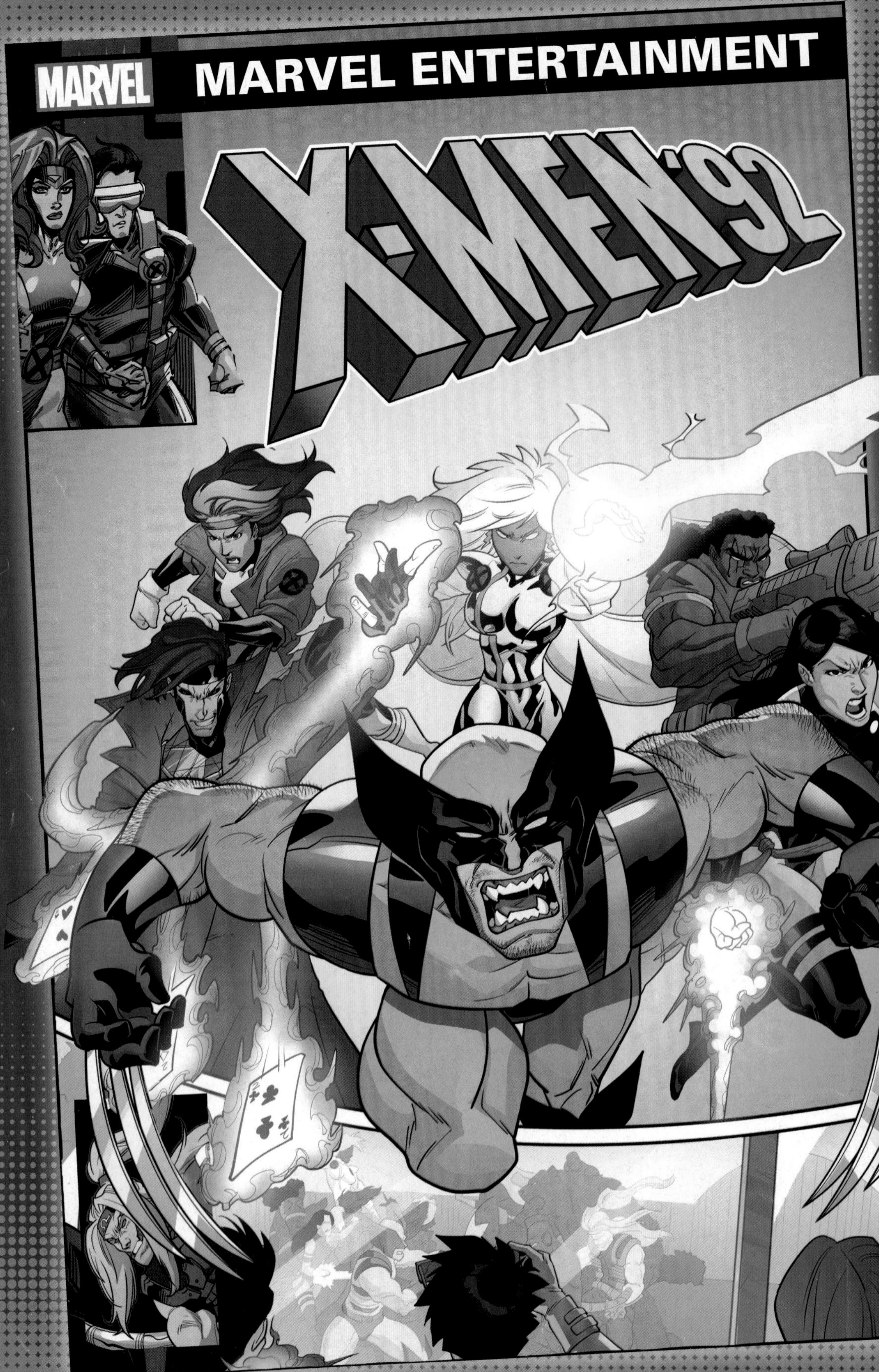

MARVEL
MARVEL ENTERTAINMENT
X-MEN '92

MARVEL ENTERTAINMENT

X-MEN '92

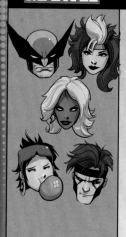

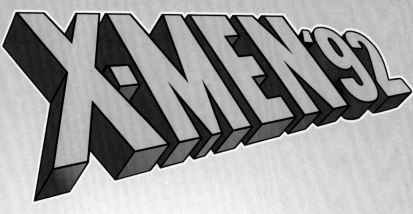

THE WORLD IS A VAMPIRE

CHRIS SIMS & CHAD BOWERS
WRITERS

ALTI FIRMANSYAH [#1-4] & CORY HAMSCHER [#5]
ARTISTS

MATT MILLA
COLOR ARTIST

VC's TRAVIS LANHAM
LETTERER

DAVID NAKAYAMA
COVER ART

HEATHER ANTOS
ASSISTANT EDITOR

JORDAN D. WHITE
EDITOR

X-MEN CREATED BY **STAN LEE & JACK KIRBY**

COLLECTION EDITOR: JENNIFER GRÜNWALD
ASSOCIATE EDITOR: SARAH BRUNSTAD
ASSOCIATE MANAGING EDITOR: KATERI WOODY
EDITOR, SPECIAL PROJECTS: MARK D. BEAZLEY
VP PRODUCTION & SPECIAL PROJECTS: JEFF YOUNGQUIST
SVP PRINT, SALES & MARKETING: DAVID GABRIEL
BOOK DESIGNER: JAY BOWEN

EDITOR IN CHIEF: AXEL ALONSO
CHIEF CREATIVE OFFICER: JOE QUESADA
PUBLISHER: DAN BUCKLEY
EXECUTIVE PRODUCER: ALAN FINE

X-MEN '92 VOL. 1: THE WORLD IS A VAMPIRE. Contains material originally published in magazine form as X-MEN '92 #1-5. First printing 2016. ISBN# 978-1-302-90049-6. Published by MARVEL WORLDWIDE, INC., a subsidiary of MARVEL ENTERTAINMENT, LLC. OFFICE OF PUBLICATION: 135 West 50th Street, New York, NY 10020. **Printed in Canada.** ALAN FINE, President, Marvel Entertainment; DAN BUCKLEY, President, TV, Publishing & Brand Management; JOE QUESADA, Chief Creative Officer; TOM BREVOORT, SVP of Publishing; DAVID BOGART, SVP of Business Affairs & Operations, Publishing & Partnership; C.B. CEBULSKI, VP of Brand Management & Development, Asia; DAVID GABRIEL, SVP of Sales & Marketing, Publishing; JEFF YOUNGQUIST, VP of Production & Special Projects; DAN CARR, Executive Director of Publishing Technology; ALEX MORALES, Director of Publishing Operations; SUSAN CRESPI, Production Manager; STAN LEE, Chairman Emeritus. For information regarding advertising in Marvel Comics or on Marvel.com, please contact Vit DeBellis, Integrated Sales Manager, at vdebellis@marvel.com. For Marvel subscription inquiries, please call 888-511-5480. **Manufactured between 9/2/2016 and 10/10/2016 by SOLISCO PRINTERS, SCOTT, QC, CANADA.**

10 9 8 7 6 5 4 3 2 1

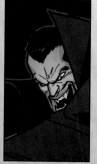

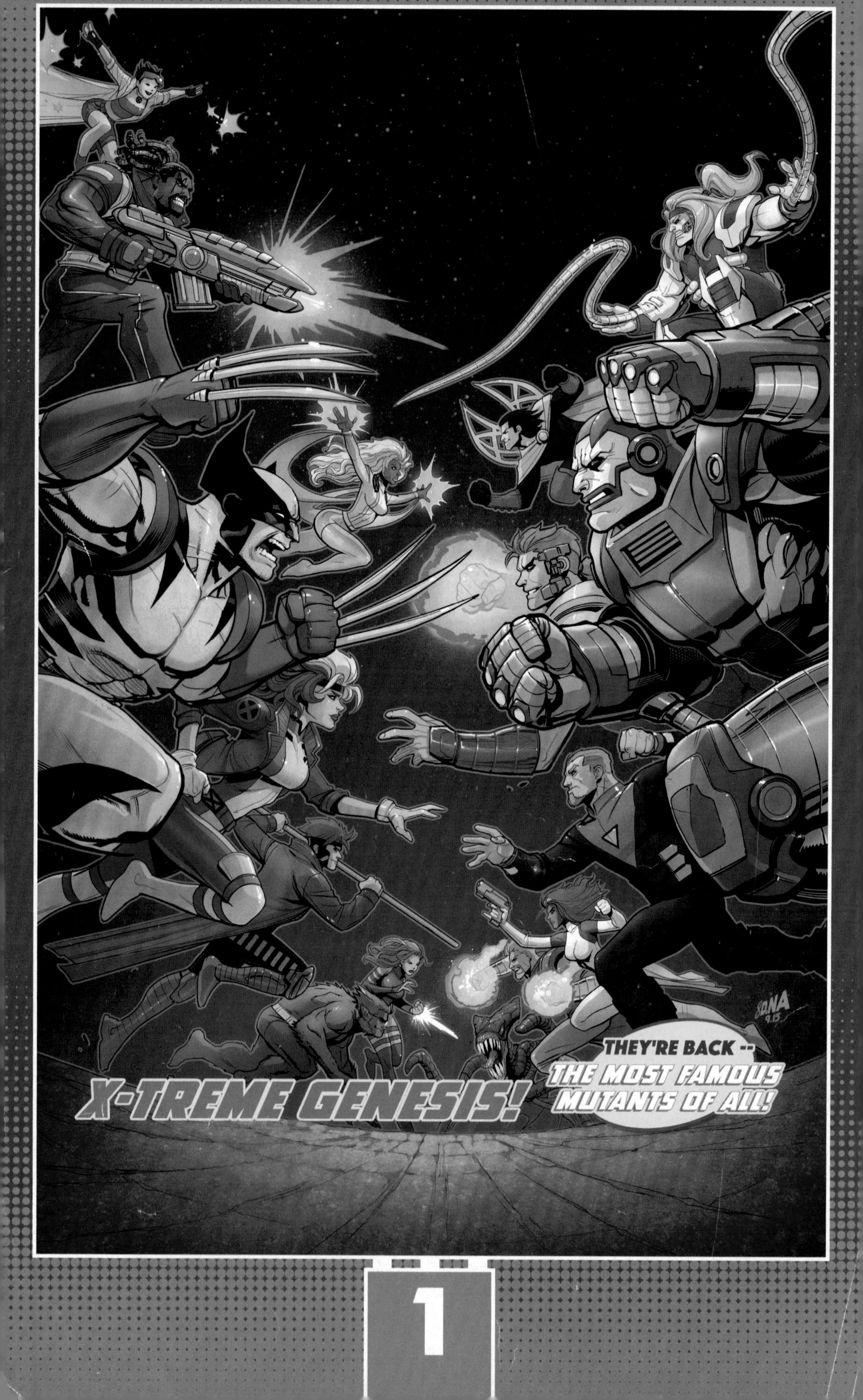
X-TREME GENESIS!
THEY'RE BACK --
THE MOST FAMOUS MUTANTS OF ALL!

1

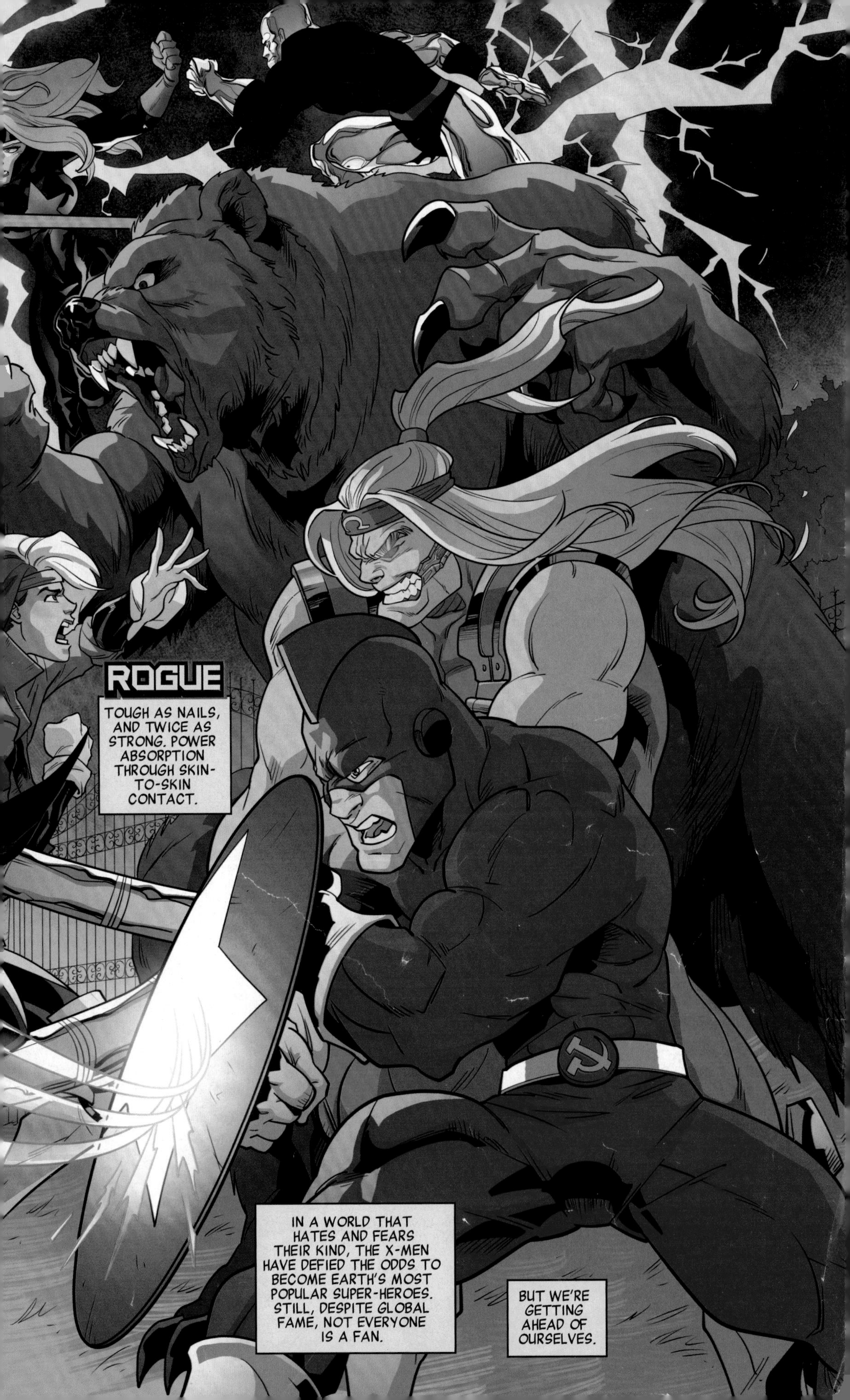
ROGUE
TOUGH AS NAILS, AND TWICE AS STRONG. POWER ABSORPTION THROUGH SKIN-TO-SKIN CONTACT.
IN A WORLD THAT HATES AND FEARS THEIR KIND, THE X-MEN HAVE DEFIED THE ODDS TO BECOME EARTH'S MOST POPULAR SUPER-HEROES. STILL, DESPITE GLOBAL FAME, NOT EVERYONE IS A FAN.
BUT WE'RE GETTING AHEAD OF OURSELVES.

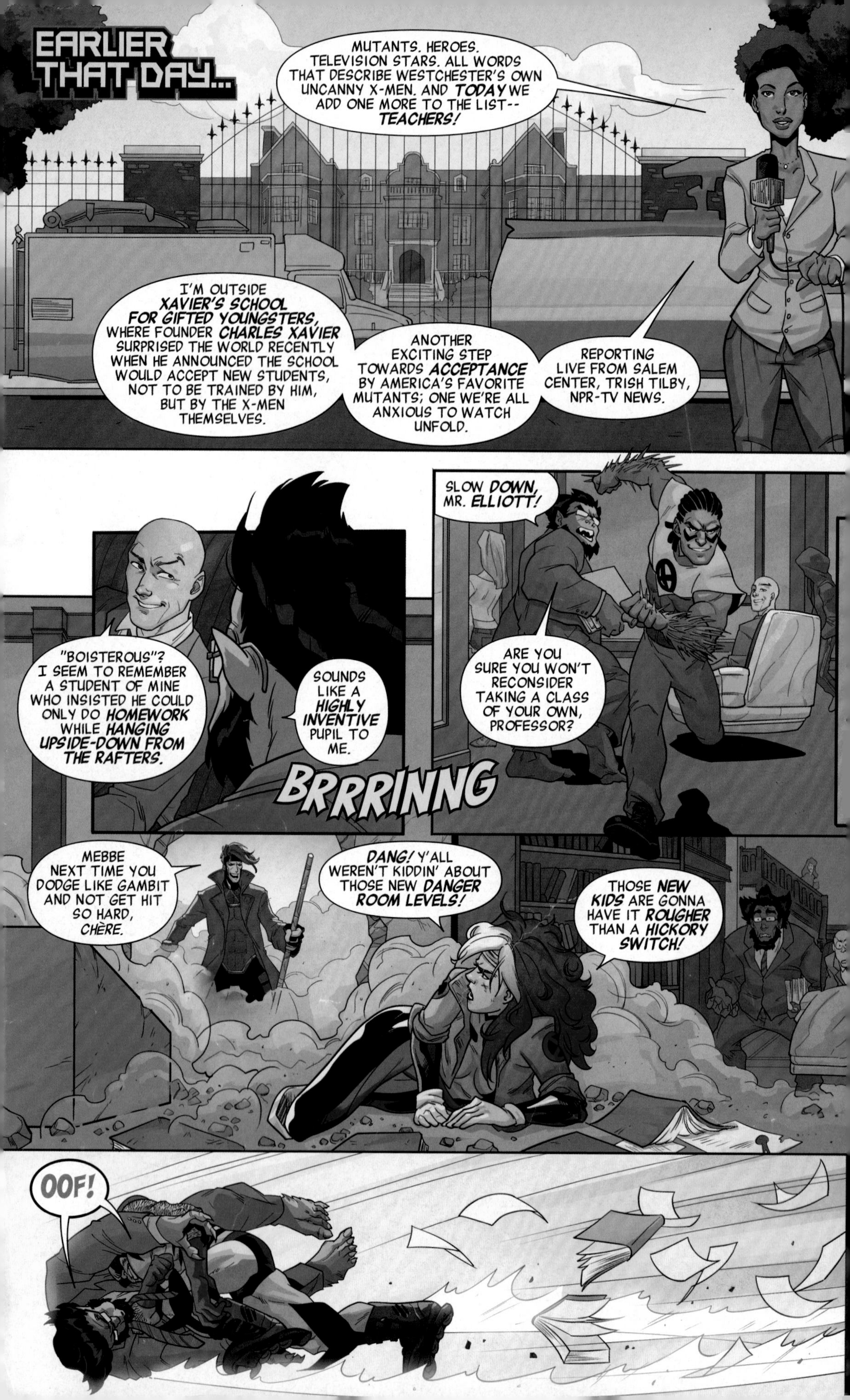
EARLIER THAT DAY...
MUTANTS. HEROES. TELEVISION STARS. ALL WORDS THAT DESCRIBE WESTCHESTER'S OWN UNCANNY X-MEN. AND TODAY WE ADD ONE MORE TO THE LIST-- TEACHERS!
I'M OUTSIDE XAVIER'S SCHOOL FOR GIFTED YOUNGSTERS, WHERE FOUNDER CHARLES XAVIER SURPRISED THE WORLD RECENTLY WHEN HE ANNOUNCED THE SCHOOL WOULD ACCEPT NEW STUDENTS, NOT TO BE TRAINED BY HIM, BUT BY THE X-MEN THEMSELVES.
ANOTHER EXCITING STEP TOWARDS ACCEPTANCE BY AMERICA'S FAVORITE MUTANTS; ONE WE'RE ALL ANXIOUS TO WATCH UNFOLD.
REPORTING LIVE FROM SALEM CENTER, TRISH TILBY, NPR-TV NEWS.
"BOISTEROUS"? I SEEM TO REMEMBER A STUDENT OF MINE WHO INSISTED HE COULD ONLY DO HOMEWORK WHILE HANGING UPSIDE-DOWN FROM THE RAFTERS.
SOUNDS LIKE A HIGHLY INVENTIVE PUPIL TO ME.
BRRRINNG
SLOW DOWN, MR. ELLIOTT!
ARE YOU SURE YOU WON'T RECONSIDER TAKING A CLASS OF YOUR OWN, PROFESSOR?
MEBBE NEXT TIME YOU DODGE LIKE GAMBIT AND NOT GET HIT SO HARD, CHÈRE.
DANG! Y'ALL WEREN'T KIDDIN' ABOUT THOSE NEW DANGER ROOM LEVELS!
THOSE NEW KIDS ARE GONNA HAVE IT ROUGHER THAN A HICKORY SWITCH!
OOF!

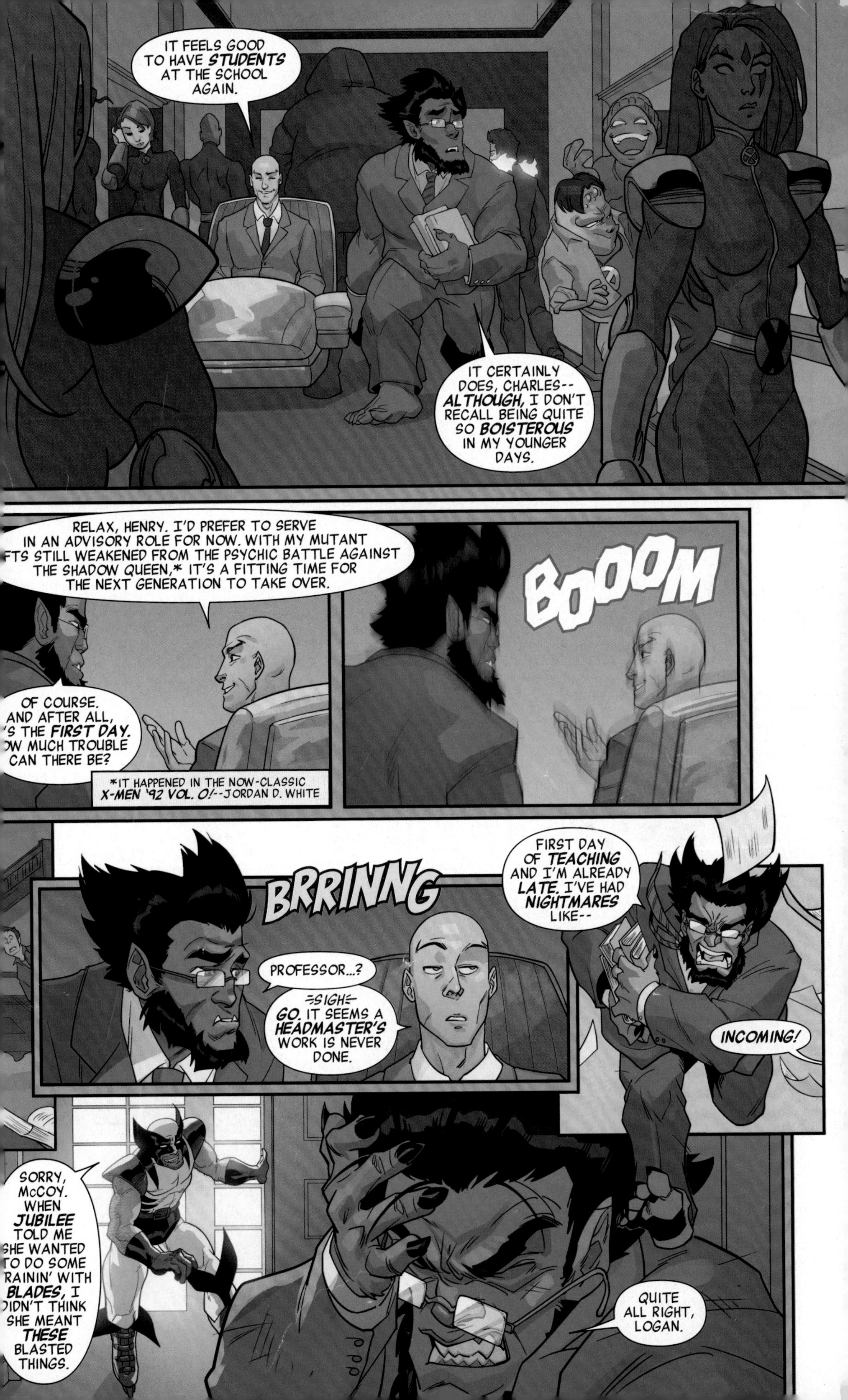
IT FEELS GOOD TO HAVE STUDENTS AT THE SCHOOL AGAIN.
IT CERTAINLY DOES, CHARLES-- ALTHOUGH, I DON'T RECALL BEING QUITE SO BOISTEROUS IN MY YOUNGER DAYS.
RELAX, HENRY. I'D PREFER TO SERVE IN AN ADVISORY ROLE FOR NOW. WITH MY MUTANT FTS STILL WEAKENED FROM THE PSYCHIC BATTLE AGAINST THE SHADOW QUEEN,* IT'S A FITTING TIME FOR THE NEXT GENERATION TO TAKE OVER.
OF COURSE. AND AFTER ALL, 'S THE FIRST DAY. OW MUCH TROUBLE CAN THERE BE?
*IT HAPPENED IN THE NOW-CLASSIC X-MEN '92 VOL. 0!--JORDAN D. WHITE
BOOOM
BRRINNG
PROFESSOR...?
=SIGH= GO. IT SEEMS A HEADMASTER'S WORK IS NEVER DONE.
FIRST DAY OF TEACHING AND I'M ALREADY LATE. I'VE HAD NIGHTMARES LIKE--
INCOMING!
SORRY, McCOY. WHEN JUBILEE TOLD ME SHE WANTED TO DO SOME RAININ' WITH BLADES, I DIDN'T THINK SHE MEANT THESE BLASTED THINGS.
QUITE ALL RIGHT, LOGAN.

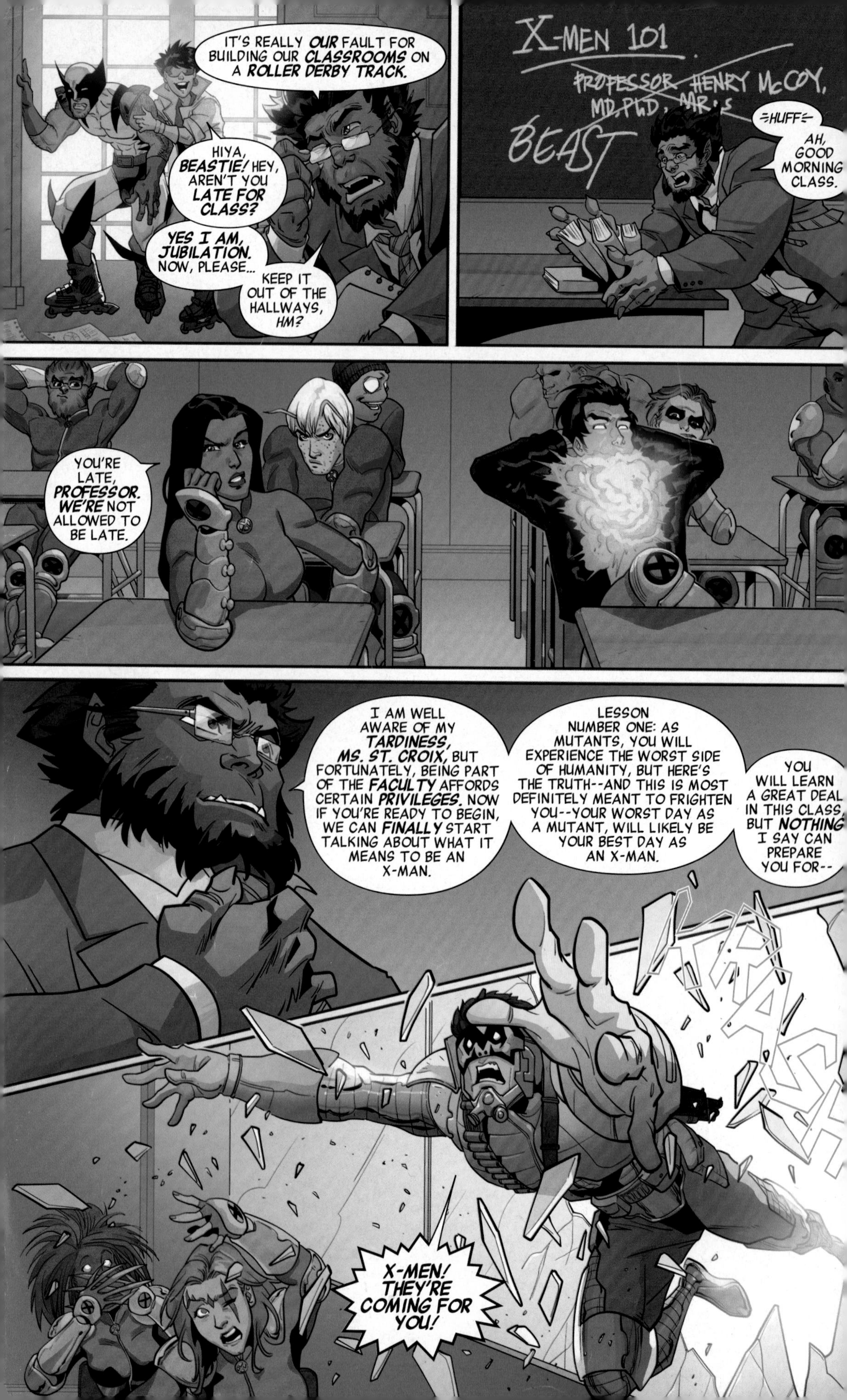
IT'S REALLY OUR FAULT FOR BUILDING OUR CLASSROOMS ON A ROLLER DERBY TRACK.
HIYA, BEASTIE! HEY, AREN'T YOU LATE FOR CLASS?
YES I AM, JUBILATION. NOW, PLEASE...
KEEP IT OUT OF THE HALLWAYS, HM?
X-MEN 101
PROFESSOR HENRY McCOY, MD, Ph.D, MR.S
BEAST
HUFF
AH, GOOD MORNING CLASS.
YOU'RE LATE, PROFESSOR. WE'RE NOT ALLOWED TO BE LATE.
I AM WELL AWARE OF MY TARDINESS, MS. ST. CROIX, BUT FORTUNATELY, BEING PART OF THE FACULTY AFFORDS CERTAIN PRIVILEGES. NOW IF YOU'RE READY TO BEGIN, WE CAN FINALLY START TALKING ABOUT WHAT IT MEANS TO BE AN X-MAN.
LESSON NUMBER ONE: AS MUTANTS, YOU WILL EXPERIENCE THE WORST SIDE OF HUMANITY, BUT HERE'S THE TRUTH--AND THIS IS MOST DEFINITELY MEANT TO FRIGHTEN YOU--YOUR WORST DAY AS A MUTANT, WILL LIKELY BE YOUR BEST DAY AS AN X-MAN.
YOU WILL LEARN A GREAT DEAL IN THIS CLASS, BUT NOTHING I SAY CAN PREPARE YOU FOR--
KRAASH
X-MEN! THEY'RE COMING FOR YOU!

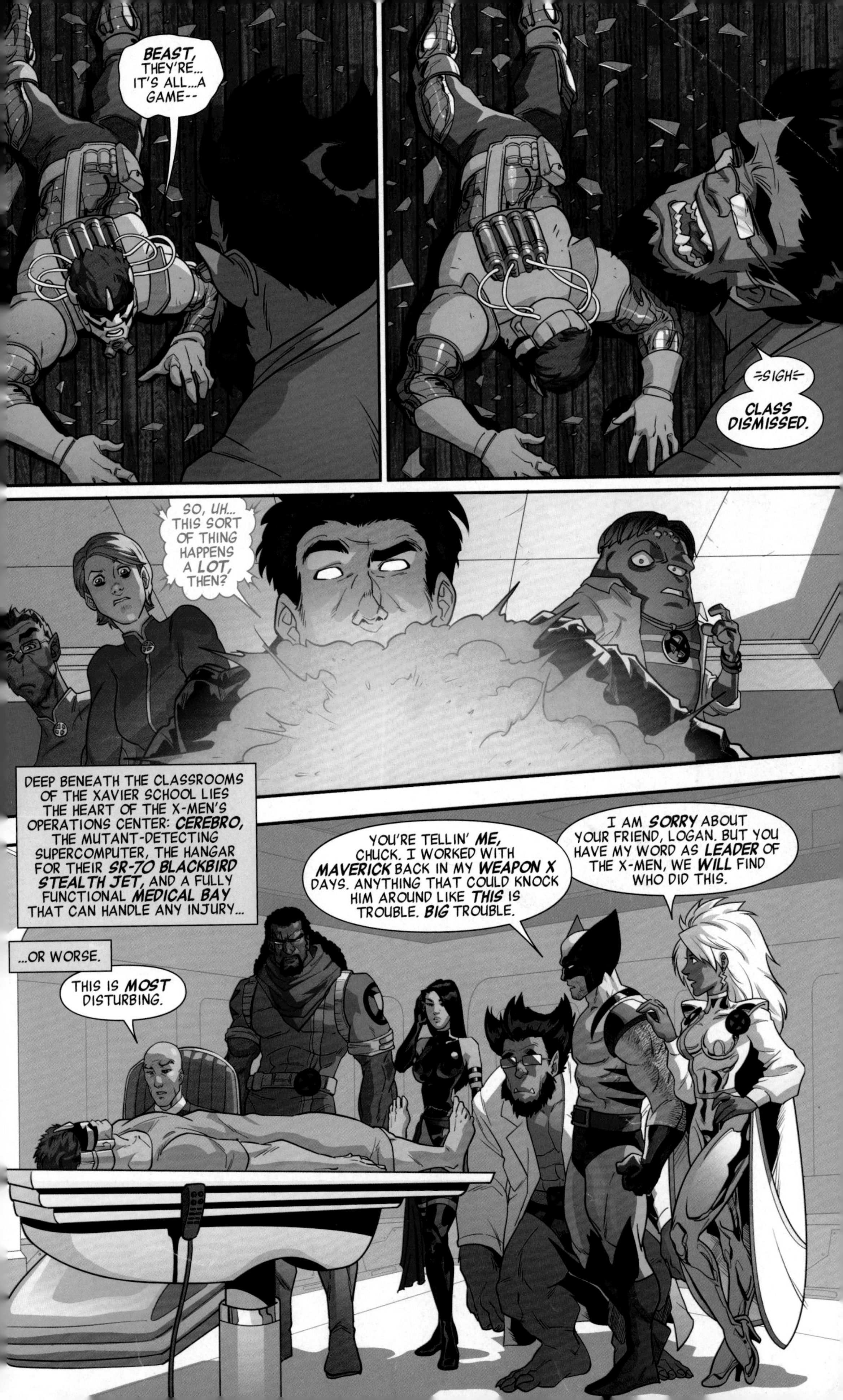
BEAST, THEY'RE... IT'S ALL...A GAME--
=SIGH=
CLASS DISMISSED.
SO, UH... THIS SORT OF THING HAPPENS A LOT, THEN?
DEEP BENEATH THE CLASSROOMS OF THE XAVIER SCHOOL LIES THE HEART OF THE X-MEN'S OPERATIONS CENTER: CEREBRO, THE MUTANT-DETECTING SUPERCOMPUTER, THE HANGAR FOR THEIR SR-70 BLACKBIRD STEALTH JET, AND A FULLY FUNCTIONAL MEDICAL BAY THAT CAN HANDLE ANY INJURY...
...OR WORSE.
THIS IS MOST DISTURBING.
YOU'RE TELLIN' ME, CHUCK. I WORKED WITH MAVERICK BACK IN MY WEAPON X DAYS. ANYTHING THAT COULD KNOCK HIM AROUND LIKE THIS IS TROUBLE. BIG TROUBLE.
I AM SORRY ABOUT YOUR FRIEND, LOGAN. BUT YOU HAVE MY WORD AS LEADER OF THE X-MEN, WE WILL FIND WHO DID THIS.

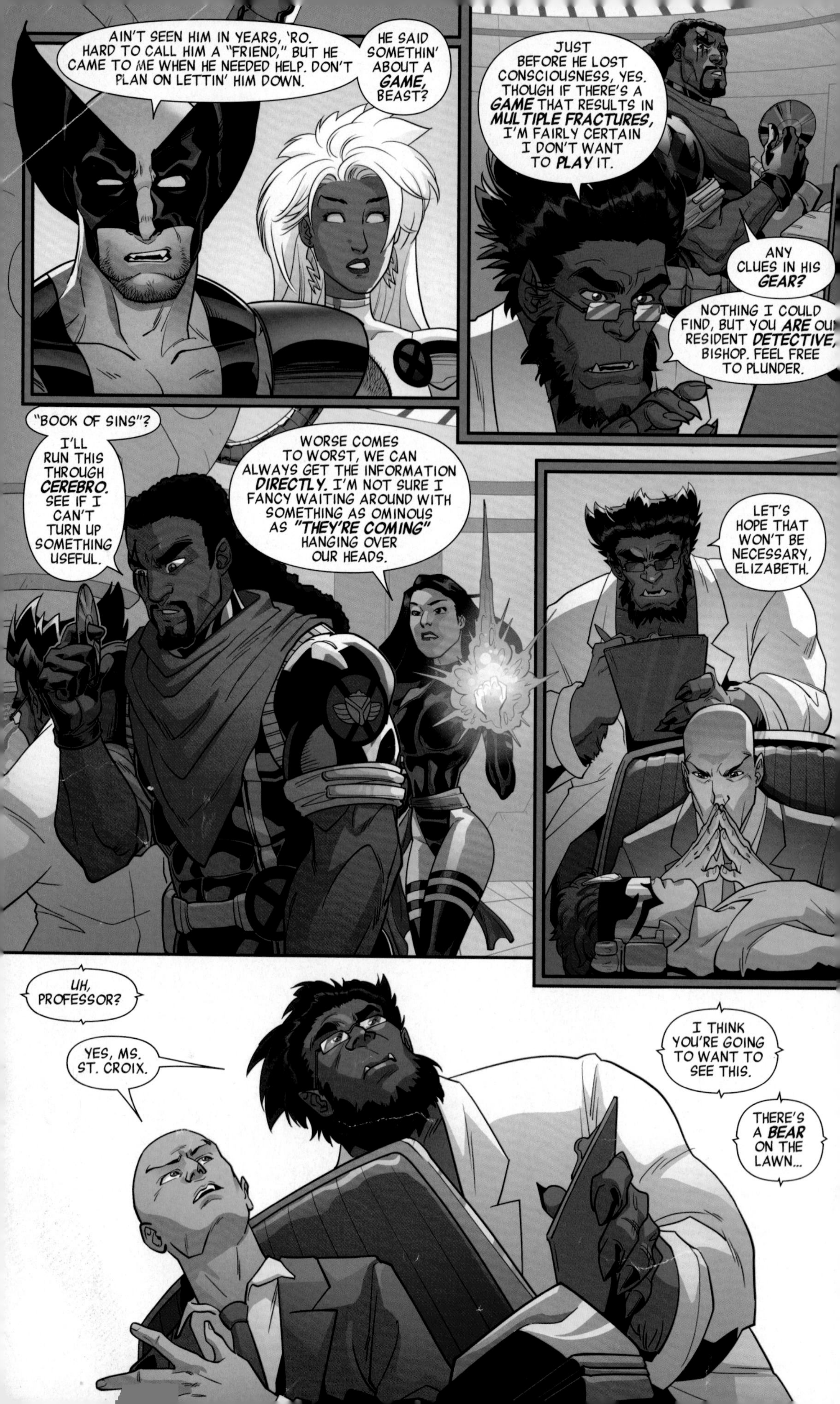
AIN'T SEEN HIM IN YEARS, 'RO. HARD TO CALL HIM A "FRIEND," BUT HE CAME TO ME WHEN HE NEEDED HELP. DON'T PLAN ON LETTIN' HIM DOWN.
HE SAID SOMETHIN' ABOUT A GAME, BEAST?
JUST BEFORE HE LOST CONSCIOUSNESS, YES. THOUGH IF THERE'S A GAME THAT RESULTS IN MULTIPLE FRACTURES, I'M FAIRLY CERTAIN I DON'T WANT TO PLAY IT.
ANY CLUES IN HIS GEAR?
NOTHING I COULD FIND, BUT YOU ARE OU RESIDENT DETECTIVE, BISHOP. FEEL FREE TO PLUNDER.
"BOOK OF SINS"?
I'LL RUN THIS THROUGH CEREBRO. SEE IF I CAN'T TURN UP SOMETHING USEFUL.
WORSE COMES TO WORST, WE CAN ALWAYS GET THE INFORMATION DIRECTLY. I'M NOT SURE I FANCY WAITING AROUND WITH SOMETHING AS OMINOUS AS "THEY'RE COMING" HANGING OVER OUR HEADS.
LET'S HOPE THAT WON'T BE NECESSARY, ELIZABETH.
UH, PROFESSOR?
YES, MS. ST. CROIX.
I THINK YOU'RE GOING TO WANT TO SEE THIS.
THERE'S A BEAR ON THE LAWN...

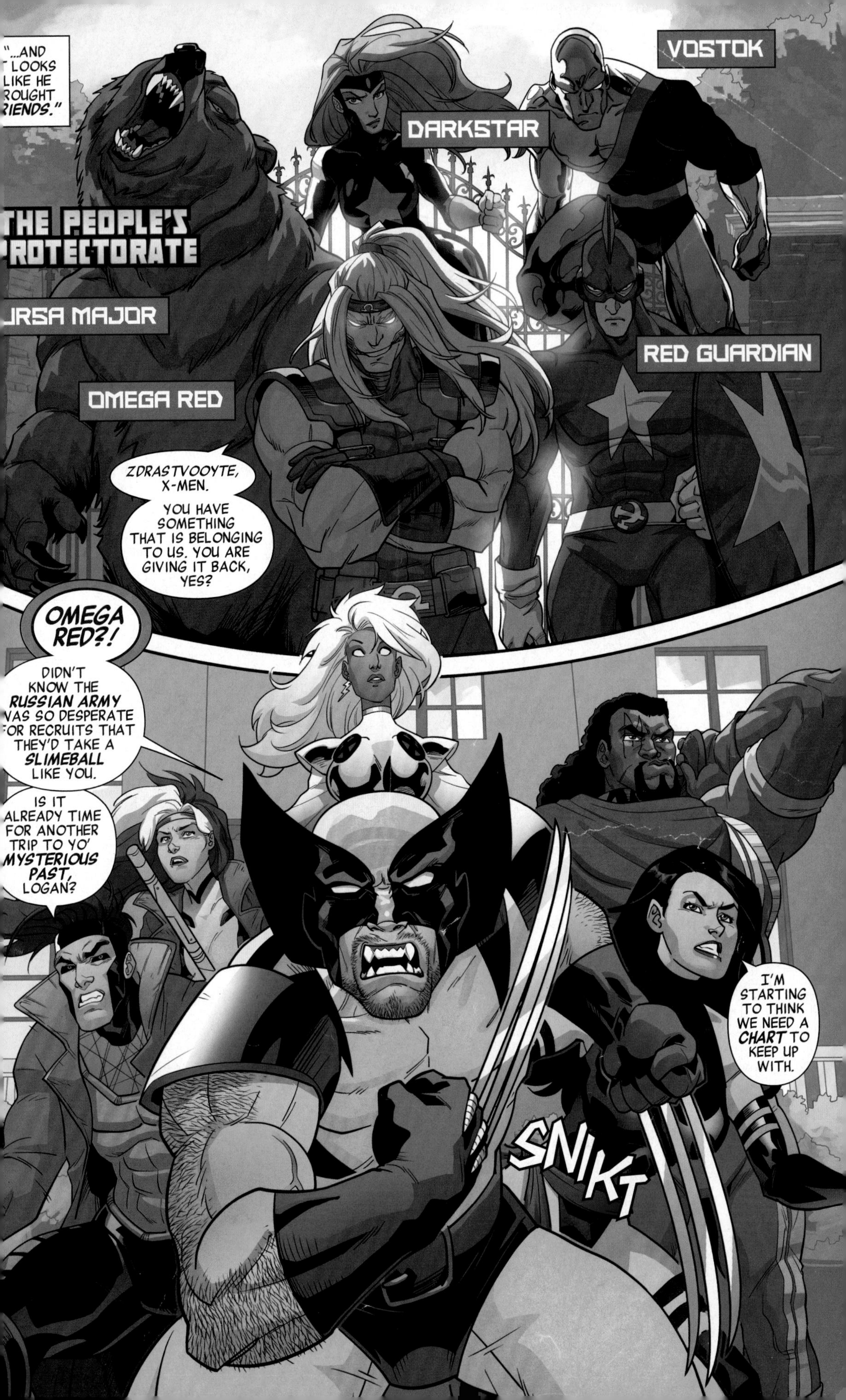

"...AND T LOOKS LIKE HE ROUGHT RIENDS."
THE PEOPLE'S ROTECTORATE
JRSA MAJOR
DARKSTAR
VOSTOK
RED GUARDIAN
OMEGA RED
ZDRASTVOOYTE, X-MEN.
YOU HAVE SOMETHING THAT IS BELONGING TO US. YOU ARE GIVING IT BACK, YES?
OMEGA RED?!
DIDN'T KNOW THE RUSSIAN ARMY VAS SO DESPERATE FOR RECRUITS THAT THEY'D TAKE A SLIMEBALL LIKE YOU.
IS IT ALREADY TIME FOR ANOTHER TRIP TO YO' MYSTERIOUS PAST, LOGAN?
I'M STARTING TO THINK WE NEED A CHART TO KEEP UP WITH.
SNIKT

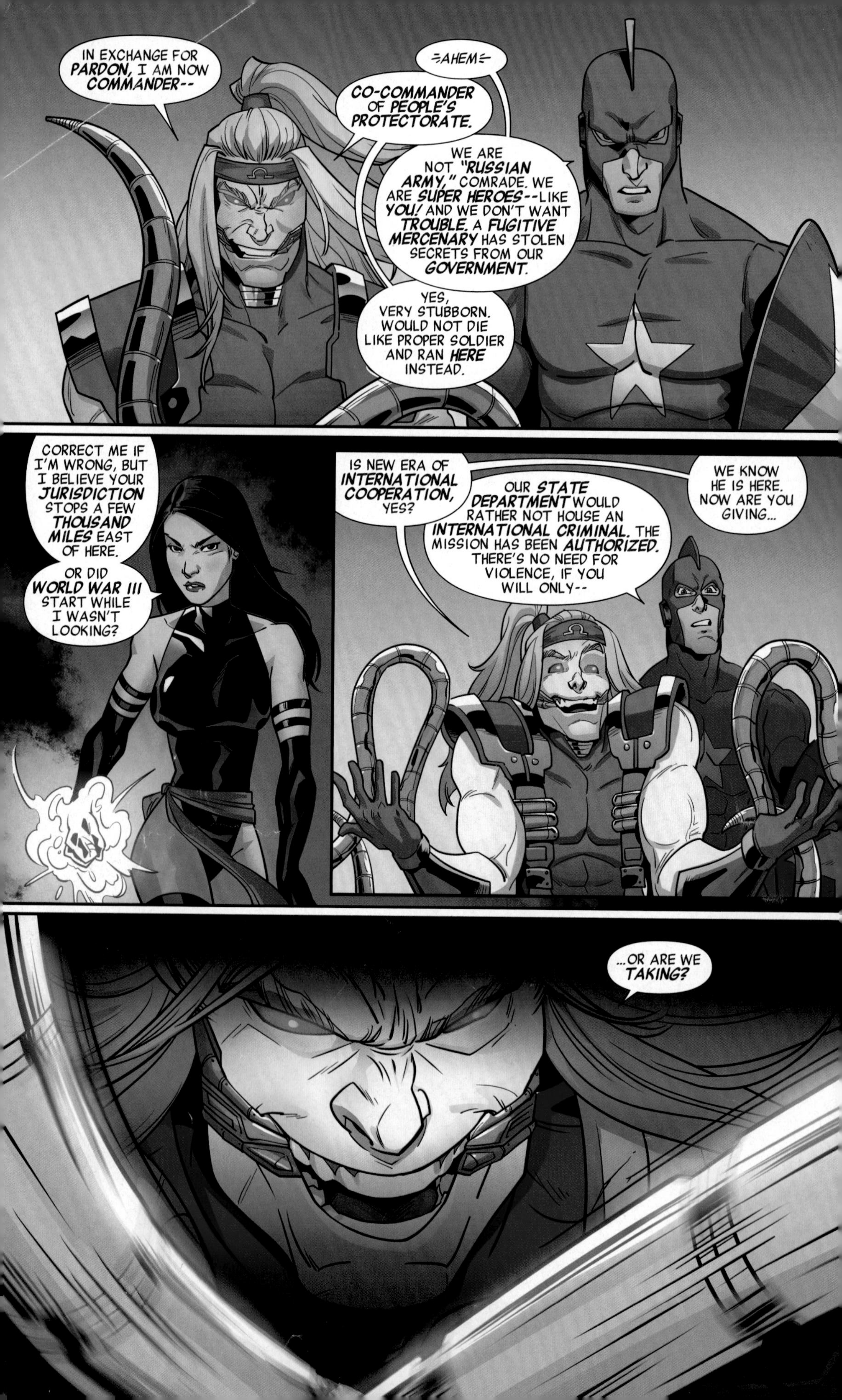

IN EXCHANGE FOR PARDON, I AM NOW COMMANDER--
AHEM
CO-COMMANDER OF PEOPLE'S PROTECTORATE.
WE ARE NOT "RUSSIAN ARMY," COMRADE. WE ARE SUPER HEROES--LIKE YOU! AND WE DON'T WANT TROUBLE. A FUGITIVE MERCENARY HAS STOLEN SECRETS FROM OUR GOVERNMENT.
YES, VERY STUBBORN. WOULD NOT DIE LIKE PROPER SOLDIER AND RAN HERE INSTEAD.
CORRECT ME IF I'M WRONG, BUT I BELIEVE YOUR JURISDICTION STOPS A FEW THOUSAND MILES EAST OF HERE.
OR DID WORLD WAR III START WHILE I WASN'T LOOKING?
IS NEW ERA OF INTERNATIONAL COOPERATION, YES?
OUR STATE DEPARTMENT WOULD RATHER NOT HOUSE AN INTERNATIONAL CRIMINAL. THE MISSION HAS BEEN AUTHORIZED. THERE'S NO NEED FOR VIOLENCE, IF YOU WILL ONLY--
WE KNOW HE IS HERE. NOW ARE YOU GIVING...
...OR ARE WE TAKING?

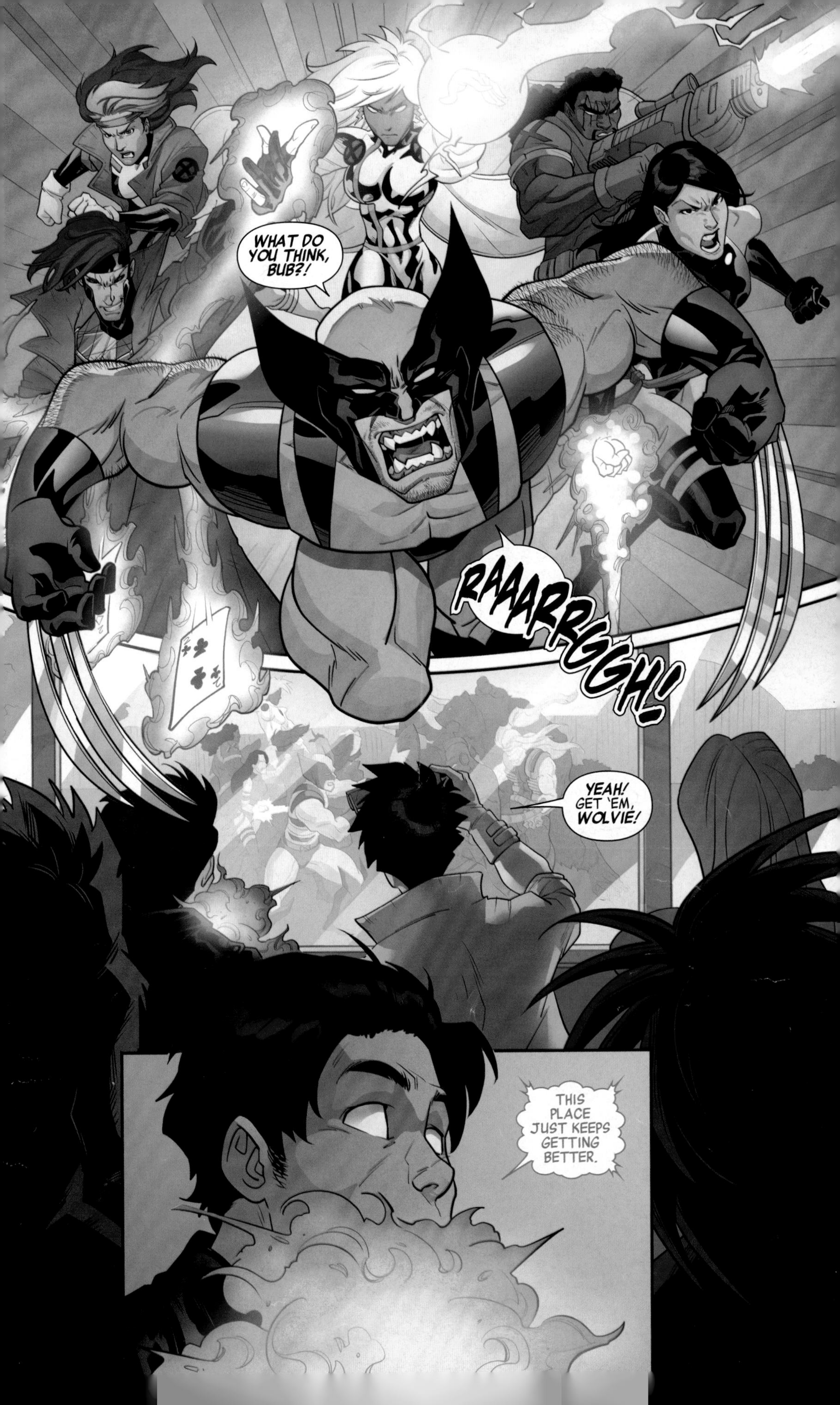

WHAT DO YOU THINK, BUB?!
RAAARRGGH!
YEAH! GET 'EM, WOLVIE!
THIS PLACE JUST KEEPS GETTING BETTER.

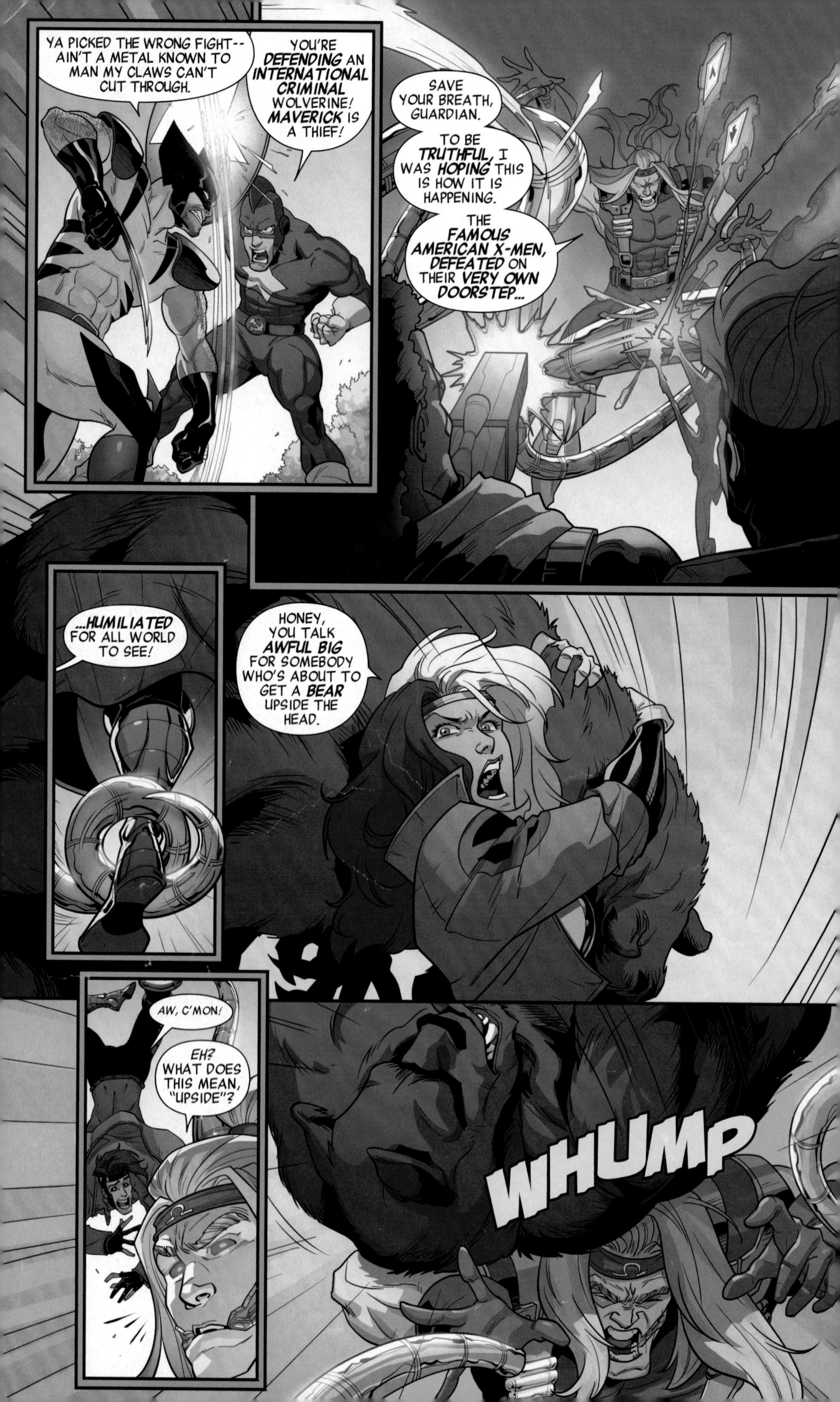
YA PICKED THE WRONG FIGHT-- AIN'T A METAL KNOWN TO MAN MY CLAWS CAN'T CUT THROUGH.
YOU'RE DEFENDING AN INTERNATIONAL CRIMINAL WOLVERINE! MAVERICK IS A THIEF!
SAVE YOUR BREATH, GUARDIAN.
TO BE TRUTHFUL, I WAS HOPING THIS IS HOW IT IS HAPPENING.
THE FAMOUS AMERICAN X-MEN, DEFEATED ON THEIR VERY OWN DOORSTEP...
...HUMILIATED FOR ALL WORLD TO SEE!
HONEY, YOU TALK AWFUL BIG FOR SOMEBODY WHO'S ABOUT TO GET A BEAR UPSIDE THE HEAD.
AW, C'MON!
EH? WHAT DOES THIS MEAN, "UPSIDE"?
WHUMP

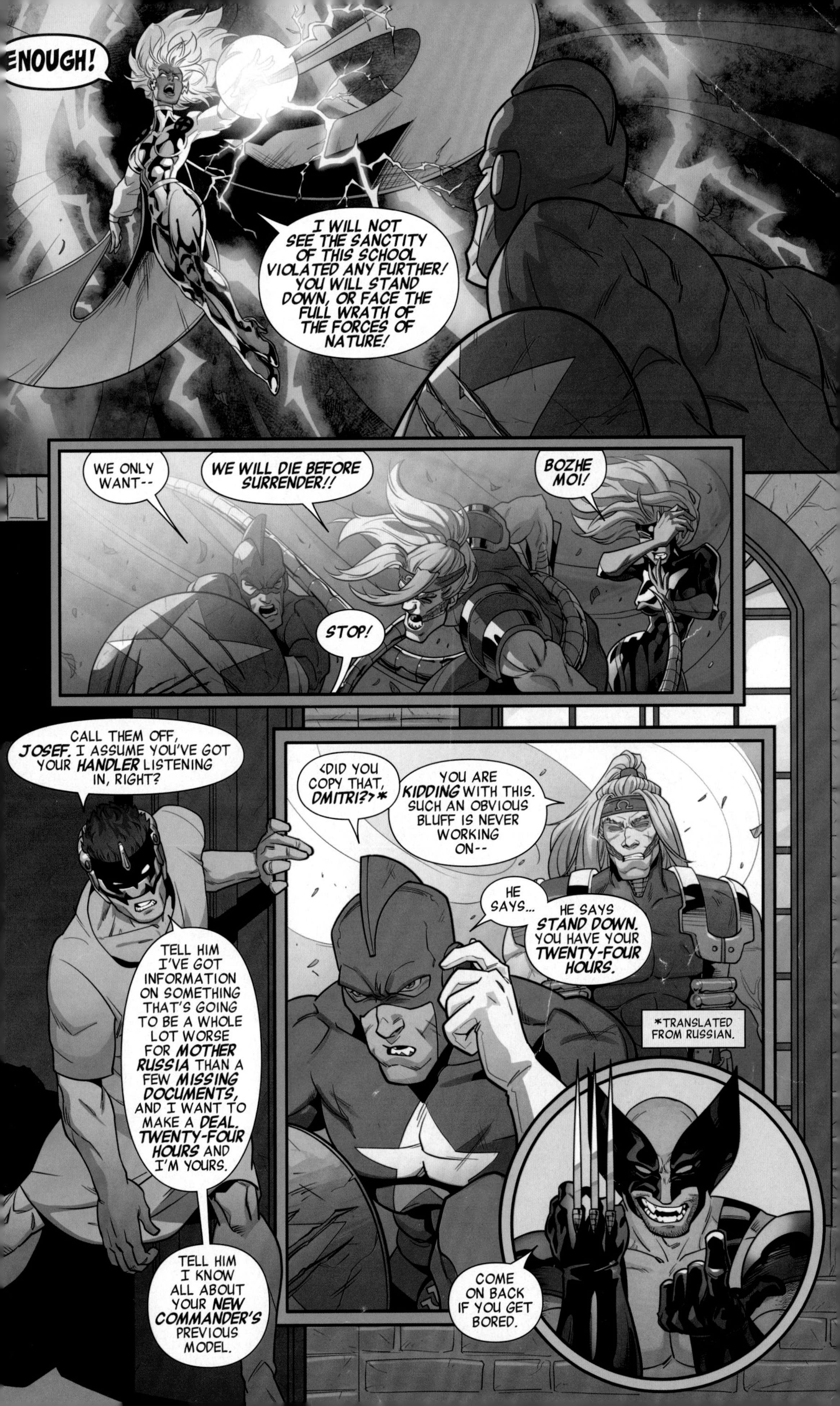

ENOUGH!
I WILL NOT SEE THE SANCTITY OF THIS SCHOOL VIOLATED ANY FURTHER! YOU WILL STAND DOWN, OR FACE THE FULL WRATH OF THE FORCES OF NATURE!
WE ONLY WANT--
WE WILL DIE BEFORE SURRENDER!!
BOZHE MOI!
STOP!
CALL THEM OFF, JOSEF. I ASSUME YOU'VE GOT YOUR HANDLER LISTENING IN, RIGHT?
TELL HIM I'VE GOT INFORMATION ON SOMETHING THAT'S GOING TO BE A WHOLE LOT WORSE FOR MOTHER RUSSIA THAN A FEW MISSING DOCUMENTS, AND I WANT TO MAKE A DEAL. TWENTY-FOUR HOURS AND I'M YOURS.
TELL HIM I KNOW ALL ABOUT YOUR NEW COMMANDER'S PREVIOUS MODEL.
<DID YOU COPY THAT, DMITRI?>*
YOU ARE KIDDING WITH THIS. SUCH AN OBVIOUS BLUFF IS NEVER WORKING ON--
HE SAYS...
HE SAYS STAND DOWN. YOU HAVE YOUR TWENTY-FOUR HOURS.
*TRANSLATED FROM RUSSIAN.
COME ON BACK IF YOU GET BORED.

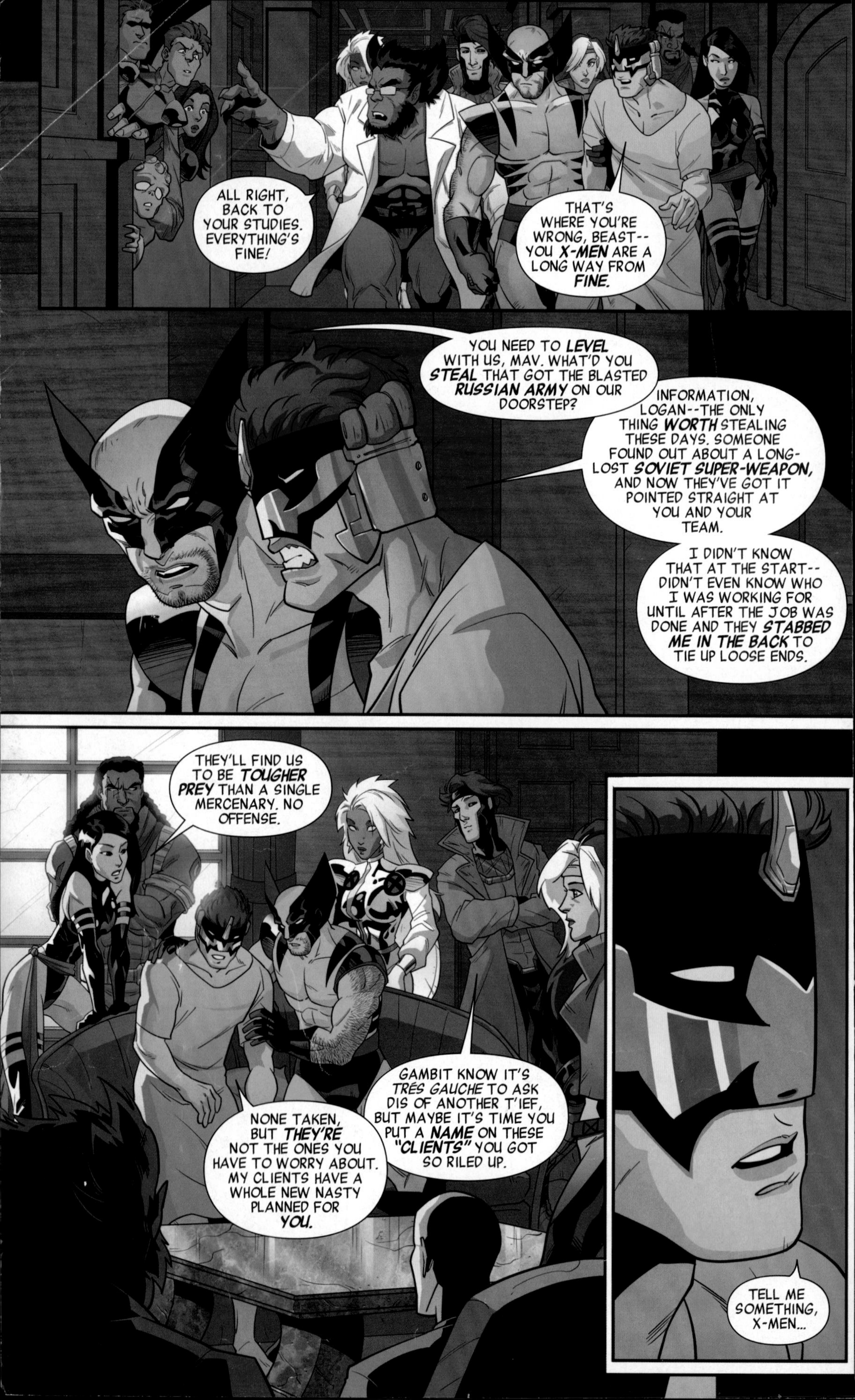
ALL RIGHT, BACK TO YOUR STUDIES. EVERYTHING'S FINE!
THAT'S WHERE YOU'RE WRONG, BEAST-- YOU X-MEN ARE A LONG WAY FROM FINE.
YOU NEED TO LEVEL WITH US, MAV. WHAT'D YOU STEAL THAT GOT THE BLASTED RUSSIAN ARMY ON OUR DOORSTEP?
INFORMATION, LOGAN--THE ONLY THING WORTH STEALING THESE DAYS. SOMEONE FOUND OUT ABOUT A LONG-LOST SOVIET SUPER-WEAPON, AND NOW THEY'VE GOT IT POINTED STRAIGHT AT YOU AND YOUR TEAM.
I DIDN'T KNOW THAT AT THE START--DIDN'T EVEN KNOW WHO I WAS WORKING FOR UNTIL AFTER THE JOB WAS DONE AND THEY STABBED ME IN THE BACK TO TIE UP LOOSE ENDS.
THEY'LL FIND US TO BE TOUGHER PREY THAN A SINGLE MERCENARY. NO OFFENSE.
NONE TAKEN, BUT THEY'RE NOT THE ONES YOU HAVE TO WORRY ABOUT. MY CLIENTS HAVE A WHOLE NEW NASTY PLANNED FOR YOU.
GAMBIT KNOW IT'S TRÉS GAUCHE TO ASK DIS OF ANOTHER T'IEF, BUT MAYBE IT'S TIME YOU PUT A NAME ON THESE "CLIENTS" YOU GOT SO RILED UP.
TELL ME SOMETHING, X-MEN...

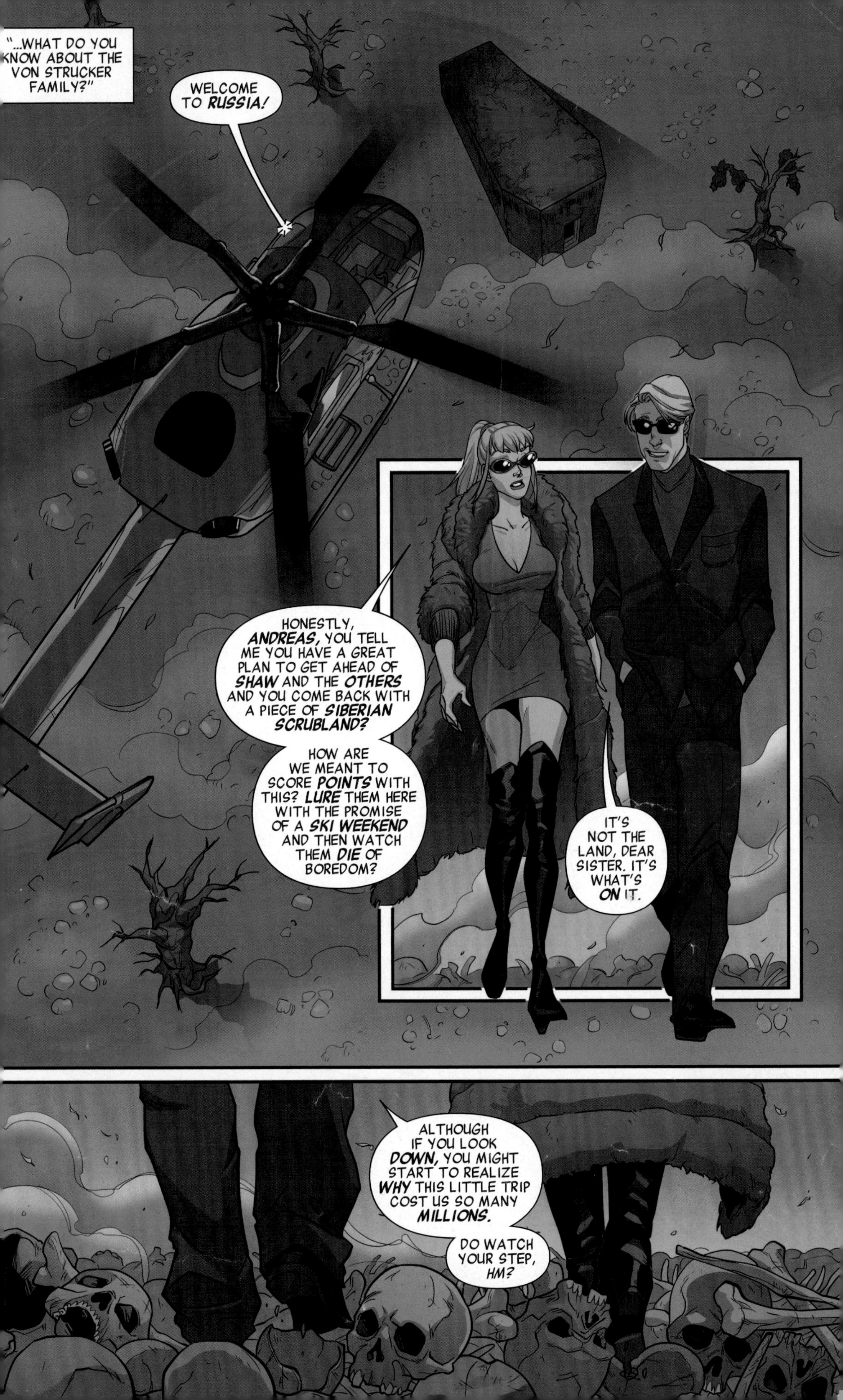
"...WHAT DO YOU KNOW ABOUT THE VON STRUCKER FAMILY?"
WELCOME TO RUSSIA!
HONESTLY, ANDREAS, YOU TELL ME YOU HAVE A GREAT PLAN TO GET AHEAD OF SHAW AND THE OTHERS AND YOU COME BACK WITH A PIECE OF SIBERIAN SCRUBLAND?
HOW ARE WE MEANT TO SCORE POINTS WITH THIS? LURE THEM HERE WITH THE PROMISE OF A SKI WEEKEND AND THEN WATCH THEM DIE OF BOREDOM?
IT'S NOT THE LAND, DEAR SISTER. IT'S WHAT'S ON IT.
ALTHOUGH IF YOU LOOK DOWN, YOU MIGHT START TO REALIZE WHY THIS LITTLE TRIP COST US SO MANY MILLIONS.
DO WATCH YOUR STEP, HM?

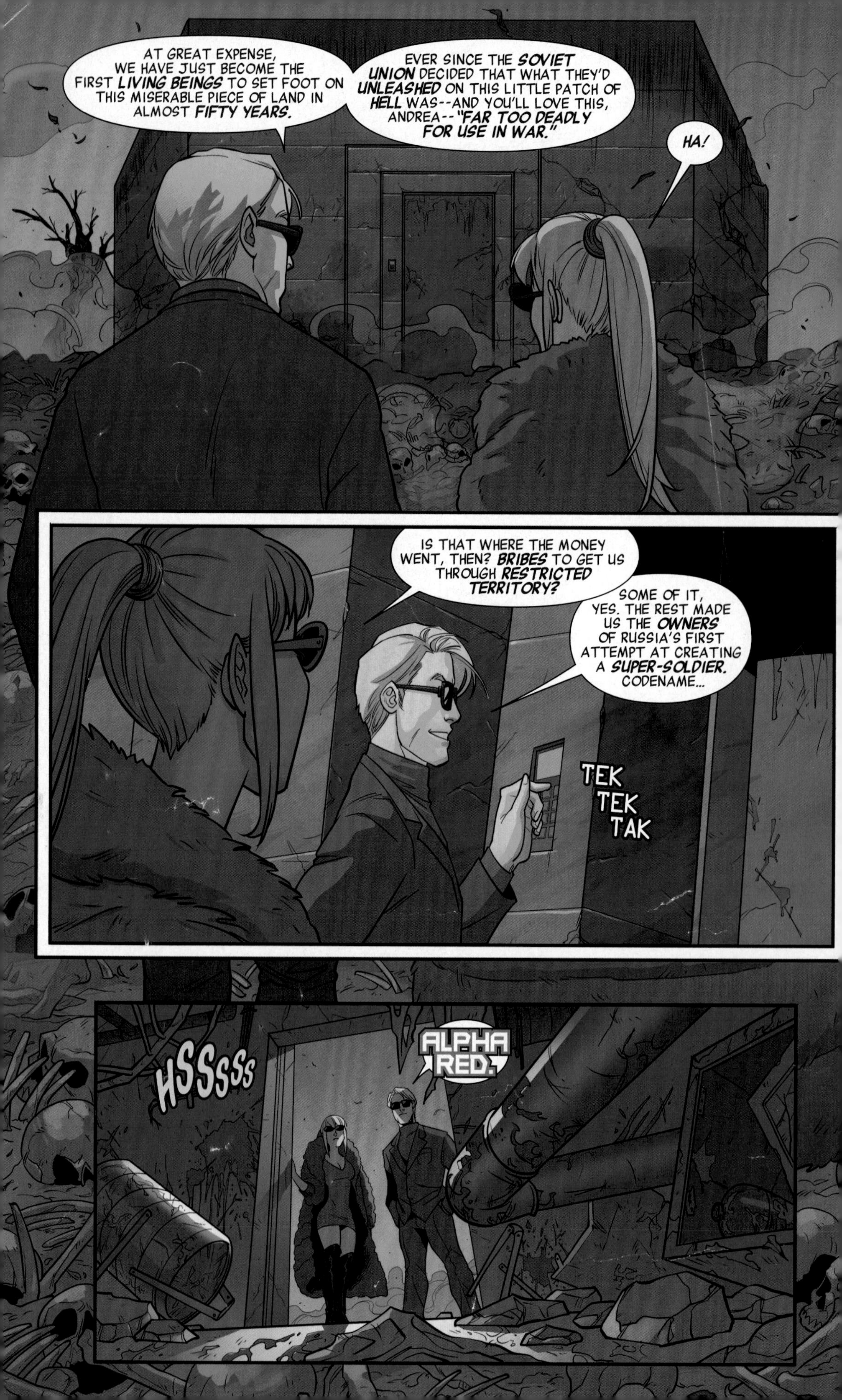
AT GREAT EXPENSE, WE HAVE JUST BECOME THE FIRST LIVING BEINGS TO SET FOOT ON THIS MISERABLE PIECE OF LAND IN ALMOST FIFTY YEARS.
EVER SINCE THE SOVIET UNION DECIDED THAT WHAT THEY'D UNLEASHED ON THIS LITTLE PATCH OF HELL WAS--AND YOU'LL LOVE THIS, ANDREA--"FAR TOO DEADLY FOR USE IN WAR."
HA!
IS THAT WHERE THE MONEY WENT, THEN? BRIBES TO GET US THROUGH RESTRICTED TERRITORY?
SOME OF IT, YES. THE REST MADE US THE OWNERS OF RUSSIA'S FIRST ATTEMPT AT CREATING A SUPER-SOLDIER. CODENAME...
TEK
TEK
TAK
HSSSSS
ALPHA RED.

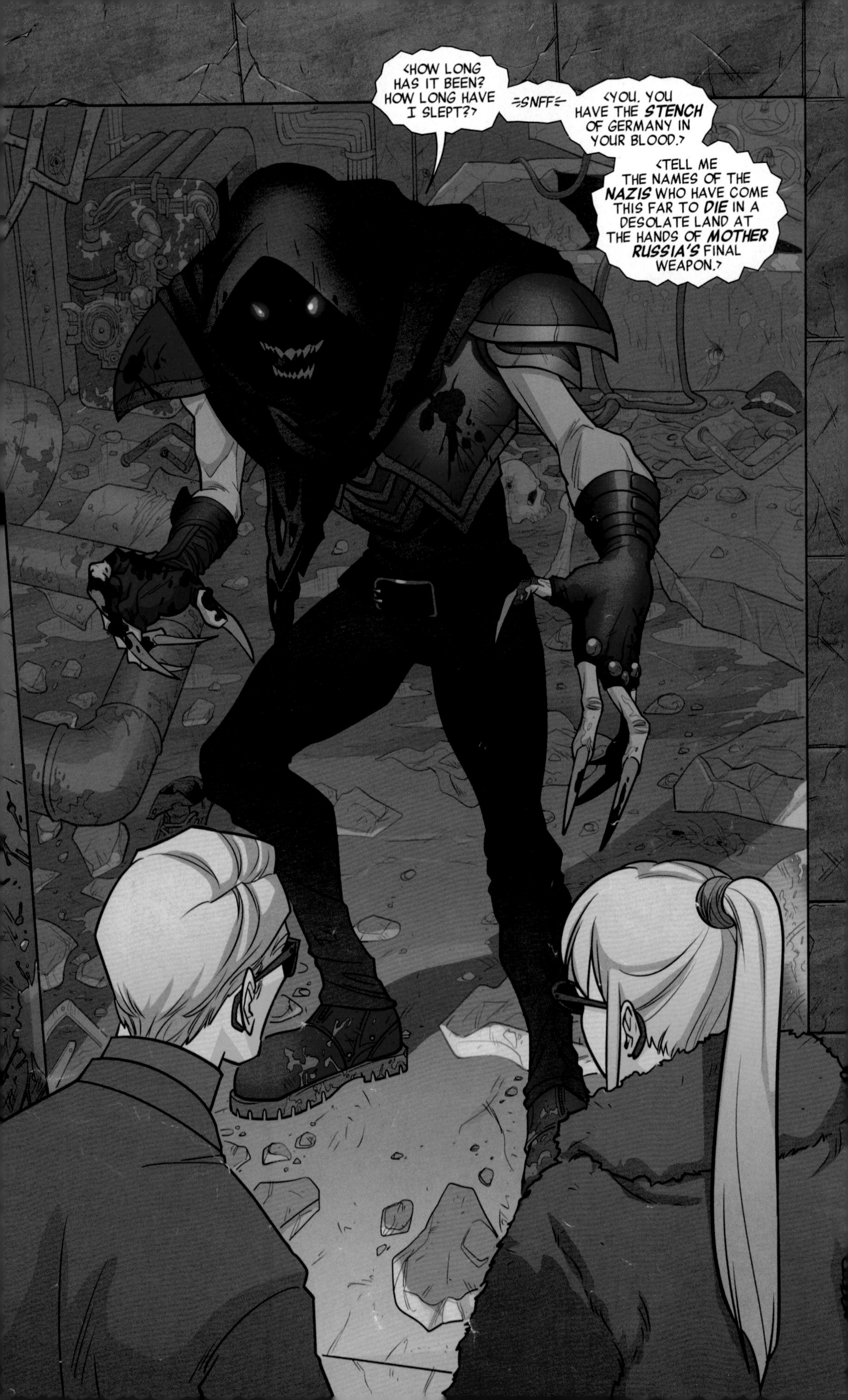
<HOW LONG HAS IT BEEN? HOW LONG HAVE I SLEPT?>
=SNFF=
<YOU. YOU HAVE THE STENCH OF GERMANY IN YOUR BLOOD.>
<TELL ME THE NAMES OF THE NAZIS WHO HAVE COME THIS FAR TO DIE IN A DESOLATE LAND AT THE HANDS OF MOTHER RUSSIA'S FINAL WEAPON.>

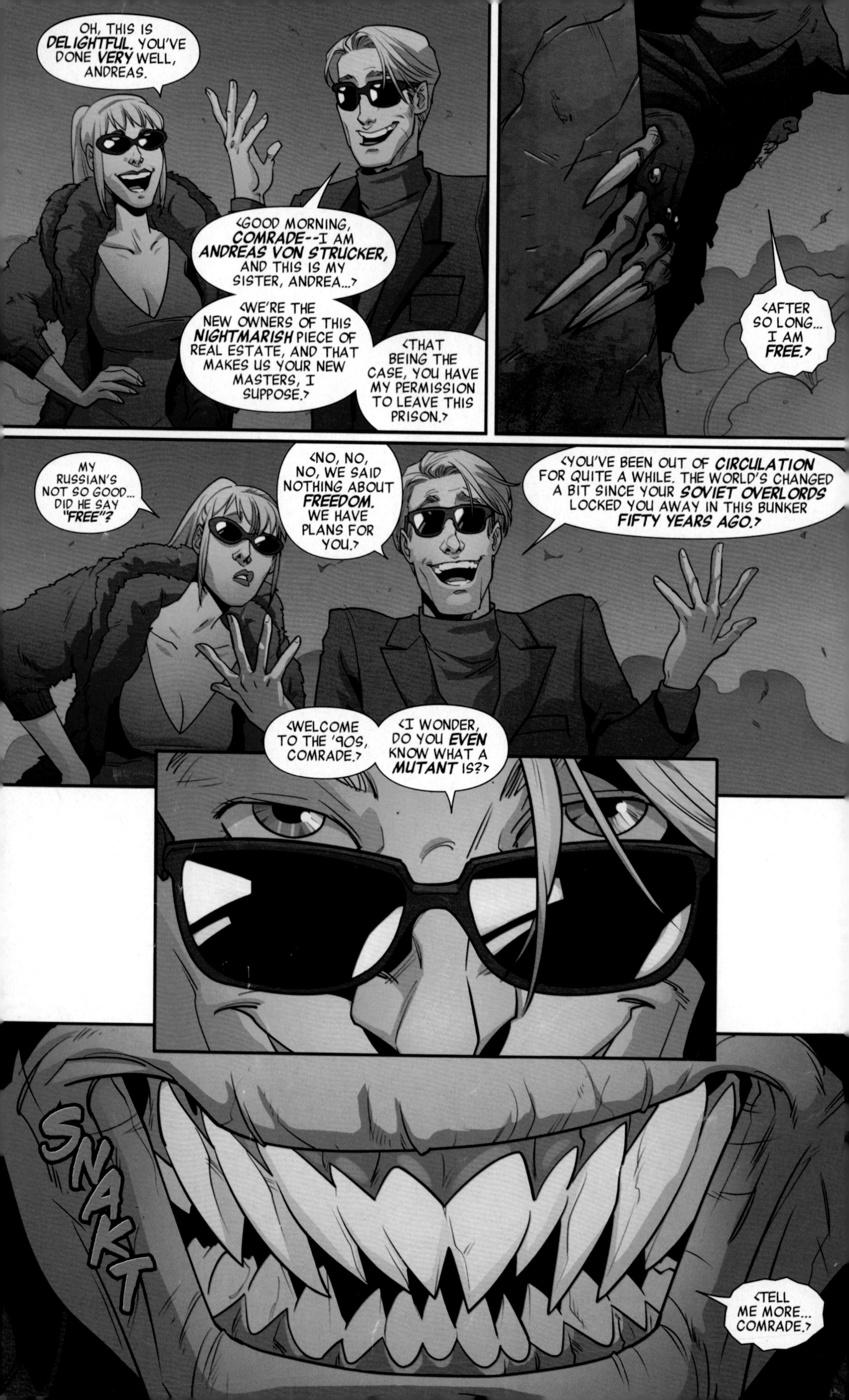
OH, THIS IS DELIGHTFUL. YOU'VE DONE VERY WELL, ANDREAS.
<GOOD MORNING, COMRADE--I AM ANDREAS VON STRUCKER, AND THIS IS MY SISTER, ANDREA...>
<WE'RE THE NEW OWNERS OF THIS NIGHTMARISH PIECE OF REAL ESTATE, AND THAT MAKES US YOUR NEW MASTERS, I SUPPOSE.>
<THAT BEING THE CASE, YOU HAVE MY PERMISSION TO LEAVE THIS PRISON.>
<AFTER SO LONG... I AM FREE.>
MY RUSSIAN'S NOT SO GOOD... DID HE SAY "FREE"?
<NO, NO, NO, WE SAID NOTHING ABOUT FREEDOM. WE HAVE PLANS FOR YOU.>
<YOU'VE BEEN OUT OF CIRCULATION FOR QUITE A WHILE. THE WORLD'S CHANGED A BIT SINCE YOUR SOVIET OVERLORDS LOCKED YOU AWAY IN THIS BUNKER FIFTY YEARS AGO.>
<WELCOME TO THE '90S, COMRADE.>
<I WONDER, DO YOU EVEN KNOW WHAT A MUTANT IS?>
SNAKT
<TELL ME MORE... COMRADE.>

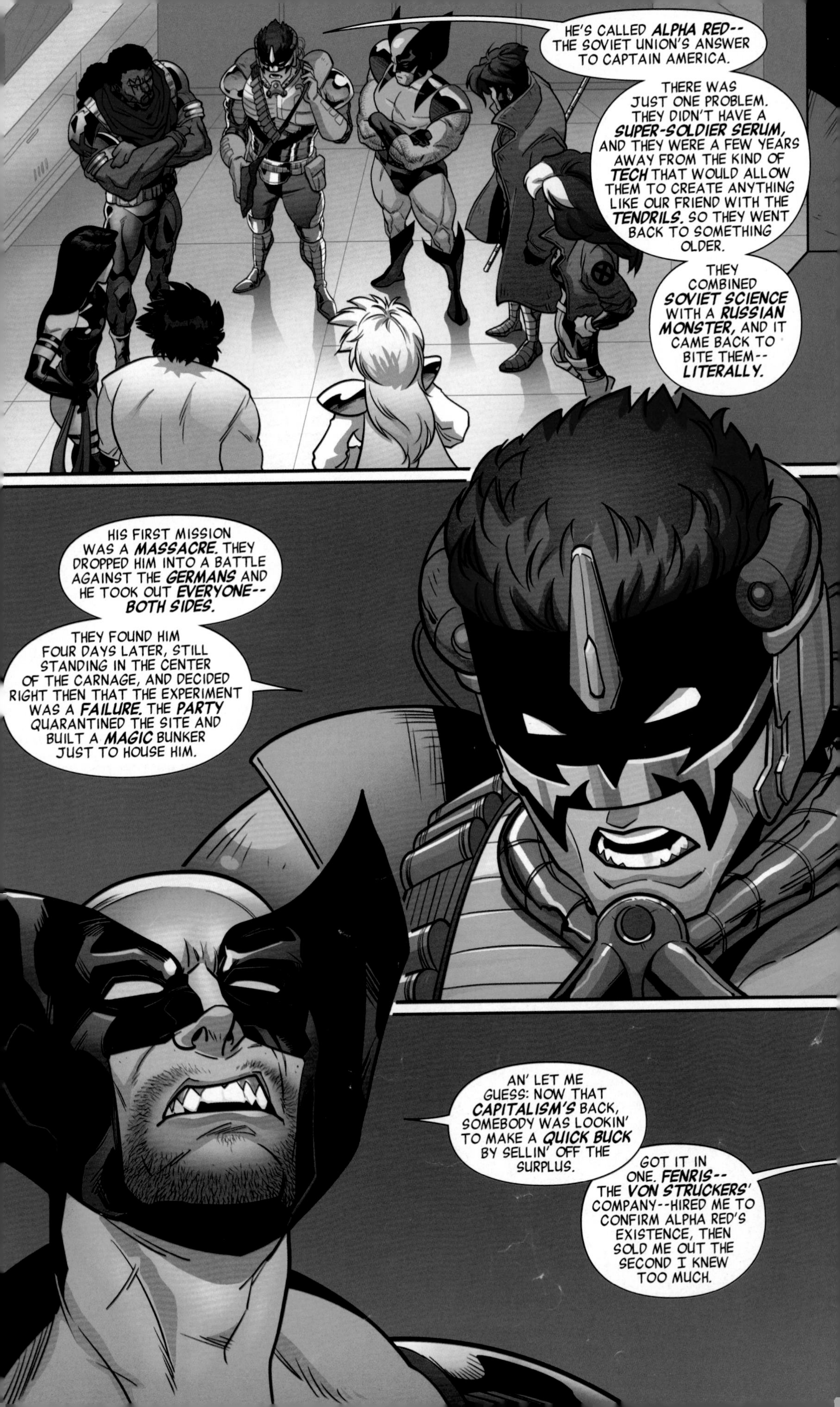
HE'S CALLED ALPHA RED-- THE SOVIET UNION'S ANSWER TO CAPTAIN AMERICA.
THERE WAS JUST ONE PROBLEM. THEY DIDN'T HAVE A SUPER-SOLDIER SERUM, AND THEY WERE A FEW YEARS AWAY FROM THE KIND OF TECH THAT WOULD ALLOW THEM TO CREATE ANYTHING LIKE OUR FRIEND WITH THE TENDRILS. SO THEY WENT BACK TO SOMETHING OLDER.
THEY COMBINED SOVIET SCIENCE WITH A RUSSIAN MONSTER, AND IT CAME BACK TO BITE THEM-- LITERALLY.
HIS FIRST MISSION WAS A MASSACRE. THEY DROPPED HIM INTO A BATTLE AGAINST THE GERMANS AND HE TOOK OUT EVERYONE-- BOTH SIDES.
THEY FOUND HIM FOUR DAYS LATER, STILL STANDING IN THE CENTER OF THE CARNAGE, AND DECIDED RIGHT THEN THAT THE EXPERIMENT WAS A FAILURE. THE PARTY QUARANTINED THE SITE AND BUILT A MAGIC BUNKER JUST TO HOUSE HIM.
AN' LET ME GUESS: NOW THAT CAPITALISM'S BACK, SOMEBODY WAS LOOKIN' TO MAKE A QUICK BUCK BY SELLIN' OFF THE SURPLUS.
GOT IT IN ONE. FENRIS-- THE VON STRUCKERS' COMPANY--HIRED ME TO CONFIRM ALPHA RED'S EXISTENCE, THEN SOLD ME OUT THE SECOND I KNEW TOO MUCH.

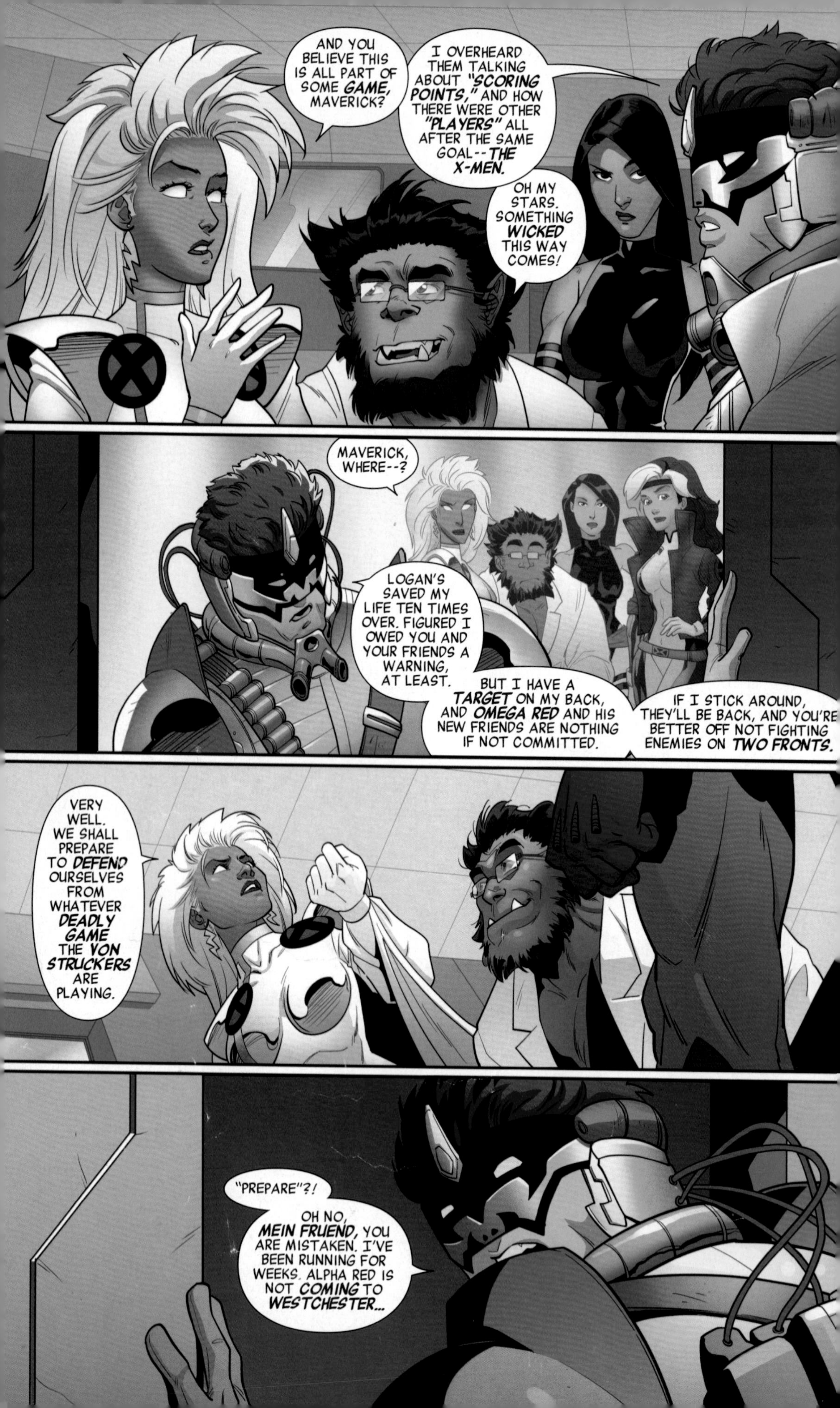
AND YOU BELIEVE THIS IS ALL PART OF SOME GAME, MAVERICK?
I OVERHEARD THEM TALKING ABOUT "SCORING POINTS," AND HOW THERE WERE OTHER "PLAYERS" ALL AFTER THE SAME GOAL--THE X-MEN.
OH MY STARS. SOMETHING WICKED THIS WAY COMES!
MAVERICK, WHERE--?
LOGAN'S SAVED MY LIFE TEN TIMES OVER. FIGURED I OWED YOU AND YOUR FRIENDS A WARNING, AT LEAST.
BUT I HAVE A TARGET ON MY BACK, AND OMEGA RED AND HIS NEW FRIENDS ARE NOTHING IF NOT COMMITTED.
IF I STICK AROUND, THEY'LL BE BACK, AND YOU'RE BETTER OFF NOT FIGHTING ENEMIES ON TWO FRONTS.
VERY WELL. WE SHALL PREPARE TO DEFEND OURSELVES FROM WHATEVER DEADLY GAME THE VON STRUCKERS ARE PLAYING.
"PREPARE"?!
OH NO, MEIN FRUEND, YOU ARE MISTAKEN. I'VE BEEN RUNNING FOR WEEKS. ALPHA RED IS NOT COMING TO WESTCHESTER...

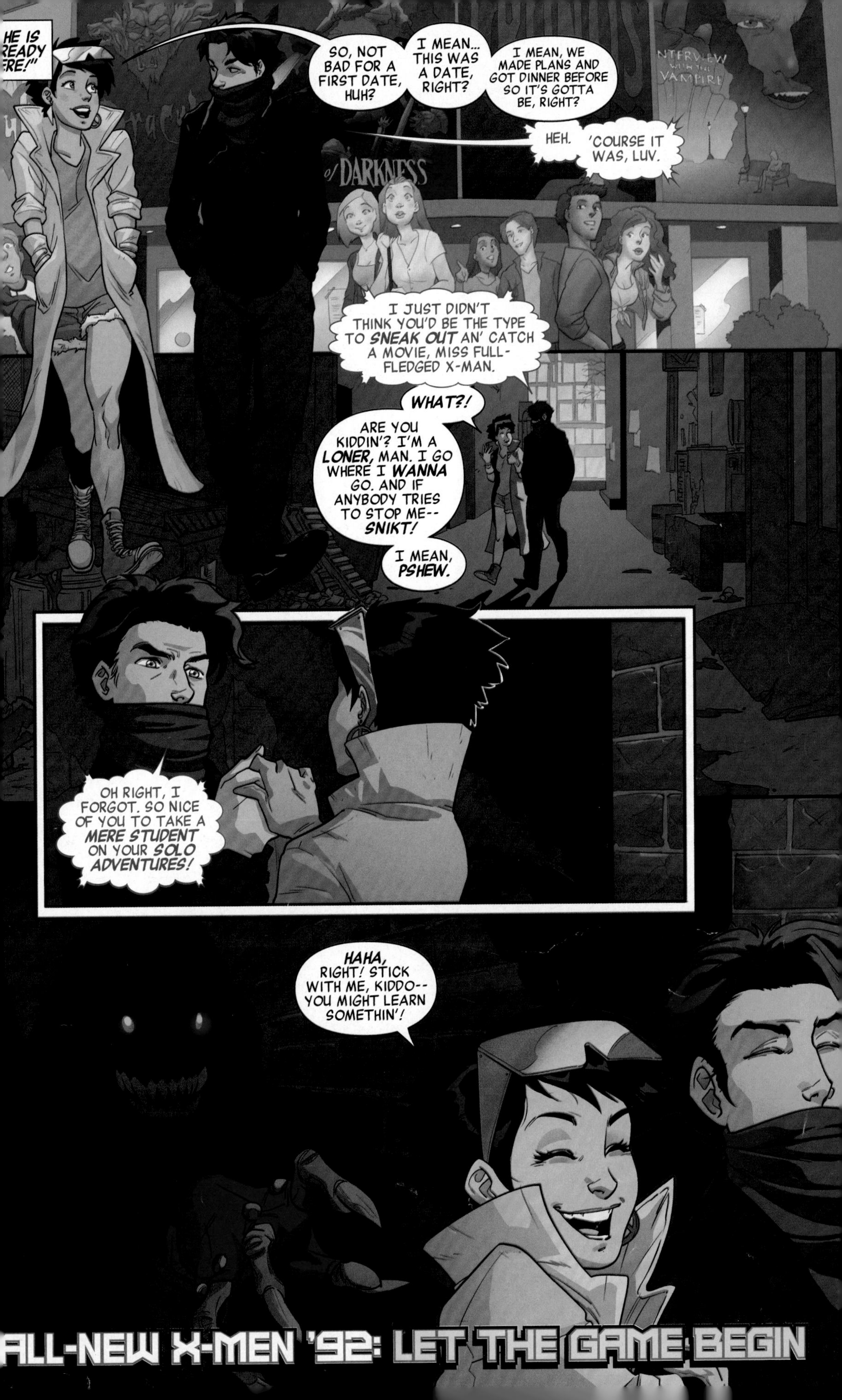
HE IS READY FRE!"
SO, NOT BAD FOR A FIRST DATE, HUH?
I MEAN... THIS WAS A DATE, RIGHT?
I MEAN, WE MADE PLANS AND GOT DINNER BEFORE SO IT'S GOTTA BE, RIGHT?
HEH. 'COURSE IT WAS, LUV.
NTERVIEW WITH THE VAMPIRE
of DARKNESS
I JUST DIDN'T THINK YOU'D BE THE TYPE TO SNEAK OUT AN' CATCH A MOVIE, MISS FULL-FLEDGED X-MAN.
WHAT?!
ARE YOU KIDDIN'? I'M A LONER, MAN. I GO WHERE I WANNA GO. AND IF ANYBODY TRIES TO STOP ME-- SNIKT!
I MEAN, PSHEW.
OH RIGHT, I FORGOT. SO NICE OF YOU TO TAKE A MERE STUDENT ON YOUR SOLO ADVENTURES!
HAHA, RIGHT! STICK WITH ME, KIDDO-- YOU MIGHT LEARN SOMETHIN'!
ALL-NEW X-MEN '92: LET THE GAME BEGIN

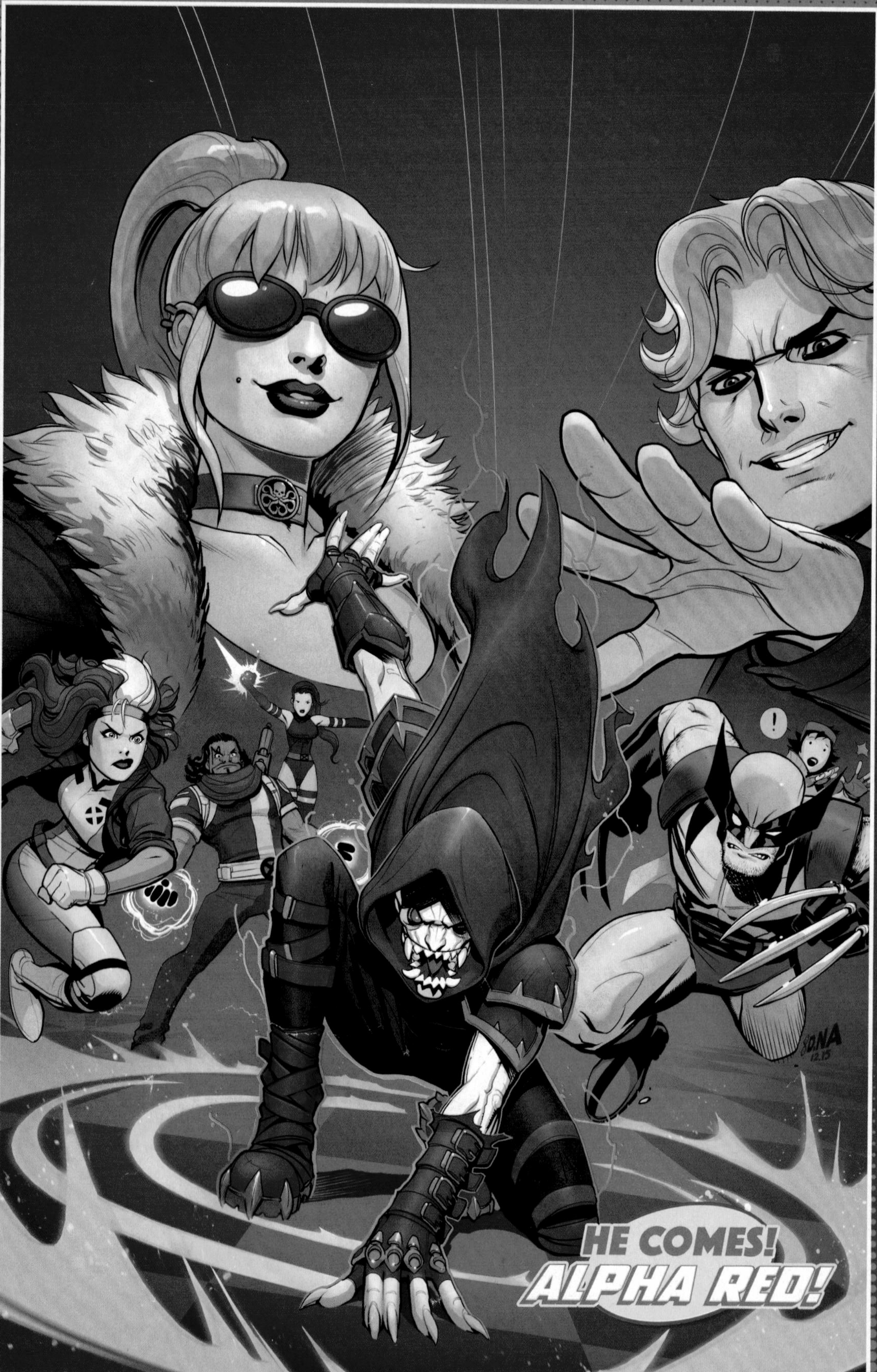

!
DNA 12.15
HE COMES!
ALPHA RED!

Z

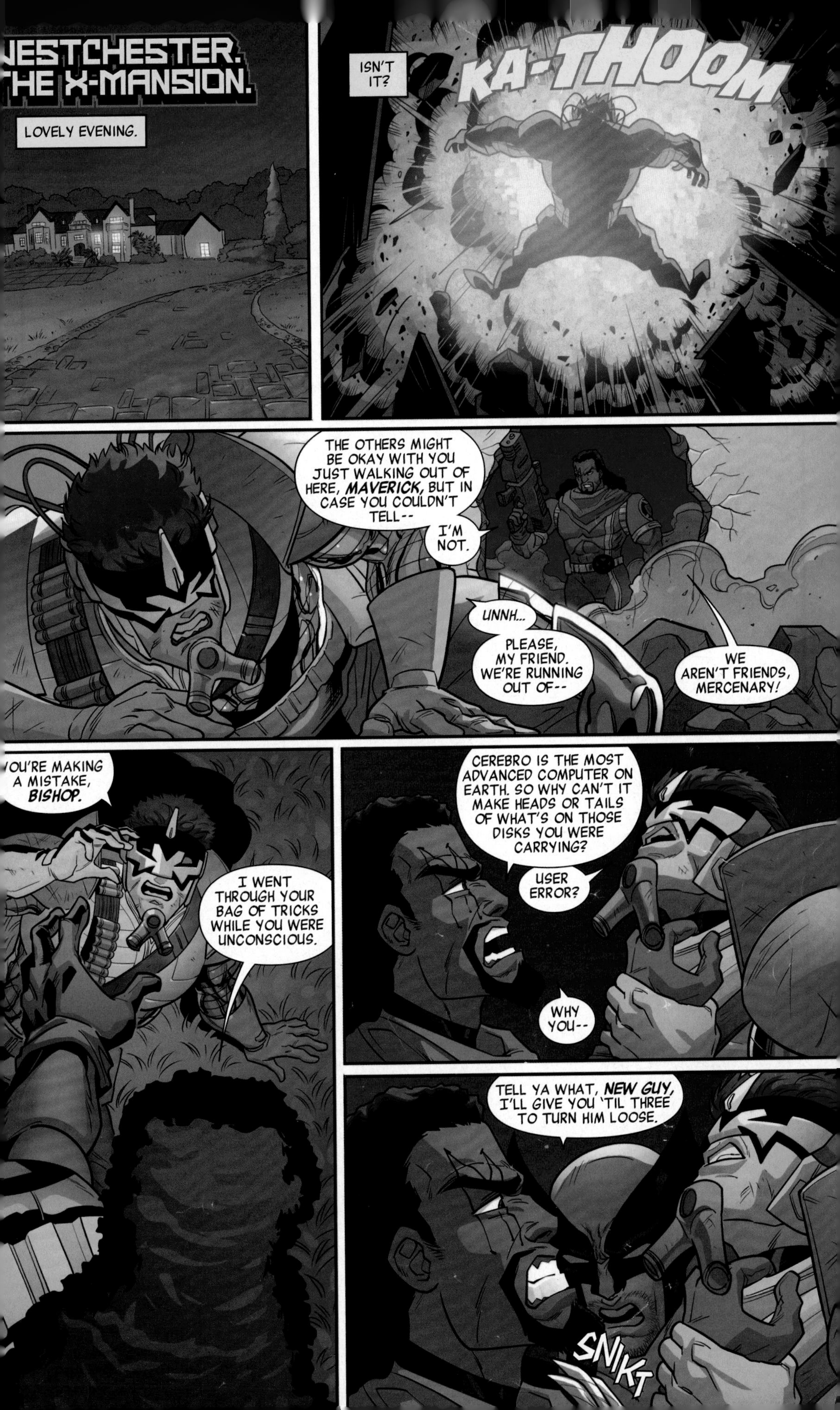

WESTCHESTER.
THE X-MANSION.
LOVELY EVENING.
ISN'T IT?
KA-THOOM
THE OTHERS MIGHT BE OKAY WITH YOU JUST WALKING OUT OF HERE, MAVERICK, BUT IN CASE YOU COULDN'T TELL--
I'M NOT.
UNNH...
PLEASE, MY FRIEND. WE'RE RUNNING OUT OF--
WE AREN'T FRIENDS, MERCENARY!
YOU'RE MAKING A MISTAKE, BISHOP.
I WENT THROUGH YOUR BAG OF TRICKS WHILE YOU WERE UNCONSCIOUS.
CEREBRO IS THE MOST ADVANCED COMPUTER ON EARTH. SO WHY CAN'T IT MAKE HEADS OR TAILS OF WHAT'S ON THOSE DISKS YOU WERE CARRYING?
USER ERROR?
WHY YOU--
TELL YA WHAT, NEW GUY, I'LL GIVE YOU 'TIL THREE TO TURN HIM LOOSE.
SNIKT

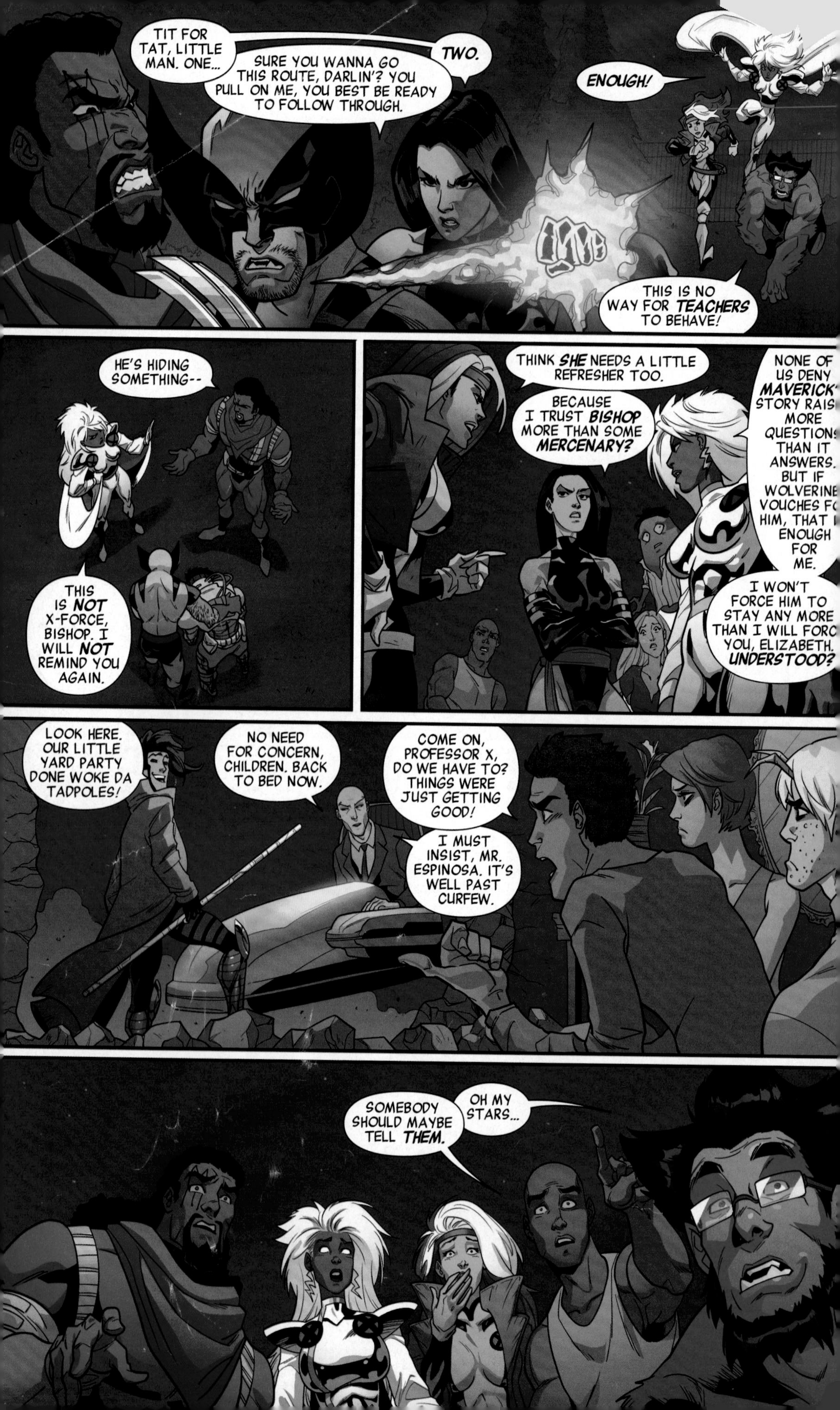

TIT FOR TAT, LITTLE MAN. ONE...
SURE YOU WANNA GO THIS ROUTE, DARLIN'? YOU PULL ON ME, YOU BEST BE READY TO FOLLOW THROUGH.
TWO.
ENOUGH!
THIS IS NO WAY FOR TEACHERS TO BEHAVE!
HE'S HIDING SOMETHING--
THIS IS NOT X-FORCE, BISHOP. I WILL NOT REMIND YOU AGAIN.
THINK SHE NEEDS A LITTLE REFRESHER TOO.
BECAUSE I TRUST BISHOP MORE THAN SOME MERCENARY?
NONE OF US DENY MAVERICK' STORY RAIS MORE QUESTION THAN IT ANSWERS. BUT IF WOLVERINE VOUCHES F HIM, THAT ENOUGH FOR ME.
I WON'T FORCE HIM TO STAY ANY MORE THAN I WILL FORC YOU, ELIZABETH. UNDERSTOOD?
LOOK HERE. OUR LITTLE YARD PARTY DONE WOKE DA TADPOLES!
NO NEED FOR CONCERN, CHILDREN. BACK TO BED NOW.
COME ON, PROFESSOR X, DO WE HAVE TO? THINGS WERE JUST GETTING GOOD!
I MUST INSIST, MR. ESPINOSA. IT'S WELL PAST CURFEW.
OH MY STARS...
SOMEBODY SHOULD MAYBE TELL THEM.

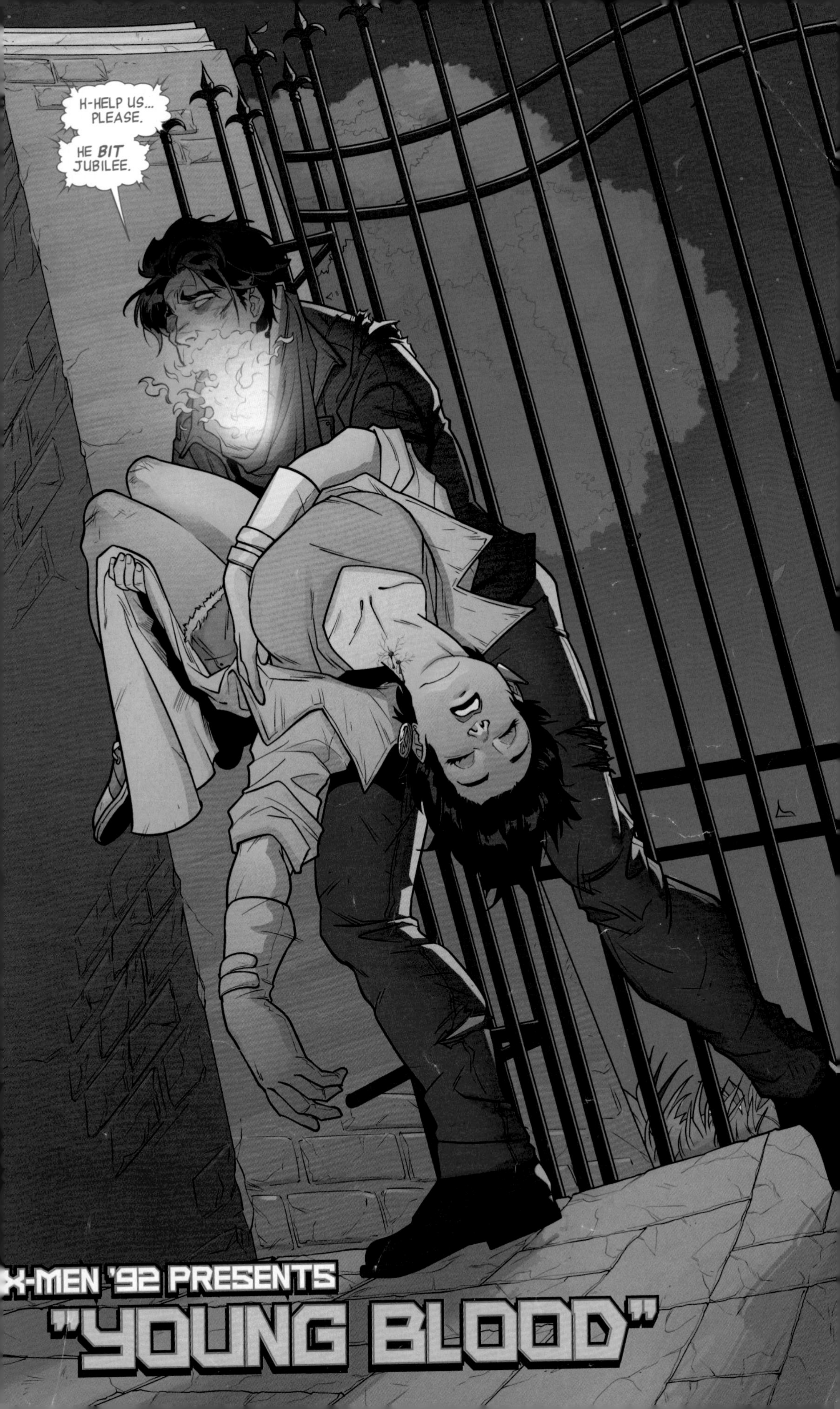

H-HELP US... PLEASE.
HE BIT JUBILEE.
X-MEN '92 PRESENTS
"YOUNG BLOOD"

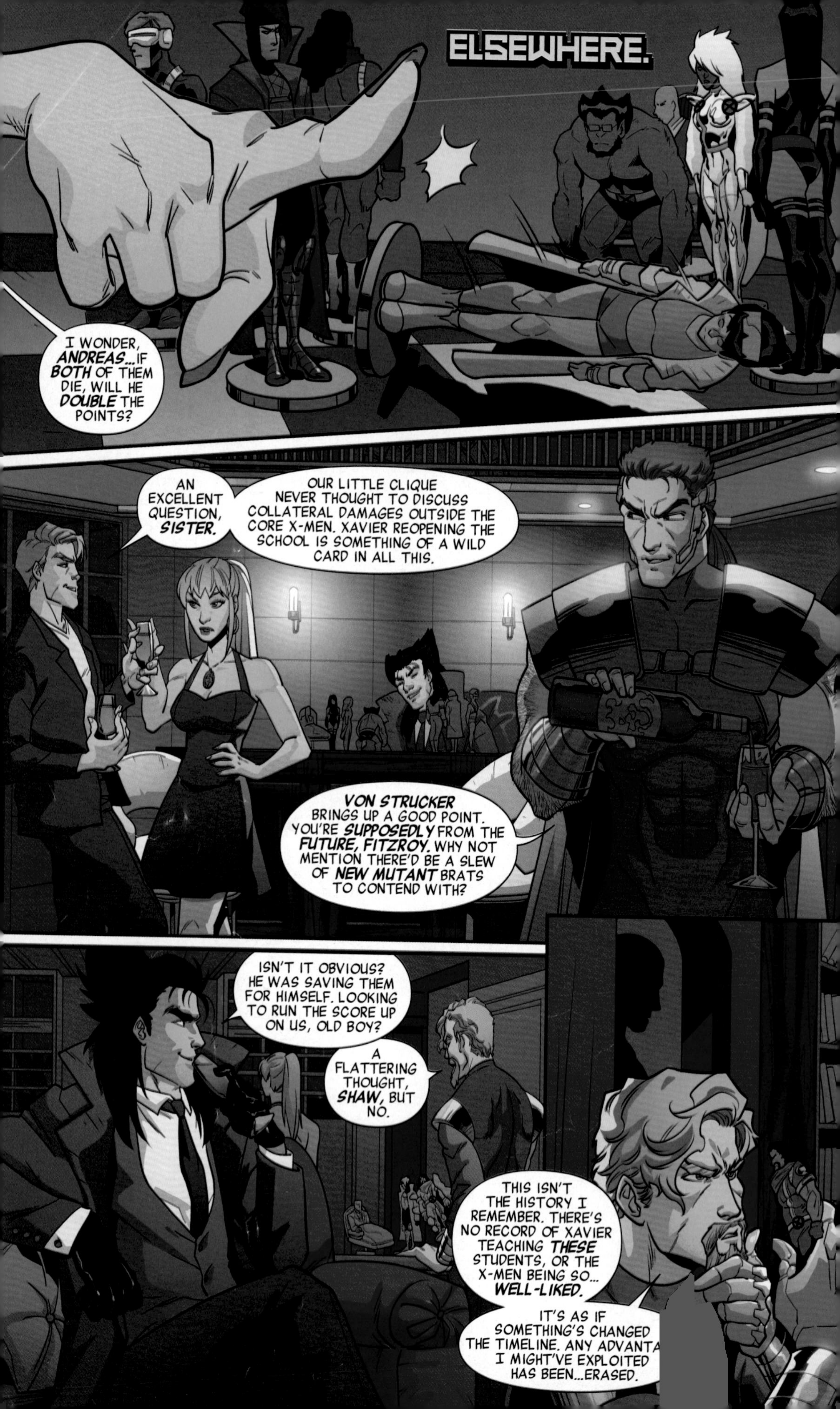
ELSEWHERE.
I WONDER, ANDREAS... IF BOTH OF THEM DIE, WILL HE DOUBLE THE POINTS?
AN EXCELLENT QUESTION, SISTER.
OUR LITTLE CLIQUE NEVER THOUGHT TO DISCUSS COLLATERAL DAMAGES OUTSIDE THE CORE X-MEN. XAVIER REOPENING THE SCHOOL IS SOMETHING OF A WILD CARD IN ALL THIS.
VON STRUCKER BRINGS UP A GOOD POINT. YOU'RE SUPPOSEDLY FROM THE FUTURE, FITZROY. WHY NOT MENTION THERE'D BE A SLEW OF NEW MUTANT BRATS TO CONTEND WITH?
ISN'T IT OBVIOUS? HE WAS SAVING THEM FOR HIMSELF. LOOKING TO RUN THE SCORE UP ON US, OLD BOY?
A FLATTERING THOUGHT, SHAW, BUT NO.
THIS ISN'T THE HISTORY I REMEMBER. THERE'S NO RECORD OF XAVIER TEACHING THESE STUDENTS, OR THE X-MEN BEING SO... WELL-LIKED.
IT'S AS IF SOMETHING'S CHANGED THE TIMELINE. ANY ADVANTA I MIGHT'VE EXPLOITED HAS BEEN...ERASED.

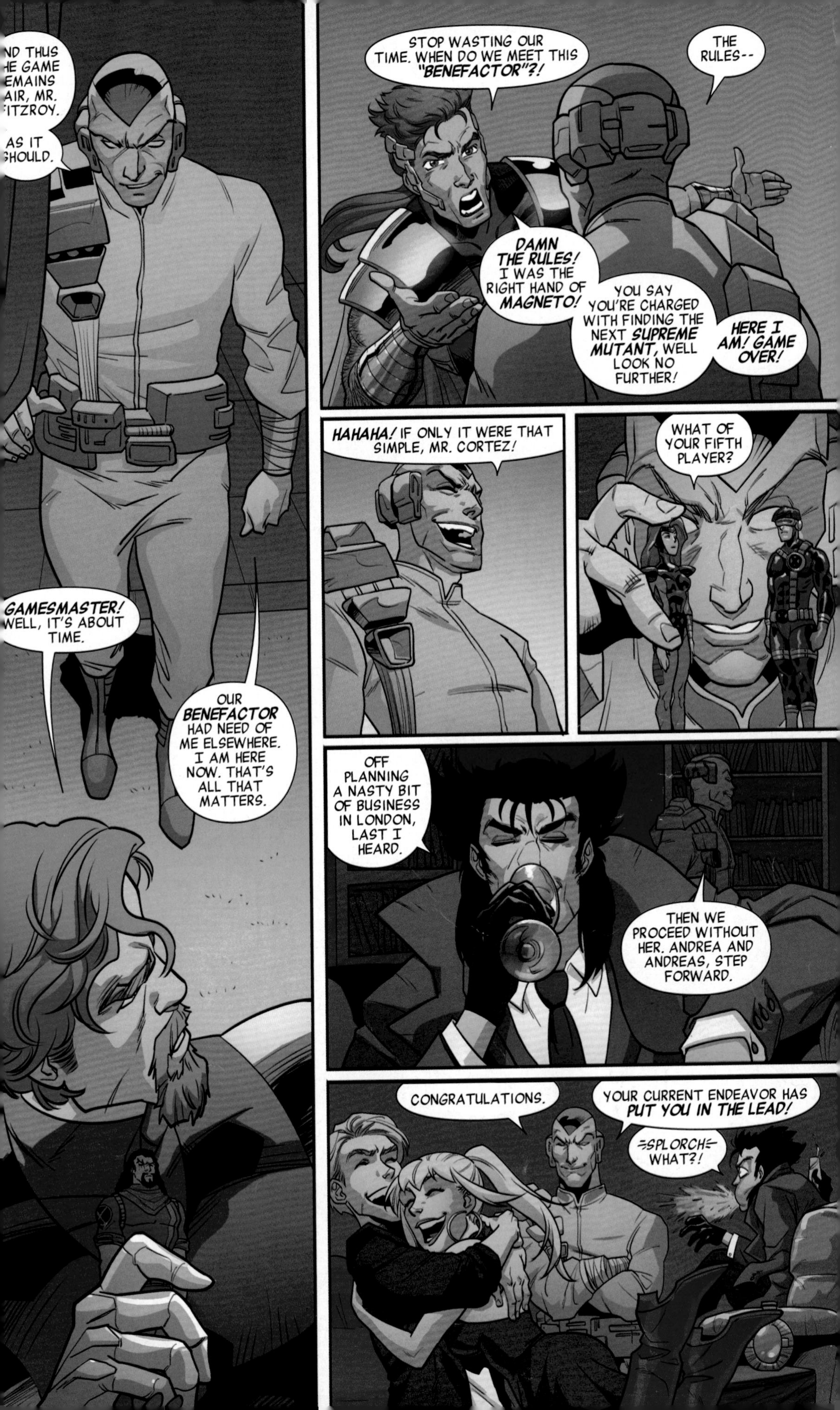
ND THUS HE GAME EMAINS AIR, MR. FITZROY.
AS IT SHOULD.
GAMESMASTER! WELL, IT'S ABOUT TIME.
OUR BENEFACTOR HAD NEED OF ME ELSEWHERE. I AM HERE NOW. THAT'S ALL THAT MATTERS.
STOP WASTING OUR TIME. WHEN DO WE MEET THIS "BENEFACTOR"?!
THE RULES--
DAMN THE RULES! I WAS THE RIGHT HAND OF MAGNETO!
YOU SAY YOU'RE CHARGED WITH FINDING THE NEXT SUPREME MUTANT, WELL LOOK NO FURTHER!
HERE I AM! GAME OVER!
HAHAHA! IF ONLY IT WERE THAT SIMPLE, MR. CORTEZ!
WHAT OF YOUR FIFTH PLAYER?
OFF PLANNING A NASTY BIT OF BUSINESS IN LONDON, LAST I HEARD.
THEN WE PROCEED WITHOUT HER. ANDREA AND ANDREAS, STEP FORWARD.
CONGRATULATIONS.
YOUR CURRENT ENDEAVOR HAS PUT YOU IN THE LEAD!
=SPLORCH= WHAT?!

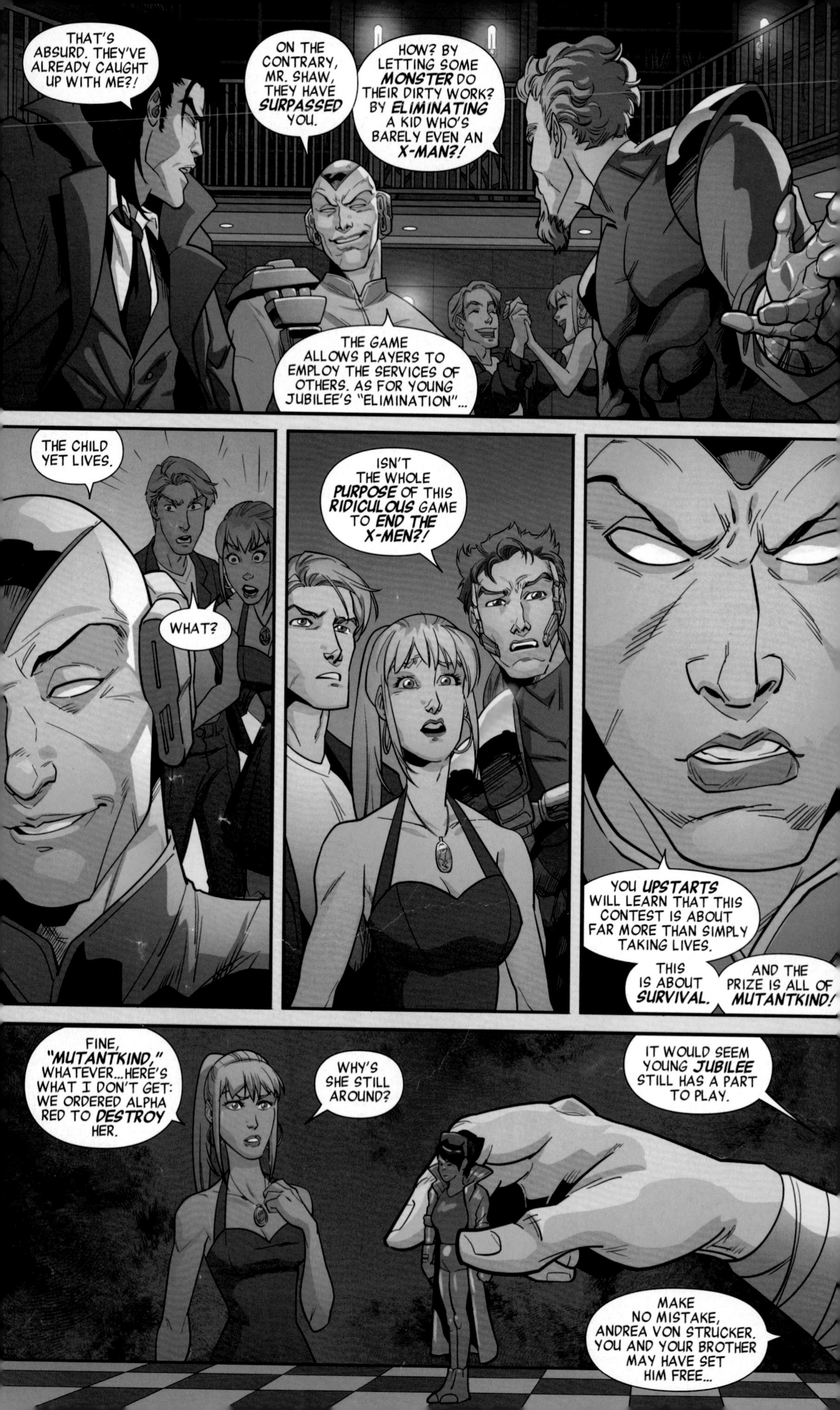
THAT'S ABSURD. THEY'VE ALREADY CAUGHT UP WITH ME?!
ON THE CONTRARY, MR. SHAW, THEY HAVE SURPASSED YOU.
HOW? BY LETTING SOME MONSTER DO THEIR DIRTY WORK? BY ELIMINATING A KID WHO'S BARELY EVEN AN X-MAN?!
THE GAME ALLOWS PLAYERS TO EMPLOY THE SERVICES OF OTHERS. AS FOR YOUNG JUBILEE'S "ELIMINATION"...
THE CHILD YET LIVES.
WHAT?
ISN'T THE WHOLE PURPOSE OF THIS RIDICULOUS GAME TO END THE X-MEN?!
YOU UPSTARTS WILL LEARN THAT THIS CONTEST IS ABOUT FAR MORE THAN SIMPLY TAKING LIVES.
THIS IS ABOUT SURVIVAL.
AND THE PRIZE IS ALL OF MUTANTKIND!
FINE, "MUTANTKIND," WHATEVER...HERE'S WHAT I DON'T GET: WE ORDERED ALPHA RED TO DESTROY HER.
WHY'S SHE STILL AROUND?
IT WOULD SEEM YOUNG JUBILEE STILL HAS A PART TO PLAY.
MAKE NO MISTAKE, ANDREA VON STRUCKER. YOU AND YOUR BROTHER MAY HAVE SET HIM FREE...

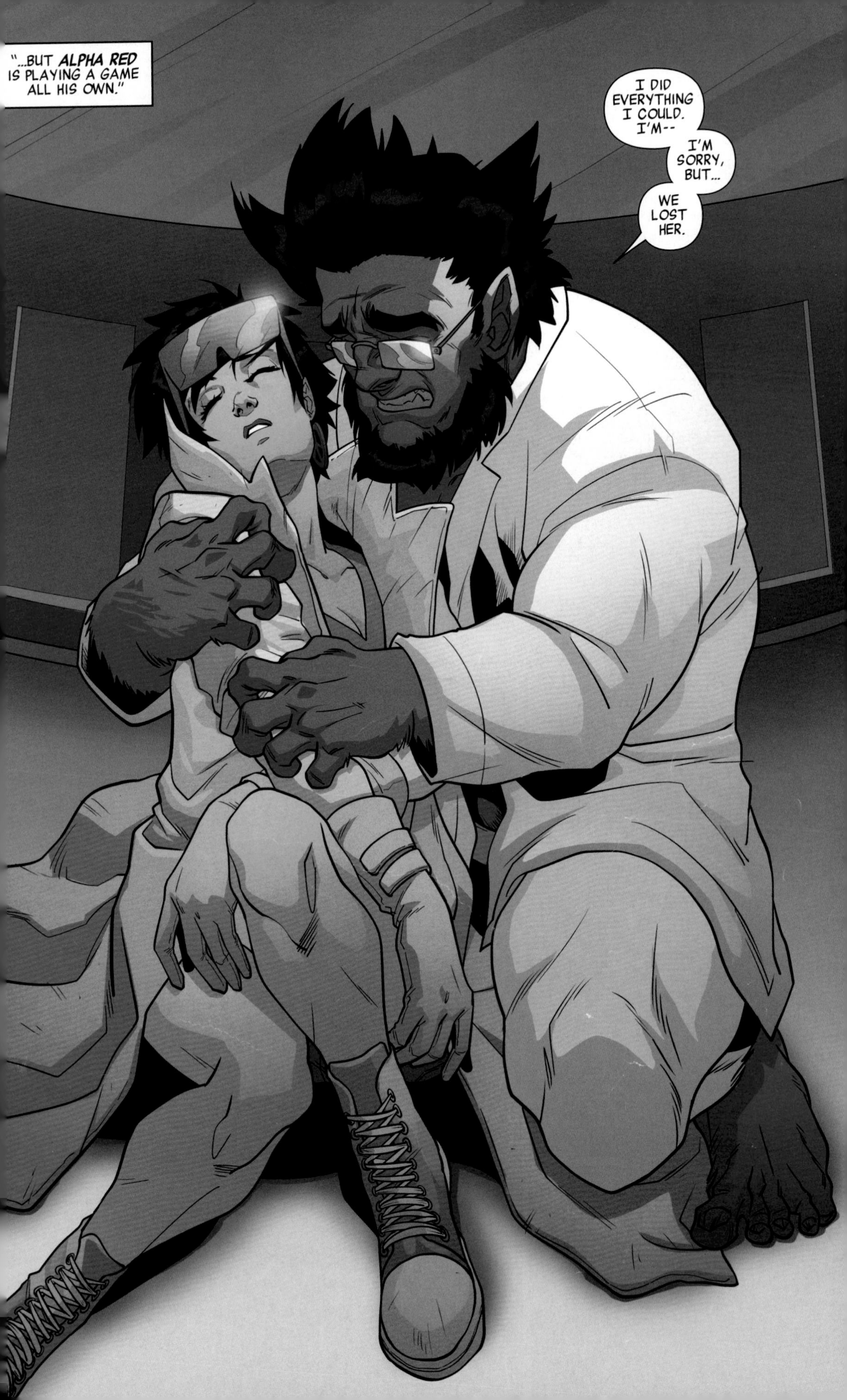
"...BUT **ALPHA RED** IS PLAYING A GAME ALL HIS OWN."
I DID EVERYTHING I COULD. I'M--
I'M SORRY, BUT...
WE LOST HER.

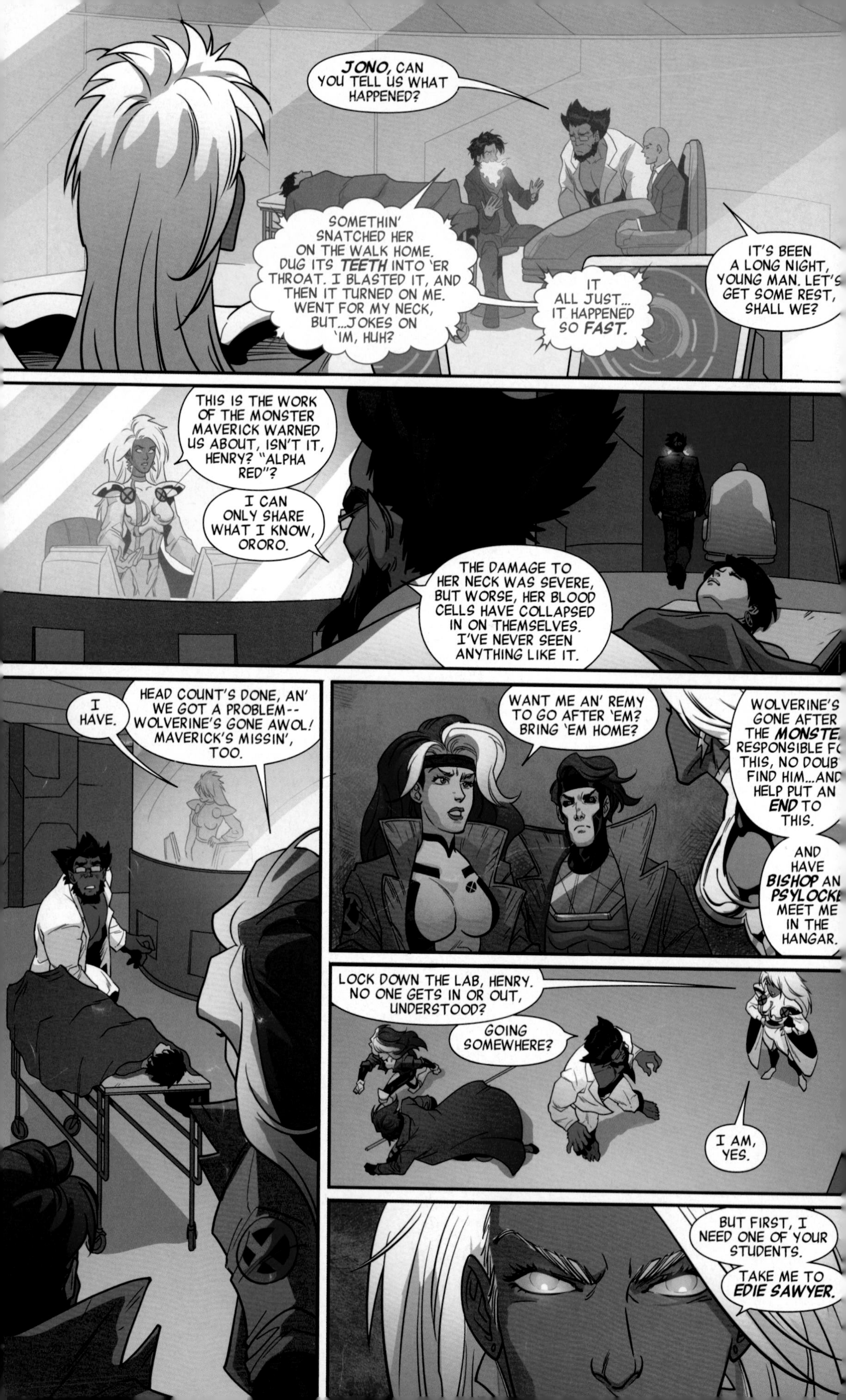

JONO, CAN YOU TELL US WHAT HAPPENED?
SOMETHIN' SNATCHED HER ON THE WALK HOME. DUG ITS TEETH INTO 'ER THROAT. I BLASTED IT, AND THEN IT TURNED ON ME. WENT FOR MY NECK, BUT...JOKES ON 'IM, HUH?
IT ALL JUST... IT HAPPENED SO FAST.
IT'S BEEN A LONG NIGHT, YOUNG MAN. LET'S GET SOME REST, SHALL WE?
THIS IS THE WORK OF THE MONSTER MAVERICK WARNED US ABOUT, ISN'T IT, HENRY? "ALPHA RED"?
I CAN ONLY SHARE WHAT I KNOW, ORORO.
THE DAMAGE TO HER NECK WAS SEVERE, BUT WORSE, HER BLOOD CELLS HAVE COLLAPSED IN ON THEMSELVES. I'VE NEVER SEEN ANYTHING LIKE IT.
HEAD COUNT'S DONE, AN' WE GOT A PROBLEM-- WOLVERINE'S GONE AWOL! MAVERICK'S MISSIN', TOO.
I HAVE.
WANT ME AN' REMY TO GO AFTER 'EM? BRING 'EM HOME?
WOLVERINE'S GONE AFTER THE MONSTE RESPONSIBLE FO THIS, NO DOUB FIND HIM...AND HELP PUT AN END TO THIS.
AND HAVE BISHOP AN PSYLOCKE MEET ME IN THE HANGAR.
LOCK DOWN THE LAB, HENRY. NO ONE GETS IN OR OUT, UNDERSTOOD?
GOING SOMEWHERE?
I AM, YES.
BUT FIRST, I NEED ONE OF YOUR STUDENTS.
TAKE ME TO EDIE SAWYER.

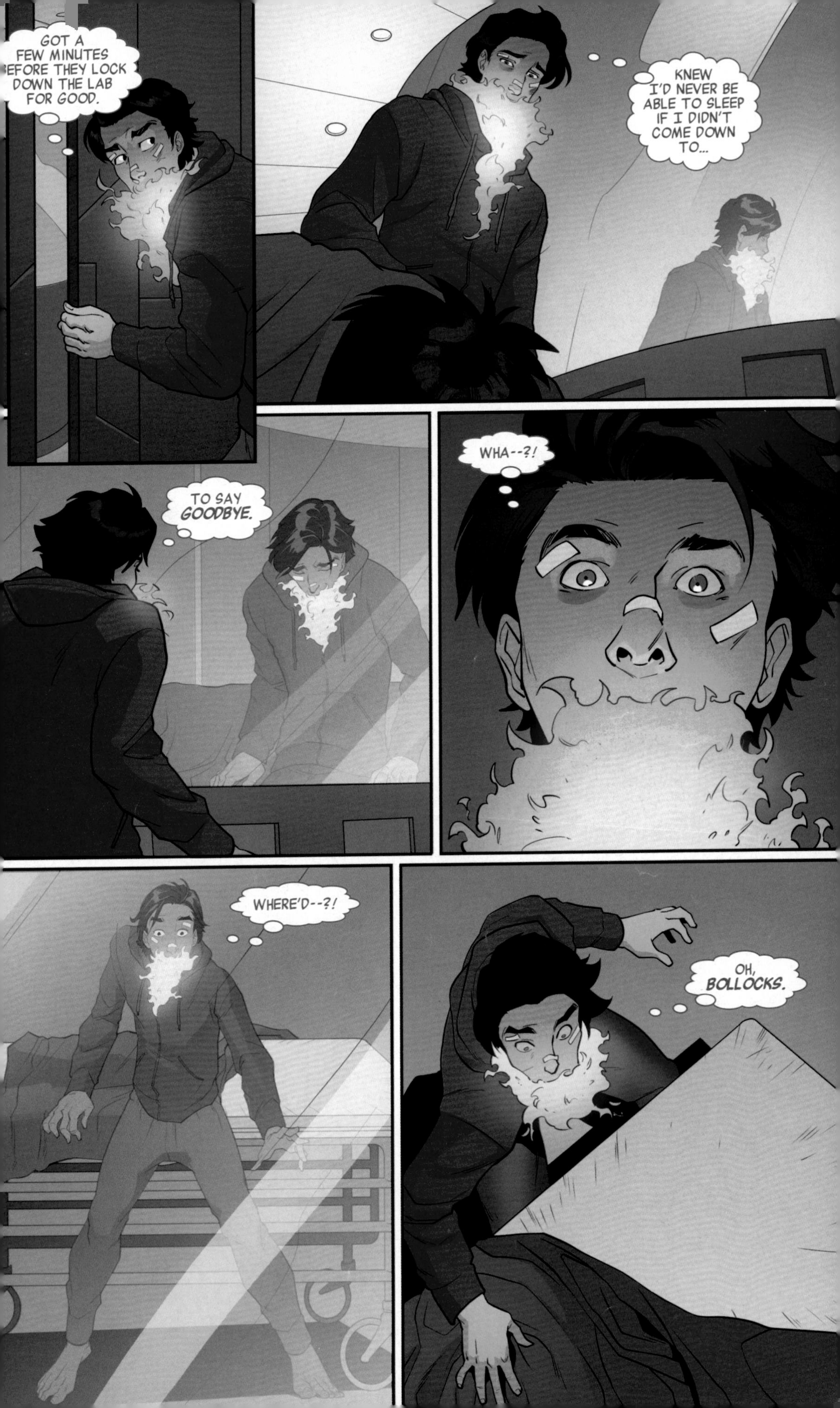
GOT A FEW MINUTES BEFORE THEY LOCK DOWN THE LAB FOR GOOD.
KNEW I'D NEVER BE ABLE TO SLEEP IF I DIDN'T COME DOWN TO...
TO SAY GOODBYE.
WHA--?!
WHERE'D--?!
OH, BOLLOCKS.

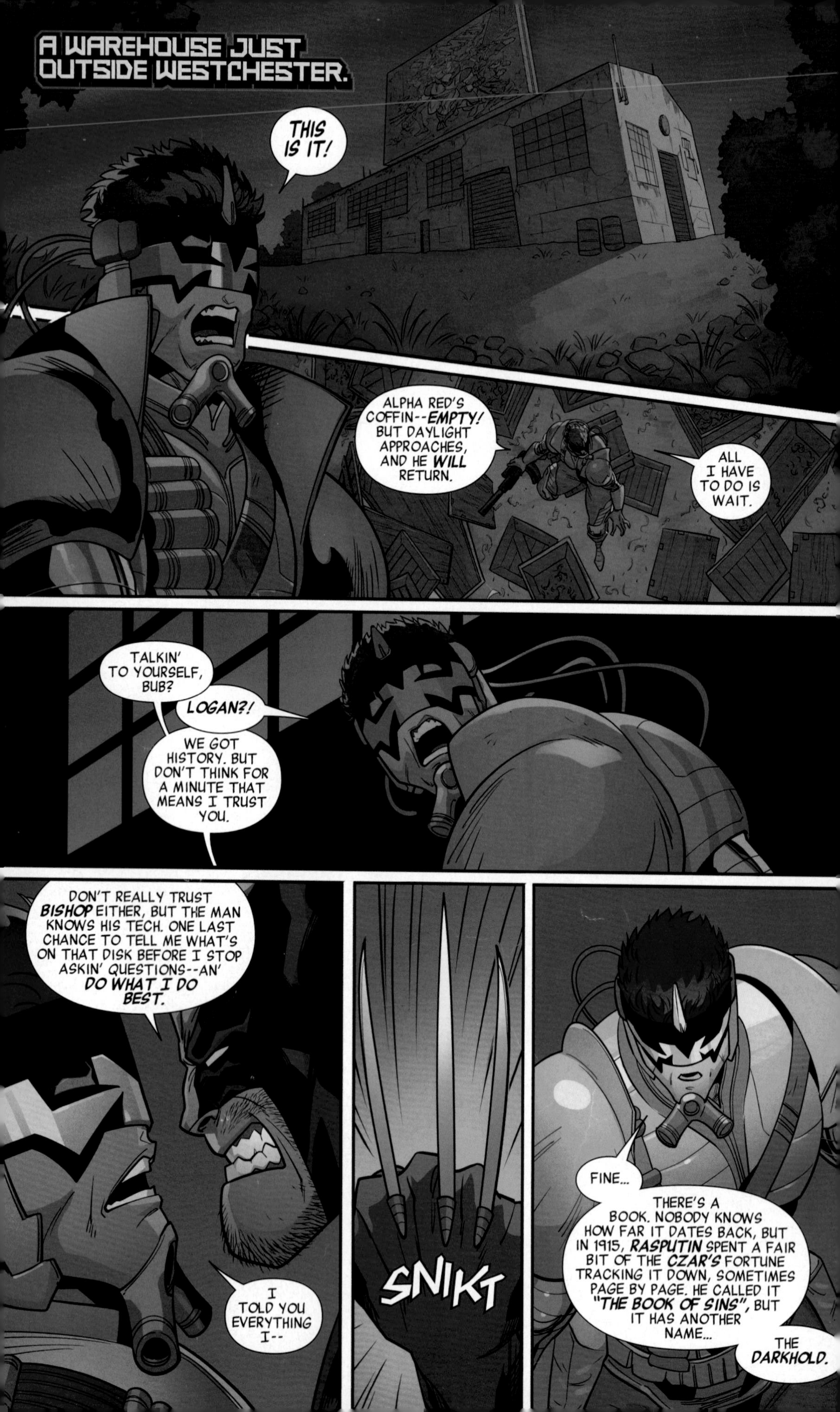
A WAREHOUSE JUST OUTSIDE WESTCHESTER.
THIS IS IT!
ALPHA RED'S COFFIN--EMPTY! BUT DAYLIGHT APPROACHES, AND HE WILL RETURN.
ALL I HAVE TO DO IS WAIT.
TALKIN' TO YOURSELF, BUB?
LOGAN?!
WE GOT HISTORY. BUT DON'T THINK FOR A MINUTE THAT MEANS I TRUST YOU.
DON'T REALLY TRUST BISHOP EITHER, BUT THE MAN KNOWS HIS TECH. ONE LAST CHANCE TO TELL ME WHAT'S ON THAT DISK BEFORE I STOP ASKIN' QUESTIONS--AN' DO WHAT I DO BEST.
I TOLD YOU EVERYTHING I--
SNIKT
FINE...
THERE'S A BOOK. NOBODY KNOWS HOW FAR IT DATES BACK, BUT IN 1915, RASPUTIN SPENT A FAIR BIT OF THE CZAR'S FORTUNE TRACKING IT DOWN, SOMETIMES PAGE BY PAGE. HE CALLED IT "THE BOOK OF SINS", BUT IT HAS ANOTHER NAME...
THE DARKHOLD.

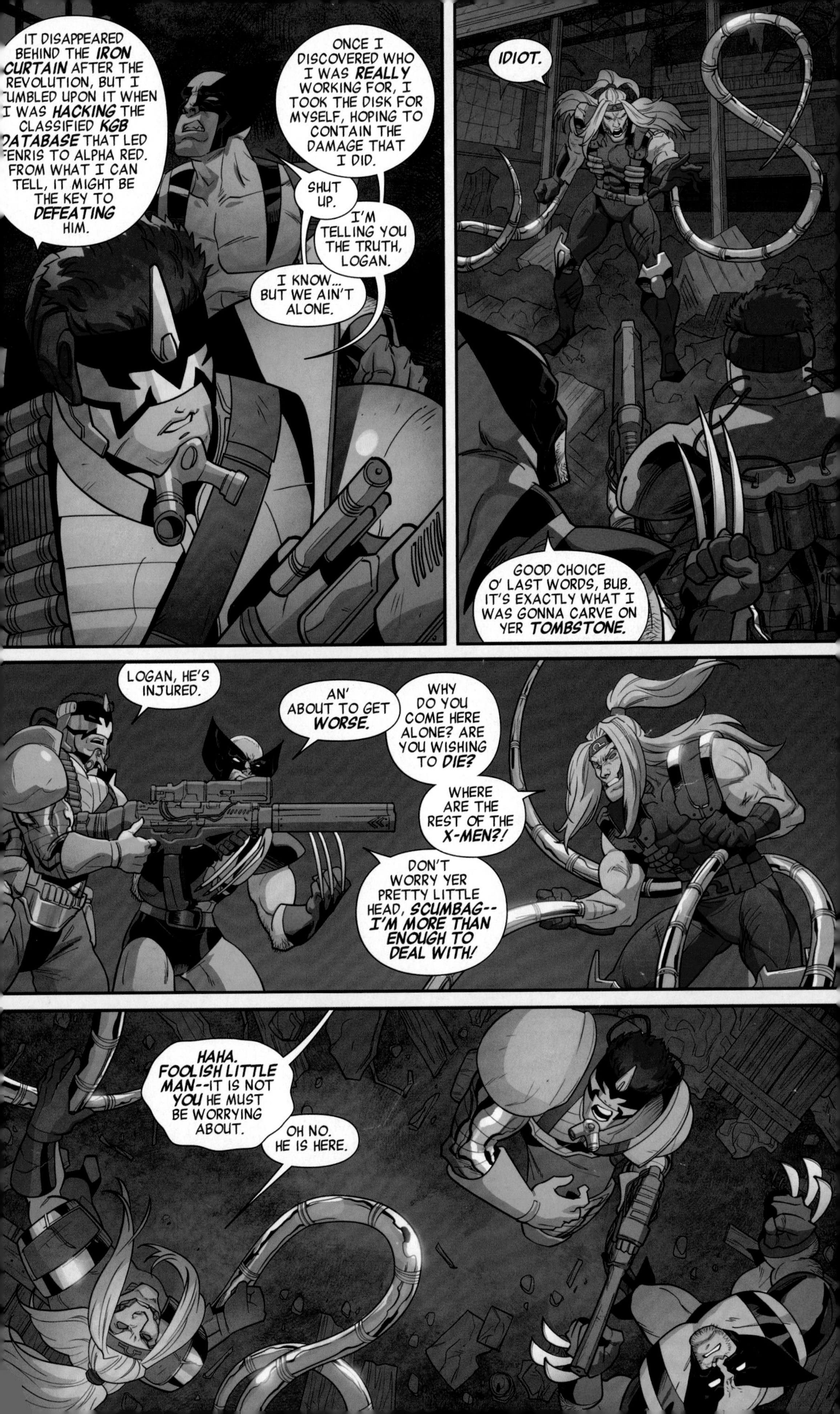

IT DISAPPEARED BEHIND THE IRON CURTAIN AFTER THE REVOLUTION, BUT I STUMBLED UPON IT WHEN I WAS HACKING THE CLASSIFIED KGB DATABASE THAT LED FENRIS TO ALPHA RED. FROM WHAT I CAN TELL, IT MIGHT BE THE KEY TO DEFEATING HIM.
ONCE I DISCOVERED WHO I WAS REALLY WORKING FOR, I TOOK THE DISK FOR MYSELF, HOPING TO CONTAIN THE DAMAGE THAT I DID.
SHUT UP.
I'M TELLING YOU THE TRUTH, LOGAN.
I KNOW... BUT WE AIN'T ALONE.
IDIOT.
GOOD CHOICE O' LAST WORDS, BUB. IT'S EXACTLY WHAT I WAS GONNA CARVE ON YER TOMBSTONE.
LOGAN, HE'S INJURED.
AN' ABOUT TO GET WORSE.
WHY DO YOU COME HERE ALONE? ARE YOU WISHING TO DIE?
WHERE ARE THE REST OF THE X-MEN?!
DON'T WORRY YER PRETTY LITTLE HEAD, SCUMBAG-- I'M MORE THAN ENOUGH TO DEAL WITH!
HAHA. FOOLISH LITTLE MAN--IT IS NOT YOU HE MUST BE WORRYING ABOUT.
OH NO. HE IS HERE.

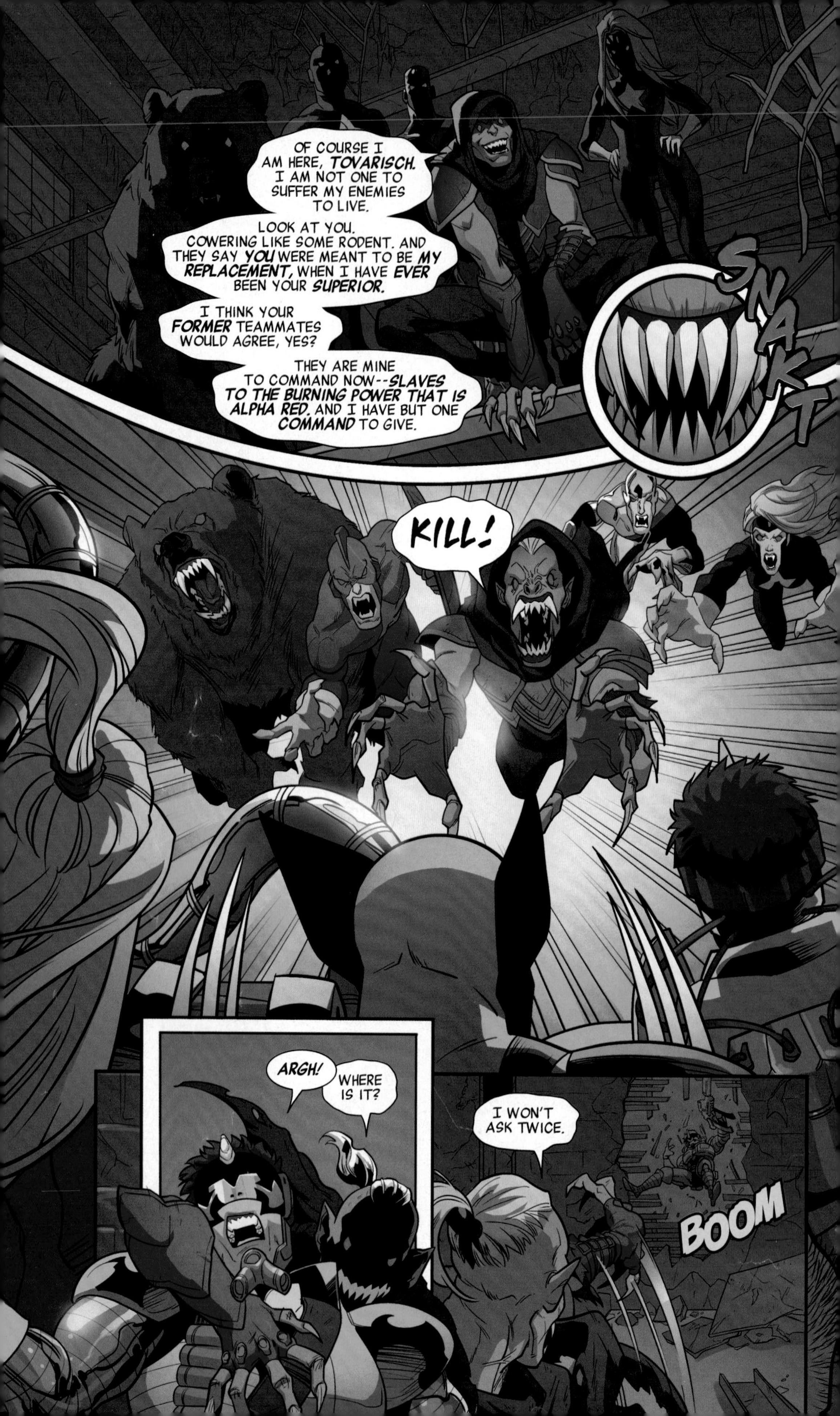
OF COURSE I AM HERE, TOVARISCH. I AM NOT ONE TO SUFFER MY ENEMIES TO LIVE.
LOOK AT YOU. COWERING LIKE SOME RODENT. AND THEY SAY YOU WERE MEANT TO BE MY REPLACEMENT, WHEN I HAVE EVER BEEN YOUR SUPERIOR.
I THINK YOUR FORMER TEAMMATES WOULD AGREE, YES?
THEY ARE MINE TO COMMAND NOW--SLAVES TO THE BURNING POWER THAT IS ALPHA RED. AND I HAVE BUT ONE COMMAND TO GIVE.
SNAKT
KILL!
ARGH!
WHERE IS IT?
I WON'T ASK TWICE.
BOOM

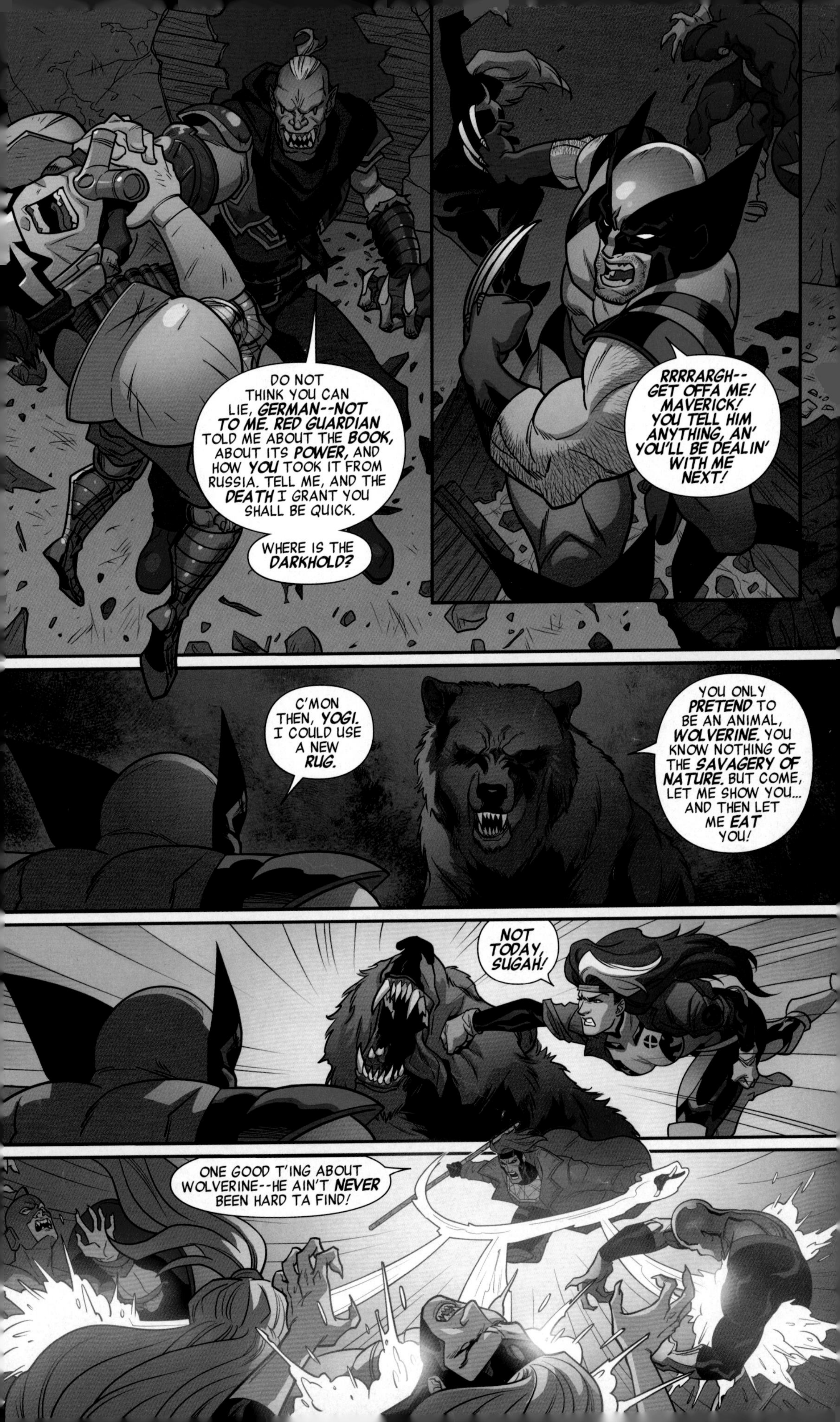
DO NOT THINK YOU CAN LIE, GERMAN--NOT TO ME. RED GUARDIAN TOLD ME ABOUT THE BOOK, ABOUT ITS POWER, AND HOW YOU TOOK IT FROM RUSSIA. TELL ME, AND THE DEATH I GRANT YOU SHALL BE QUICK.
WHERE IS THE DARKHOLD?
RRRRARGH--GET OFFA ME! MAVERICK! YOU TELL HIM ANYTHING, AN' YOU'LL BE DEALIN' WITH ME NEXT!
C'MON THEN, YOGI. I COULD USE A NEW RUG.
YOU ONLY PRETEND TO BE AN ANIMAL, WOLVERINE. YOU KNOW NOTHING OF THE SAVAGERY OF NATURE. BUT COME, LET ME SHOW YOU... AND THEN LET ME EAT YOU!
NOT TODAY, SUGAH!
ONE GOOD T'ING ABOUT WOLVERINE--HE AIN'T NEVER BEEN HARD TA FIND!

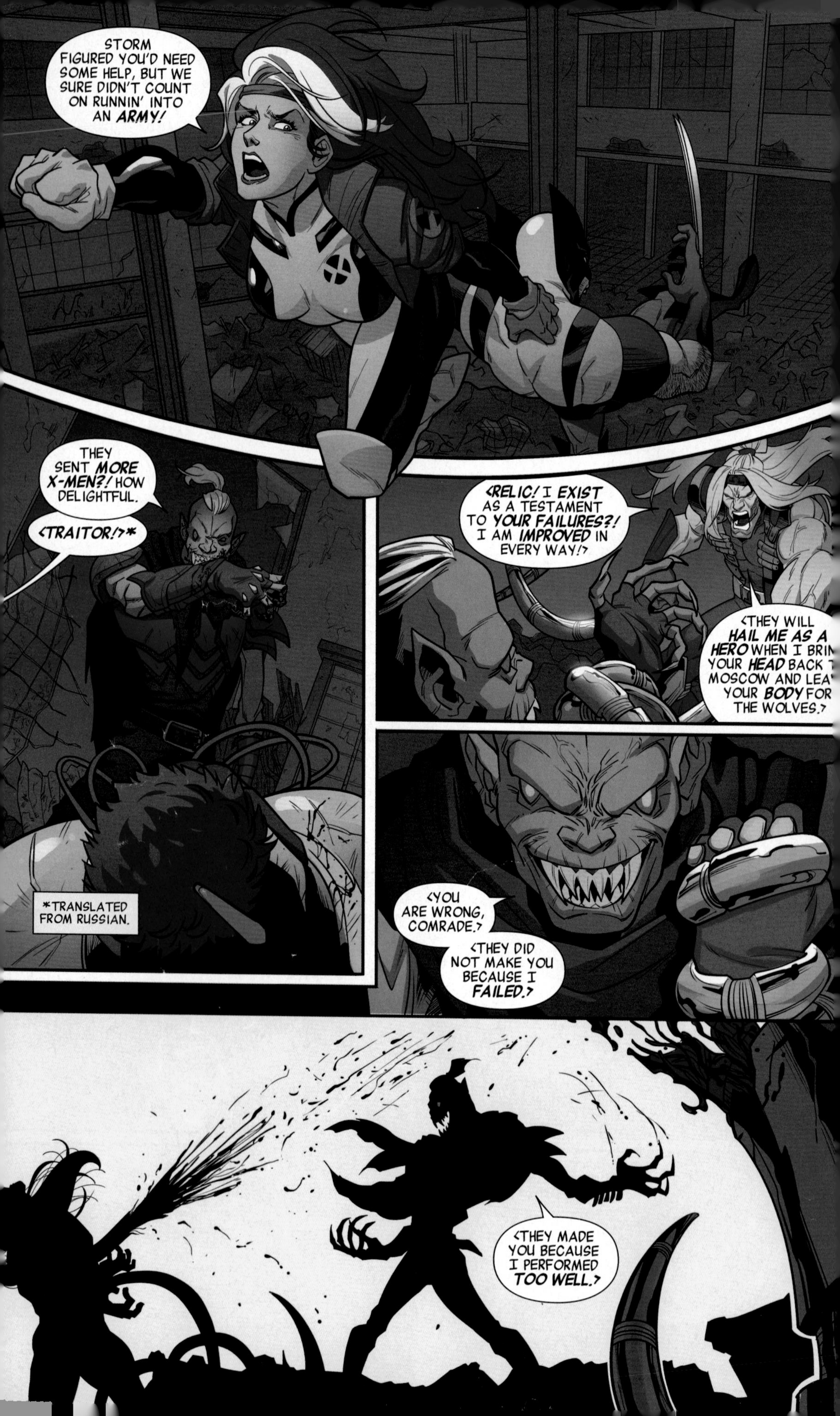
STORM FIGURED YOU'D NEED SOME HELP, BUT WE SURE DIDN'T COUNT ON RUNNIN' INTO AN ARMY!
THEY SENT MORE X-MEN?! HOW DELIGHTFUL.
<TRAITOR!>*
*TRANSLATED FROM RUSSIAN.
<RELIC! I EXIST AS A TESTAMENT TO YOUR FAILURES?! I AM IMPROVED IN EVERY WAY!>
<YOU ARE WRONG, COMRADE.>
<THEY DID NOT MAKE YOU BECAUSE I FAILED.>
<THEY MADE YOU BECAUSE I PERFORMED TOO WELL.>

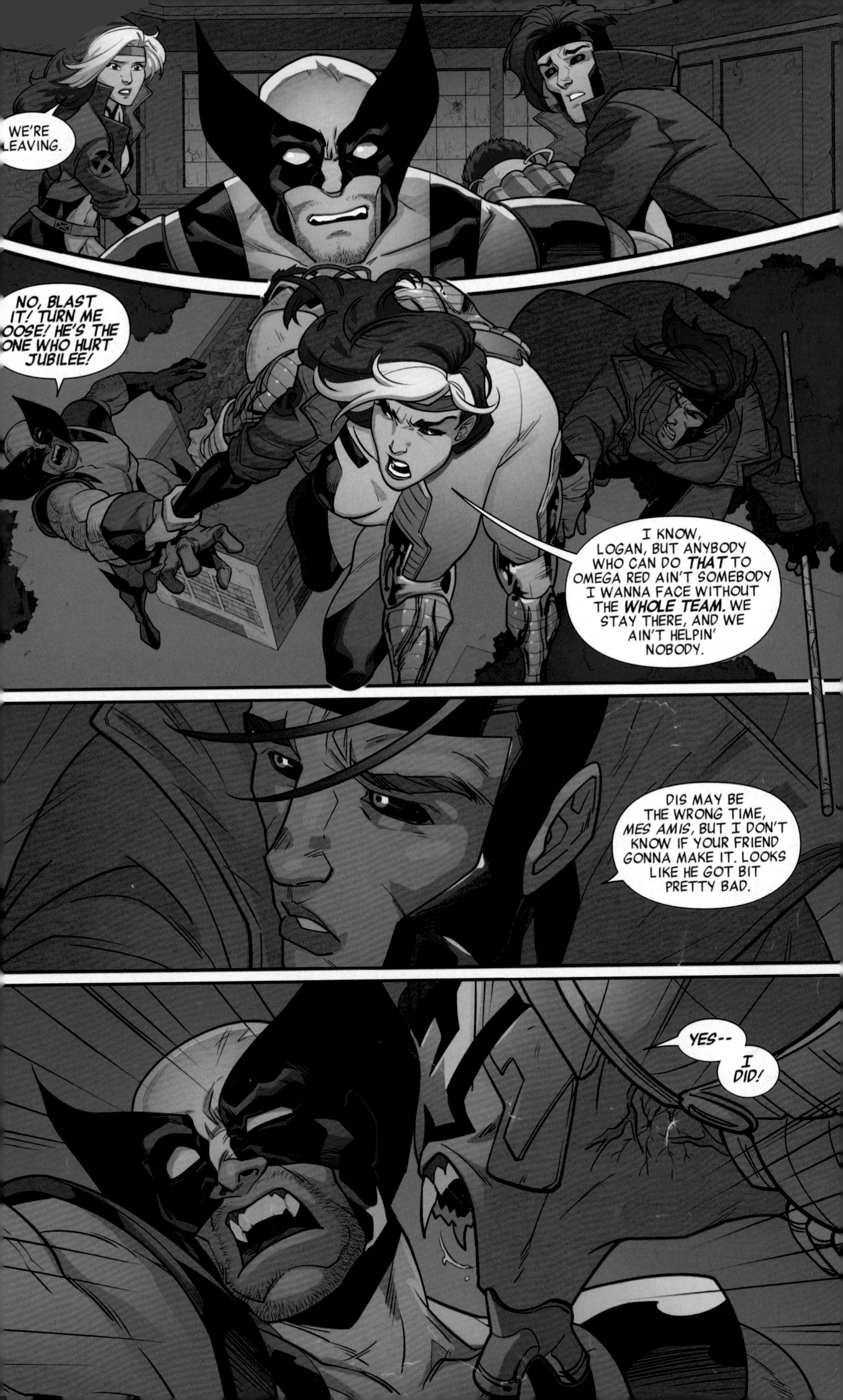
WE'RE LEAVING.
NO, BLAST IT! TURN ME LOOSE! HE'S THE ONE WHO HURT JUBILEE!
I KNOW, LOGAN, BUT ANYBODY WHO CAN DO THAT TO OMEGA RED AIN'T SOMEBODY I WANNA FACE WITHOUT THE WHOLE TEAM. WE STAY THERE, AND WE AIN'T HELPIN' NOBODY.
DIS MAY BE THE WRONG TIME, MES AMIS, BUT I DON'T KNOW IF YOUR FRIEND GONNA MAKE IT. LOOKS LIKE HE GOT BIT PRETTY BAD.
YES-- I DID!

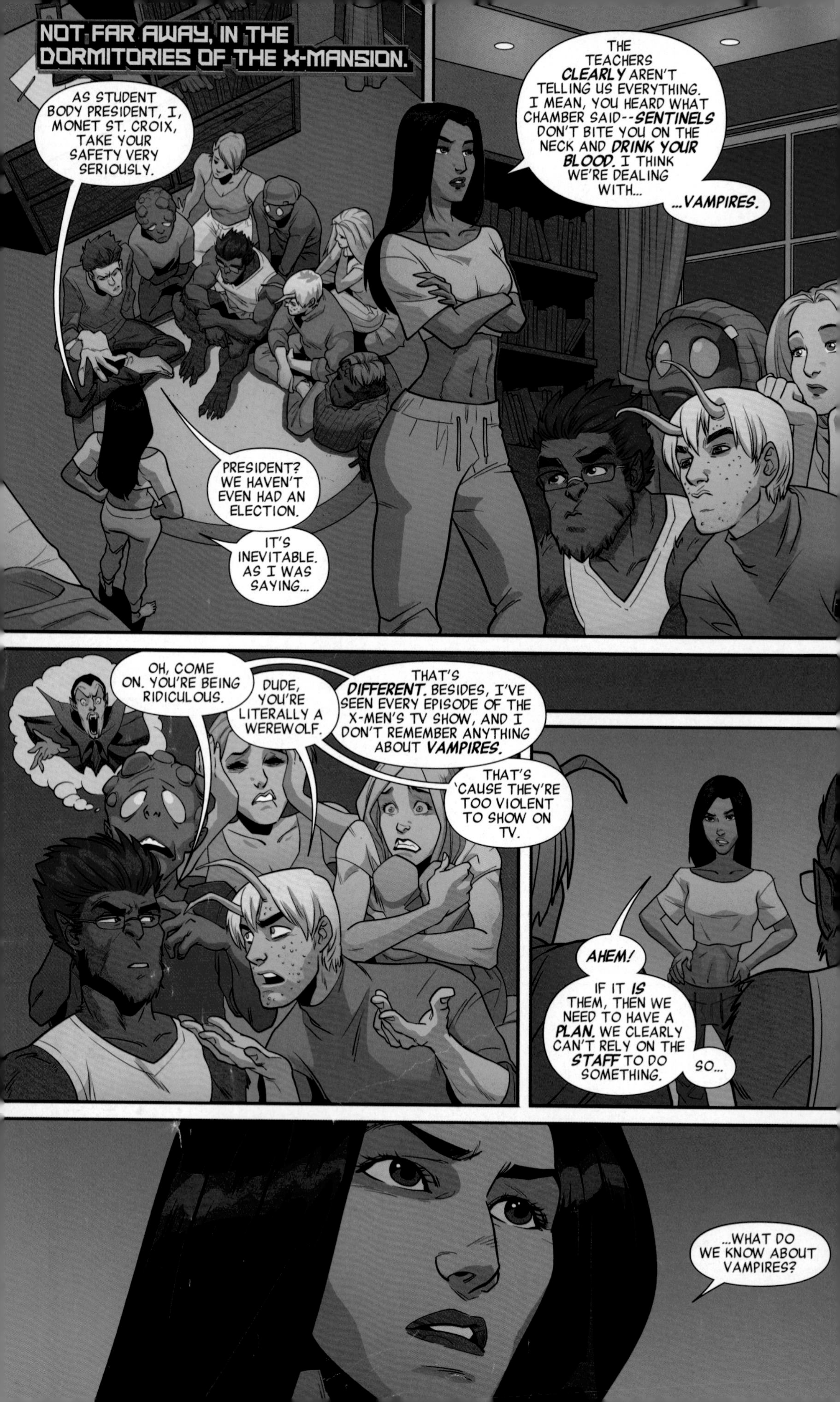

NOT FAR AWAY, IN THE DORMITORIES OF THE X-MANSION.
AS STUDENT BODY PRESIDENT, I, MONET ST. CROIX, TAKE YOUR SAFETY VERY SERIOUSLY.
PRESIDENT? WE HAVEN'T EVEN HAD AN ELECTION.
IT'S INEVITABLE. AS I WAS SAYING...
THE TEACHERS CLEARLY AREN'T TELLING US EVERYTHING. I MEAN, YOU HEARD WHAT CHAMBER SAID--SENTINELS DON'T BITE YOU ON THE NECK AND DRINK YOUR BLOOD. I THINK WE'RE DEALING WITH...
...VAMPIRES.
OH, COME ON. YOU'RE BEING RIDICULOUS.
DUDE, YOU'RE LITERALLY A WEREWOLF.
THAT'S DIFFERENT. BESIDES, I'VE SEEN EVERY EPISODE OF THE X-MEN'S TV SHOW, AND I DON'T REMEMBER ANYTHING ABOUT VAMPIRES.
THAT'S 'CAUSE THEY'RE TOO VIOLENT TO SHOW ON TV.
AHEM!
IF IT IS THEM, THEN WE NEED TO HAVE A PLAN. WE CLEARLY CAN'T RELY ON THE STAFF TO DO SOMETHING.
SO...
...WHAT DO WE KNOW ABOUT VAMPIRES?

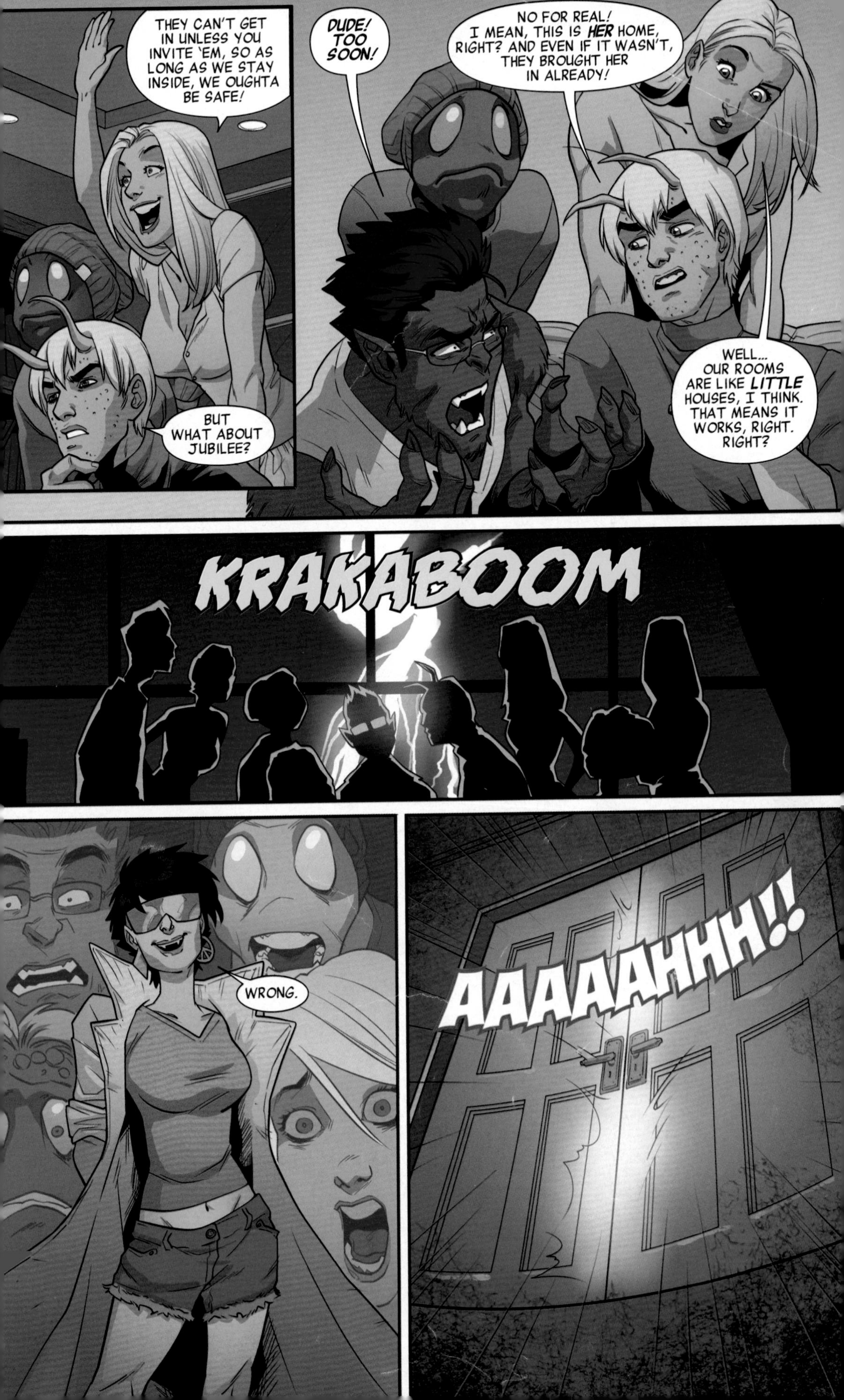
THEY CAN'T GET IN UNLESS YOU INVITE 'EM, SO AS LONG AS WE STAY INSIDE, WE OUGHTA BE SAFE!
BUT WHAT ABOUT JUBILEE?
DUDE! TOO SOON!
NO FOR REAL! I MEAN, THIS IS HER HOME, RIGHT? AND EVEN IF IT WASN'T, THEY BROUGHT HER IN ALREADY!
WELL... OUR ROOMS ARE LIKE LITTLE HOUSES, I THINK. THAT MEANS IT WORKS, RIGHT. RIGHT?
KRAKABOOM
WRONG.
AAAAAHHH!!

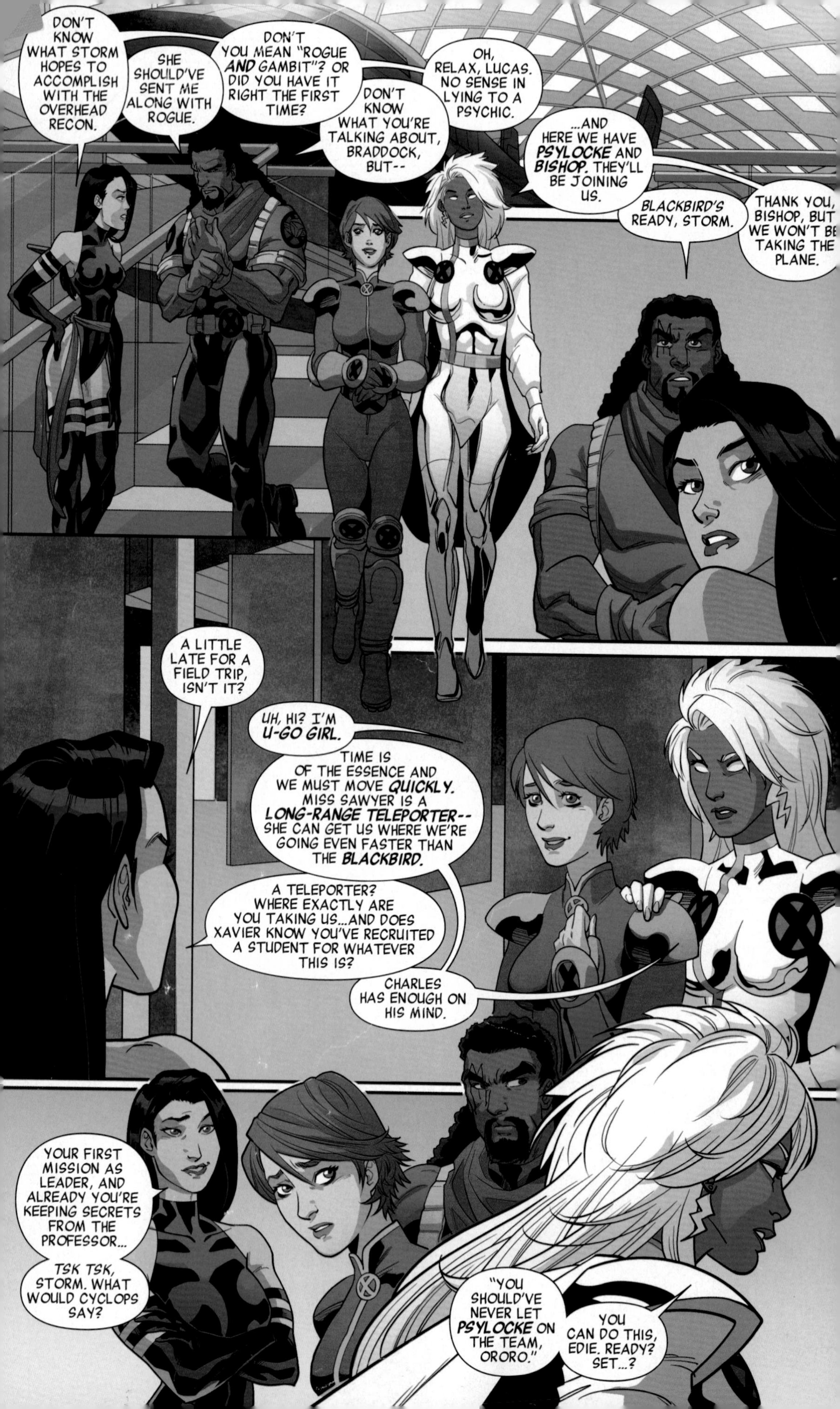
DON'T KNOW WHAT STORM HOPES TO ACCOMPLISH WITH THE OVERHEAD RECON.
SHE SHOULD'VE SENT ME ALONG WITH ROGUE.
DON'T YOU MEAN "ROGUE AND GAMBIT"? OR DID YOU HAVE IT RIGHT THE FIRST TIME?
DON'T KNOW WHAT YOU'RE TALKING ABOUT, BRADDOCK, BUT--
OH, RELAX, LUCAS. NO SENSE IN LYING TO A PSYCHIC.
...AND HERE WE HAVE PSYLOCKE AND BISHOP. THEY'LL BE JOINING US.
BLACKBIRD'S READY, STORM.
THANK YOU, BISHOP, BUT WE WON'T BE TAKING THE PLANE.
A LITTLE LATE FOR A FIELD TRIP, ISN'T IT?
UH, HI? I'M U-GO GIRL.
TIME IS OF THE ESSENCE AND WE MUST MOVE QUICKLY. MISS SAWYER IS A LONG-RANGE TELEPORTER-- SHE CAN GET US WHERE WE'RE GOING EVEN FASTER THAN THE BLACKBIRD.
A TELEPORTER? WHERE EXACTLY ARE YOU TAKING US...AND DOES XAVIER KNOW YOU'VE RECRUITED A STUDENT FOR WHATEVER THIS IS?
CHARLES HAS ENOUGH ON HIS MIND.
YOUR FIRST MISSION AS LEADER, AND ALREADY YOU'RE KEEPING SECRETS FROM THE PROFESSOR...
TSK TSK, STORM. WHAT WOULD CYCLOPS SAY?
"YOU SHOULD'VE NEVER LET PSYLOCKE ON THE TEAM, ORORO."
YOU CAN DO THIS, EDIE. READY? SET...?

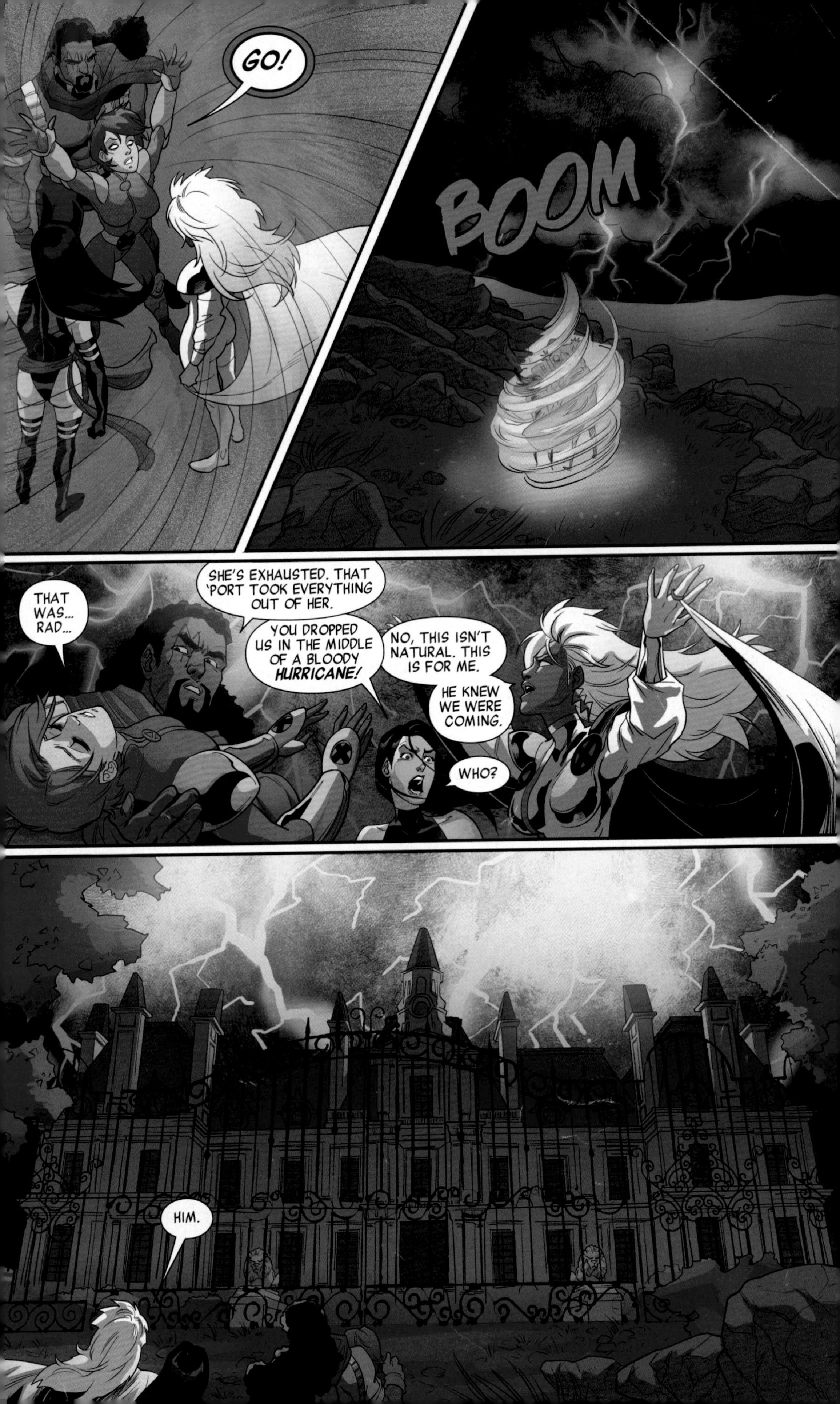
GO!
BOOM
THAT WAS... RAD...
SHE'S EXHAUSTED. THAT 'PORT TOOK EVERYTHING OUT OF HER.
YOU DROPPED US IN THE MIDDLE OF A BLOODY HURRICANE!
NO, THIS ISN'T NATURAL. THIS IS FOR ME.
HE KNEW WE WERE COMING.
WHO?
HIM.

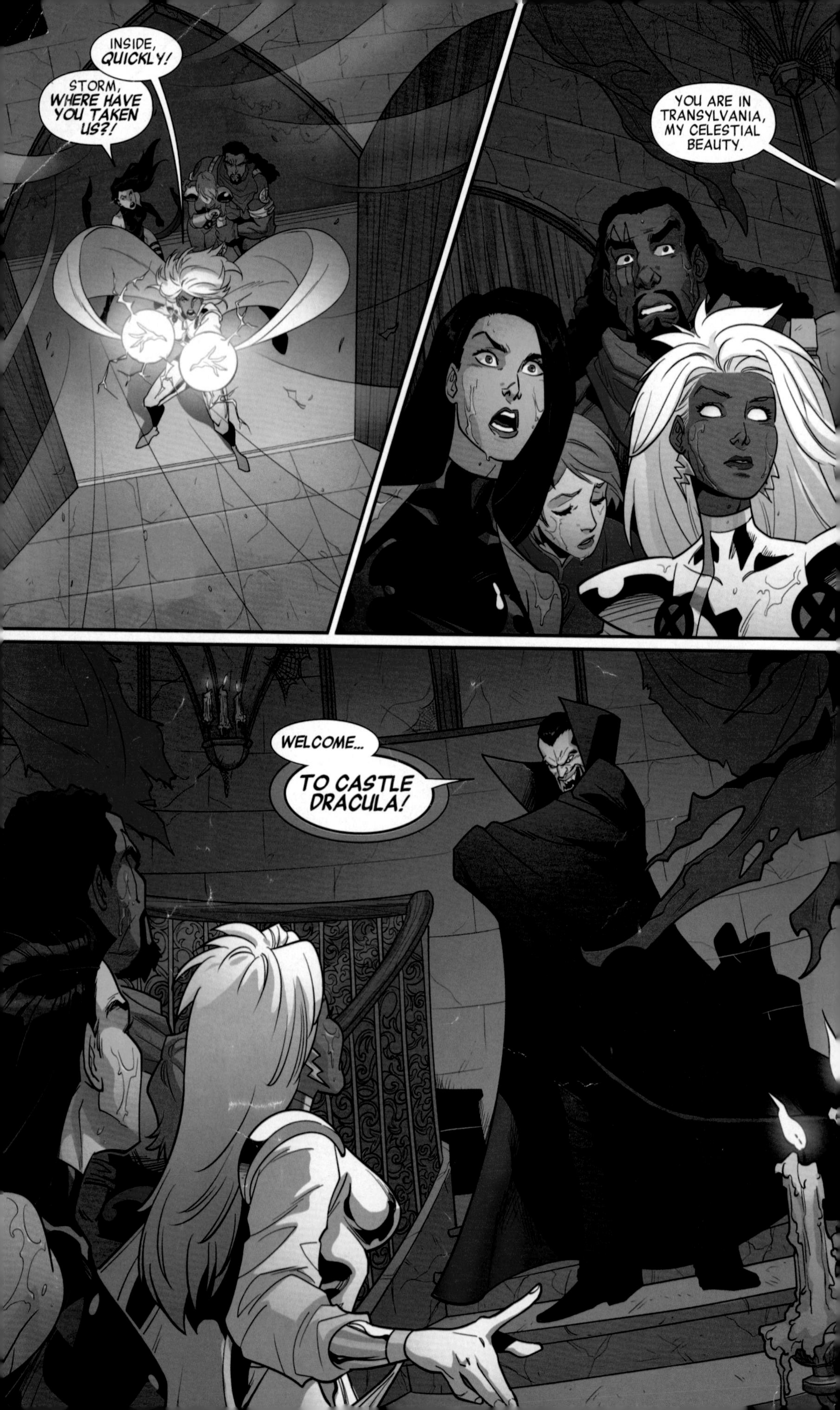
INSIDE, QUICKLY!
STORM, WHERE HAVE YOU TAKEN US?!
YOU ARE IN TRANSYLVANIA, MY CELESTIAL BEAUTY.
WELCOME...
TO CASTLE DRACULA!

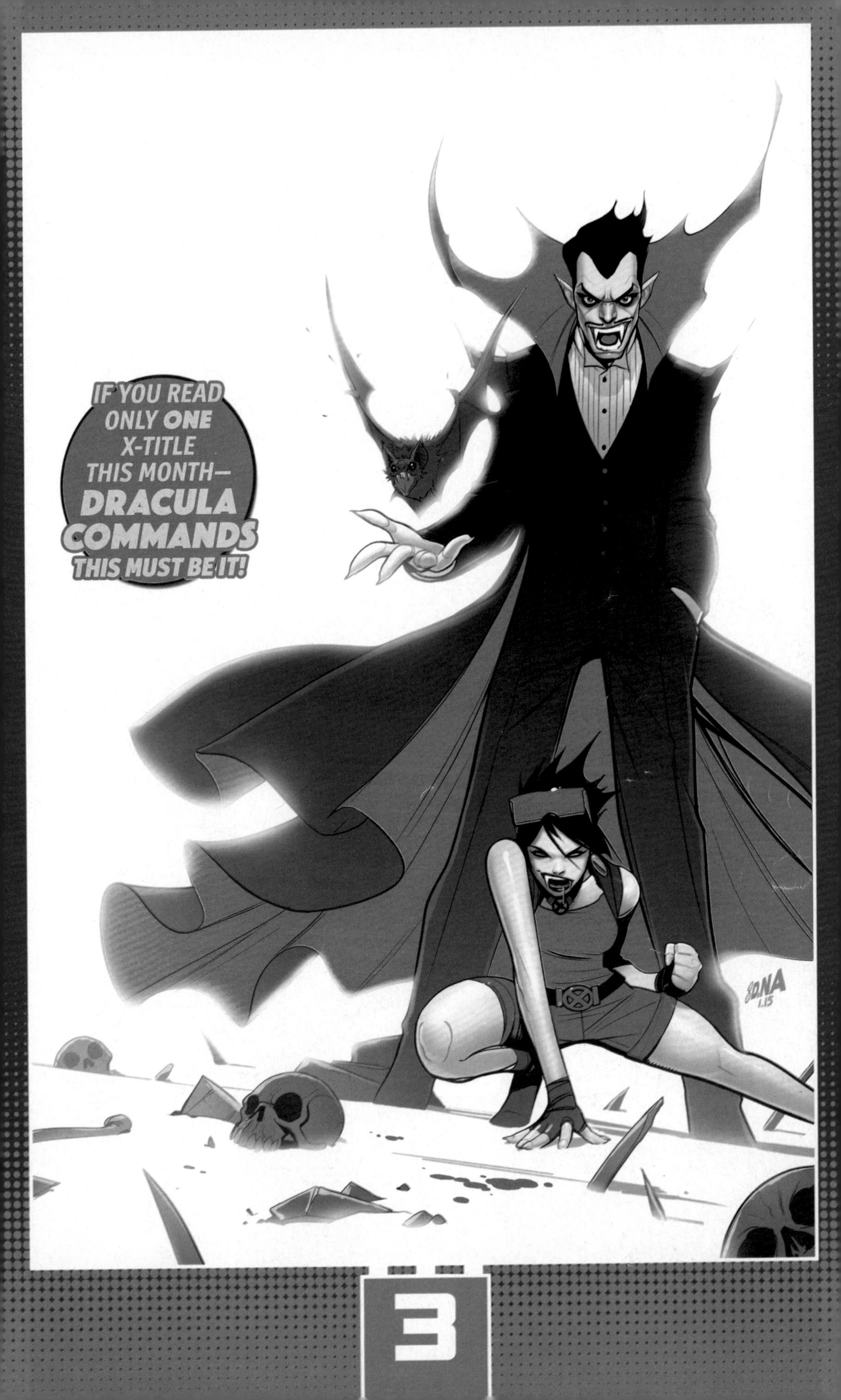
IF YOU READ ONLY ONE X-TITLE THIS MONTH—DRACULA COMMANDS THIS MUST BE IT!
3

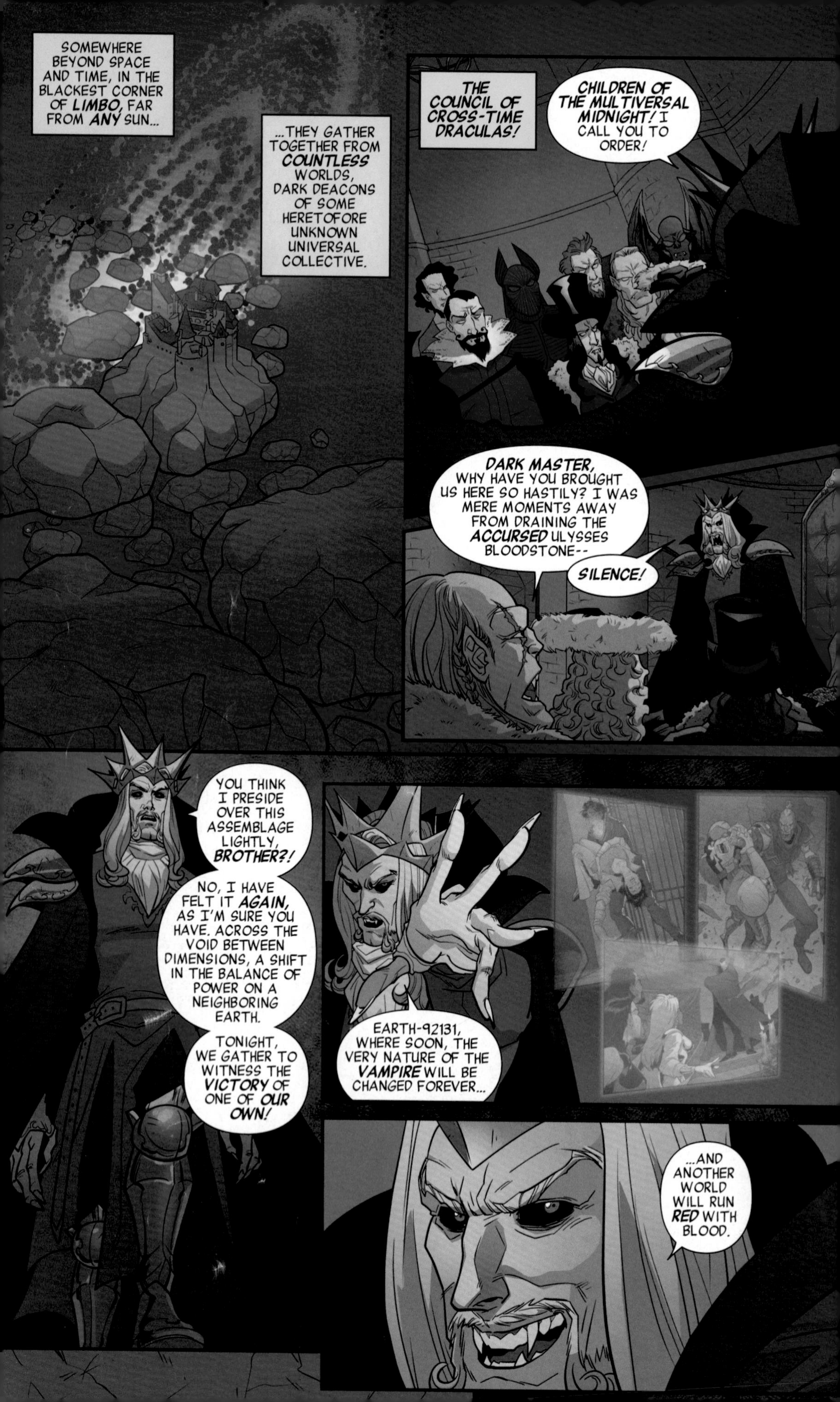

SOMEWHERE BEYOND SPACE AND TIME, IN THE BLACKEST CORNER OF LIMBO, FAR FROM ANY SUN...
...THEY GATHER TOGETHER FROM COUNTLESS WORLDS, DARK DEACONS OF SOME HERETOFORE UNKNOWN UNIVERSAL COLLECTIVE.
THE COUNCIL OF CROSS-TIME DRACULAS!
CHILDREN OF THE MULTIVERSAL MIDNIGHT! I CALL YOU TO ORDER!
DARK MASTER, WHY HAVE YOU BROUGHT US HERE SO HASTILY? I WAS MERE MOMENTS AWAY FROM DRAINING THE ACCURSED ULYSSES BLOODSTONE--
SILENCE!
YOU THINK I PRESIDE OVER THIS ASSEMBLAGE LIGHTLY, BROTHER?!
NO, I HAVE FELT IT AGAIN, AS I'M SURE YOU HAVE. ACROSS THE VOID BETWEEN DIMENSIONS, A SHIFT IN THE BALANCE OF POWER ON A NEIGHBORING EARTH.
TONIGHT, WE GATHER TO WITNESS THE VICTORY OF ONE OF OUR OWN!
EARTH-92131, WHERE SOON, THE VERY NATURE OF THE VAMPIRE WILL BE CHANGED FOREVER...
...AND ANOTHER WORLD WILL RUN RED WITH BLOOD.

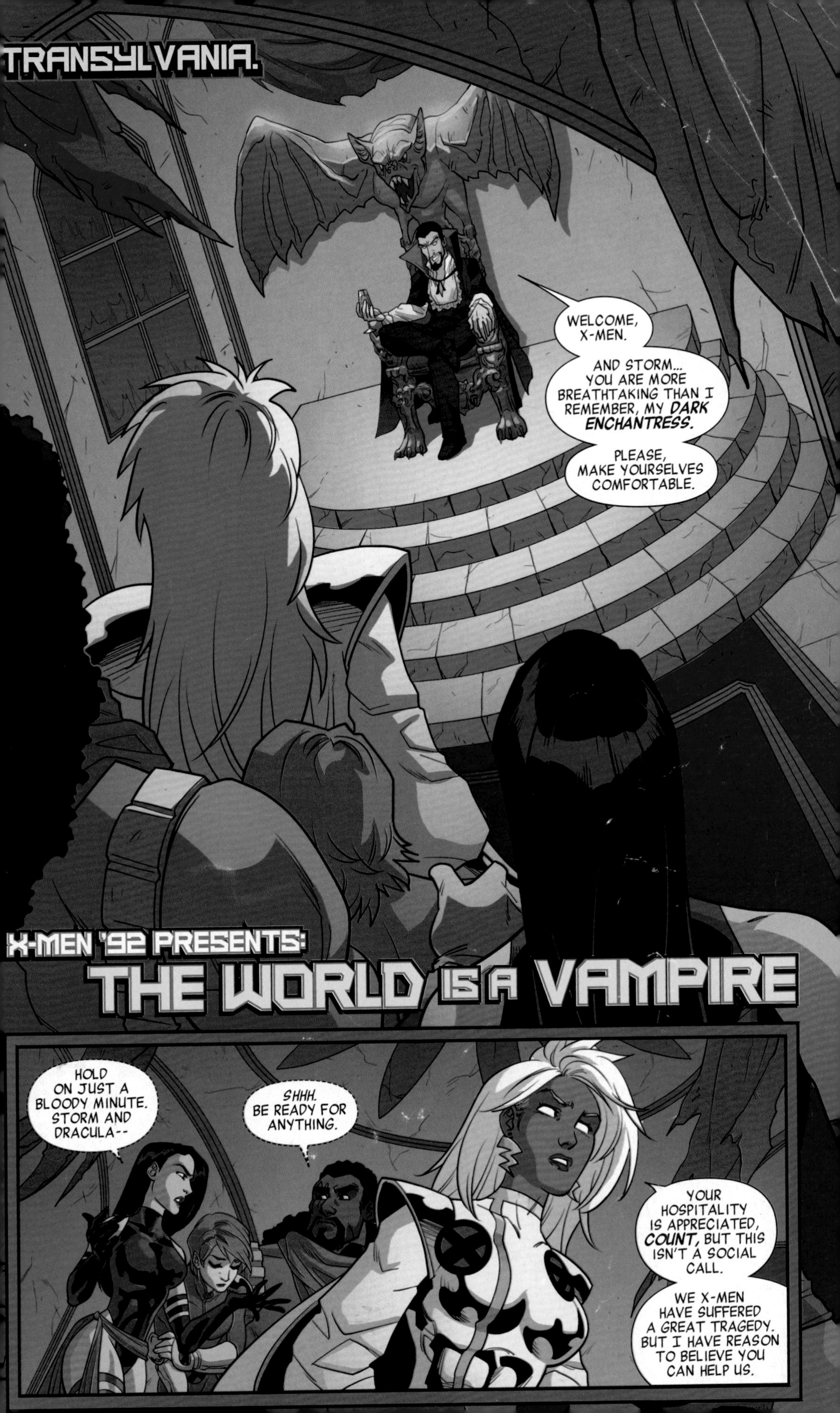

TRANSYLVANIA.
WELCOME, X-MEN.
AND STORM... YOU ARE MORE BREATHTAKING THAN I REMEMBER, MY DARK ENCHANTRESS.
PLEASE, MAKE YOURSELVES COMFORTABLE.
X-MEN '92 PRESENTS:
THE WORLD IS A VAMPIRE
HOLD ON JUST A BLOODY MINUTE. STORM AND DRACULA--
SHHH. BE READY FOR ANYTHING.
YOUR HOSPITALITY IS APPRECIATED, COUNT, BUT THIS ISN'T A SOCIAL CALL.
WE X-MEN HAVE SUFFERED A GREAT TRAGEDY. BUT I HAVE REASON TO BELIEVE YOU CAN HELP US.

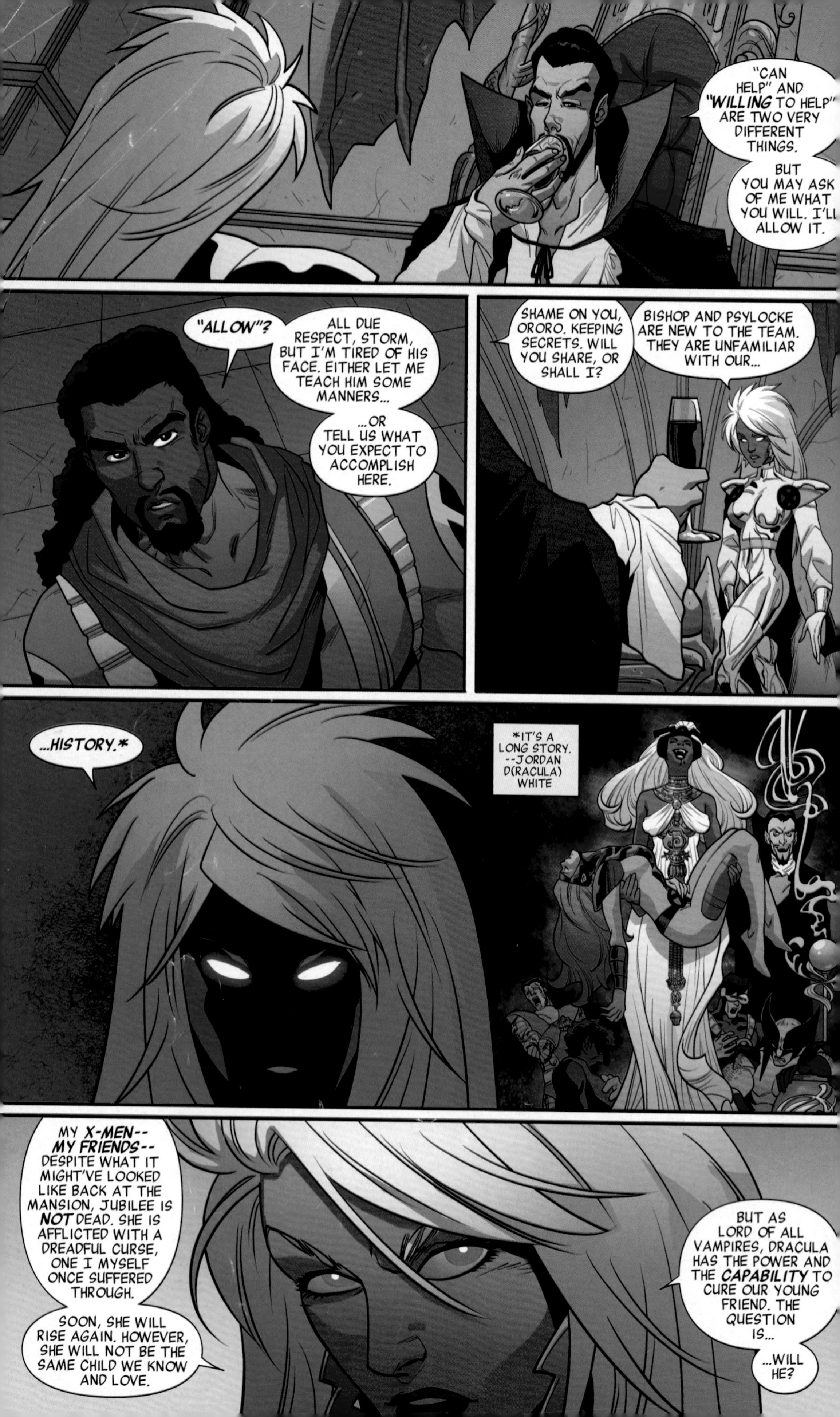
"CAN HELP" AND "WILLING TO HELP" ARE TWO VERY DIFFERENT THINGS.
BUT YOU MAY ASK OF ME WHAT YOU WILL. I'LL ALLOW IT.
"ALLOW"?
ALL DUE RESPECT, STORM, BUT I'M TIRED OF HIS FACE. EITHER LET ME TEACH HIM SOME MANNERS...
...OR TELL US WHAT YOU EXPECT TO ACCOMPLISH HERE.
SHAME ON YOU, ORORO. KEEPING SECRETS. WILL YOU SHARE, OR SHALL I?
BISHOP AND PSYLOCKE ARE NEW TO THE TEAM. THEY ARE UNFAMILIAR WITH OUR...
...HISTORY.*
*IT'S A LONG STORY. --JORDAN D(RACULA) WHITE
MY X-MEN-- MY FRIENDS-- DESPITE WHAT IT MIGHT'VE LOOKED LIKE BACK AT THE MANSION, JUBILEE IS NOT DEAD. SHE IS AFFLICTED WITH A DREADFUL CURSE, ONE I MYSELF ONCE SUFFERED THROUGH.
SOON, SHE WILL RISE AGAIN. HOWEVER, SHE WILL NOT BE THE SAME CHILD WE KNOW AND LOVE.
BUT AS LORD OF ALL VAMPIRES, DRACULA HAS THE POWER AND THE CAPABILITY TO CURE OUR YOUNG FRIEND. THE QUESTION IS...
...WILL HE?

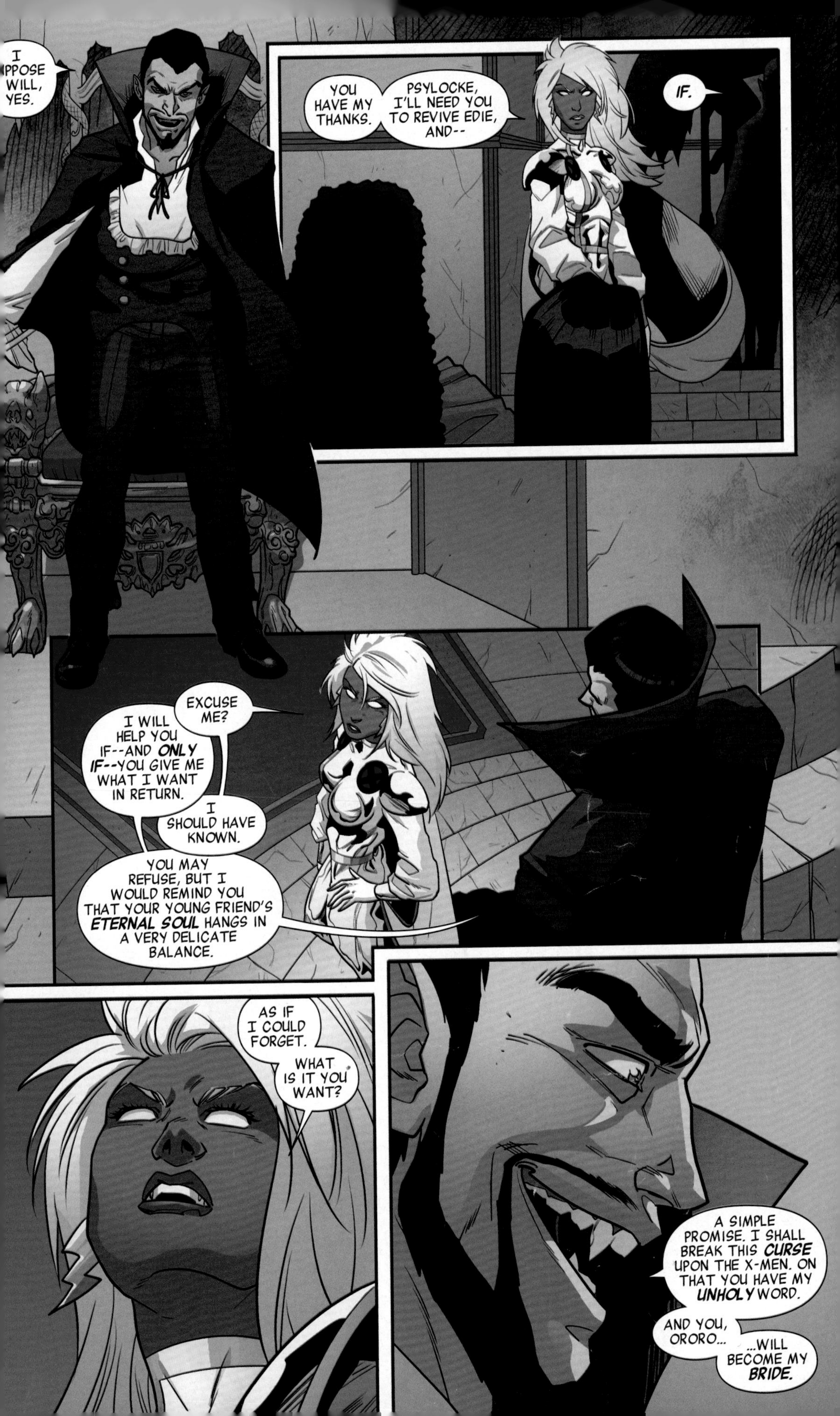
I
PPOSE
WILL,
YES.
YOU HAVE MY THANKS.
PSYLOCKE, I'LL NEED YOU TO REVIVE EDIE, AND--
IF.
I WILL HELP YOU IF--AND ONLY IF--YOU GIVE ME WHAT I WANT IN RETURN.
EXCUSE ME?
I SHOULD HAVE KNOWN.
YOU MAY REFUSE, BUT I WOULD REMIND YOU THAT YOUR YOUNG FRIEND'S ETERNAL SOUL HANGS IN A VERY DELICATE BALANCE.
AS IF I COULD FORGET.
WHAT IS IT YOU WANT?
A SIMPLE PROMISE. I SHALL BREAK THIS CURSE UPON THE X-MEN. ON THAT YOU HAVE MY UNHOLY WORD.
AND YOU, ORORO...
...WILL BECOME MY BRIDE.

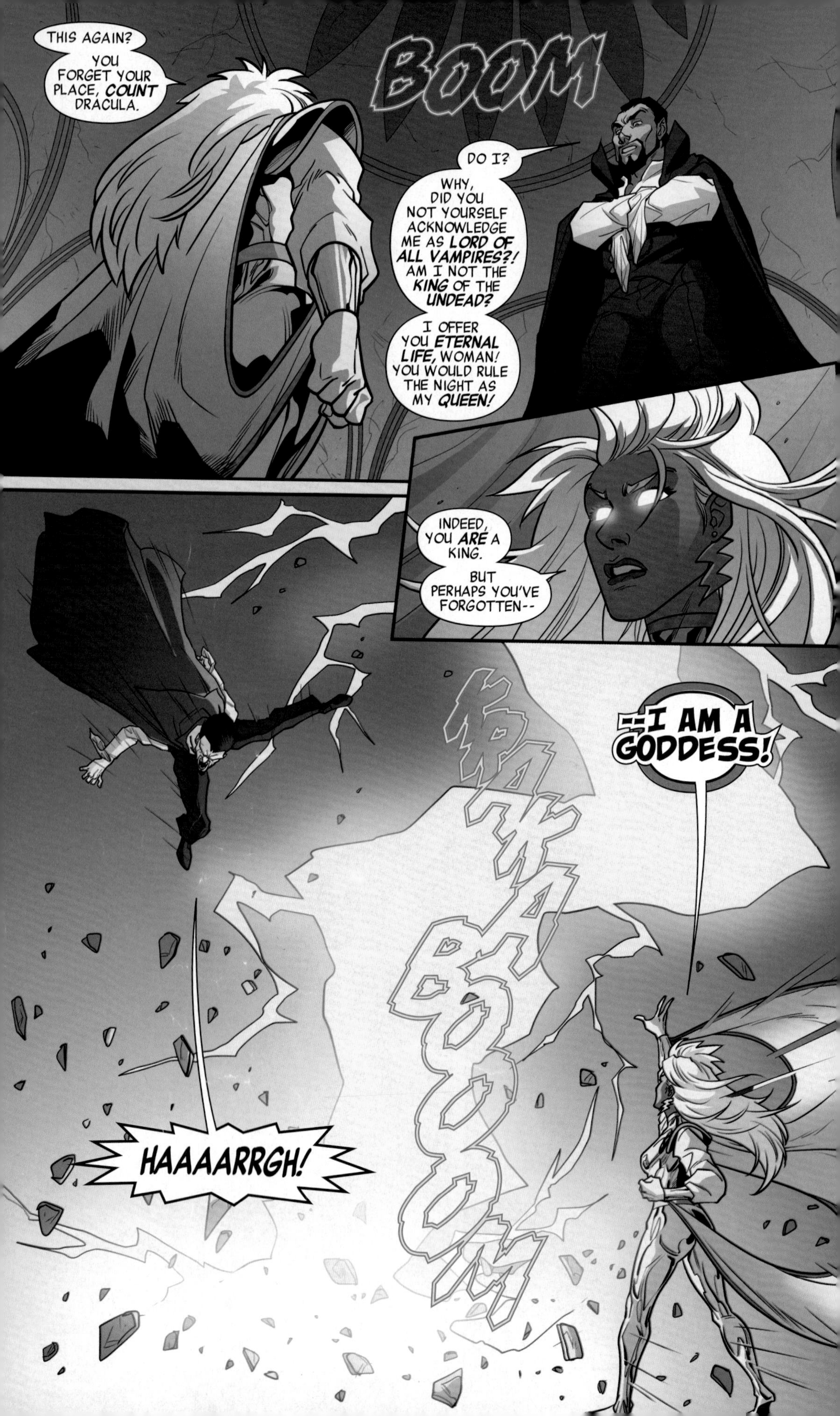
THIS AGAIN? YOU FORGET YOUR PLACE, COUNT DRACULA.
BOOM
DO I?
WHY, DID YOU NOT YOURSELF ACKNOWLEDGE ME AS LORD OF ALL VAMPIRES?! AM I NOT THE KING OF THE UNDEAD?
I OFFER YOU ETERNAL LIFE, WOMAN! YOU WOULD RULE THE NIGHT AS MY QUEEN!
INDEED, YOU ARE A KING.
BUT PERHAPS YOU'VE FORGOTTEN--
--I AM A GODDESS!
KRAKABOOM
HAAAARRGH!

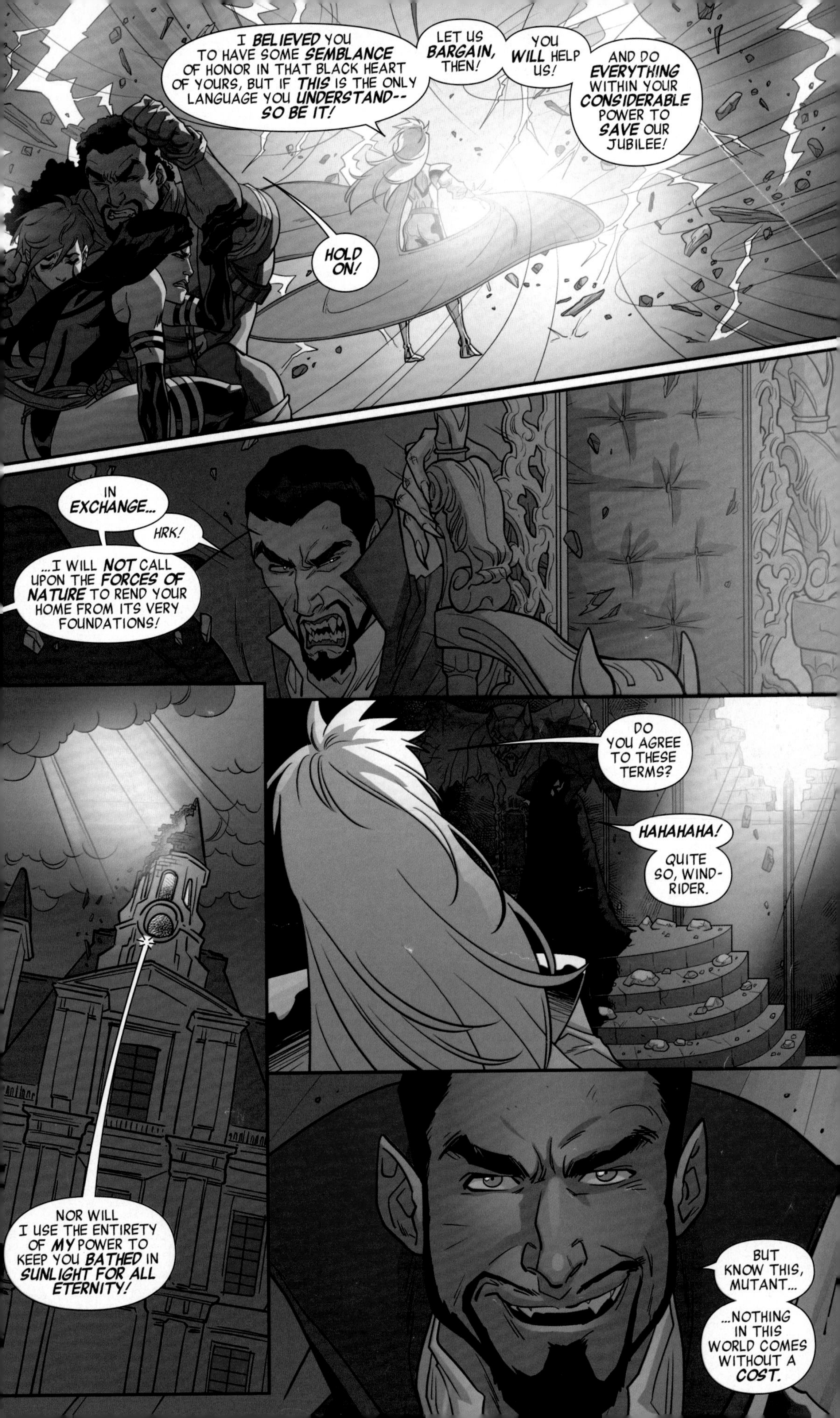
I BELIEVED YOU TO HAVE SOME SEMBLANCE OF HONOR IN THAT BLACK HEART OF YOURS, BUT IF THIS IS THE ONLY LANGUAGE YOU UNDERSTAND-- SO BE IT!
LET US BARGAIN, THEN!
YOU WILL HELP US!
AND DO EVERYTHING WITHIN YOUR CONSIDERABLE POWER TO SAVE OUR JUBILEE!
HOLD ON!
IN EXCHANGE...
HRK!
...I WILL NOT CALL UPON THE FORCES OF NATURE TO REND YOUR HOME FROM ITS VERY FOUNDATIONS!
NOR WILL I USE THE ENTIRETY OF MY POWER TO KEEP YOU BATHED IN SUNLIGHT FOR ALL ETERNITY!
DO YOU AGREE TO THESE TERMS?
HAHAHAHA!
QUITE SO, WIND-RIDER.
BUT KNOW THIS, MUTANT...
...NOTHING IN THIS WORLD COMES WITHOUT A COST.

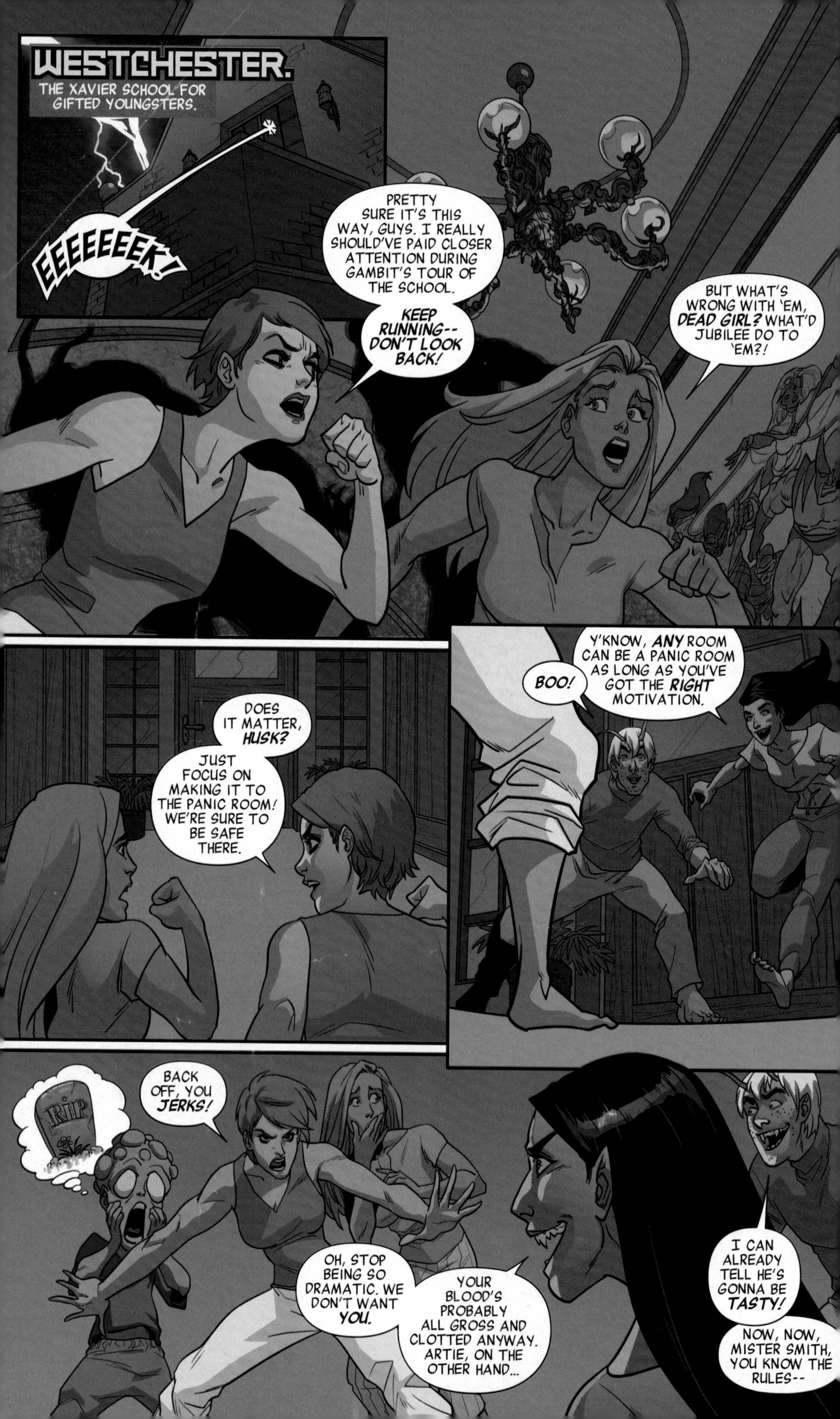
WESTCHESTER.
THE XAVIER SCHOOL FOR GIFTED YOUNGSTERS.
EEEEEEEK!
PRETTY SURE IT'S THIS WAY, GUYS. I REALLY SHOULD'VE PAID CLOSER ATTENTION DURING GAMBIT'S TOUR OF THE SCHOOL.
KEEP RUNNING-- DON'T LOOK BACK!
BUT WHAT'S WRONG WITH 'EM, DEAD GIRL? WHAT'D JUBILEE DO TO 'EM?!
DOES IT MATTER, HUSK?
JUST FOCUS ON MAKING IT TO THE PANIC ROOM! WE'RE SURE TO BE SAFE THERE.
BOO!
Y'KNOW, ANY ROOM CAN BE A PANIC ROOM AS LONG AS YOU'VE GOT THE RIGHT MOTIVATION.
RIP
BACK OFF, YOU JERKS!
OH, STOP BEING SO DRAMATIC. WE DON'T WANT YOU.
YOUR BLOOD'S PROBABLY ALL GROSS AND CLOTTED ANYWAY. ARTIE, ON THE OTHER HAND...
I CAN ALREADY TELL HE'S GONNA BE TASTY!
NOW, NOW, MISTER SMITH, YOU KNOW THE RULES--

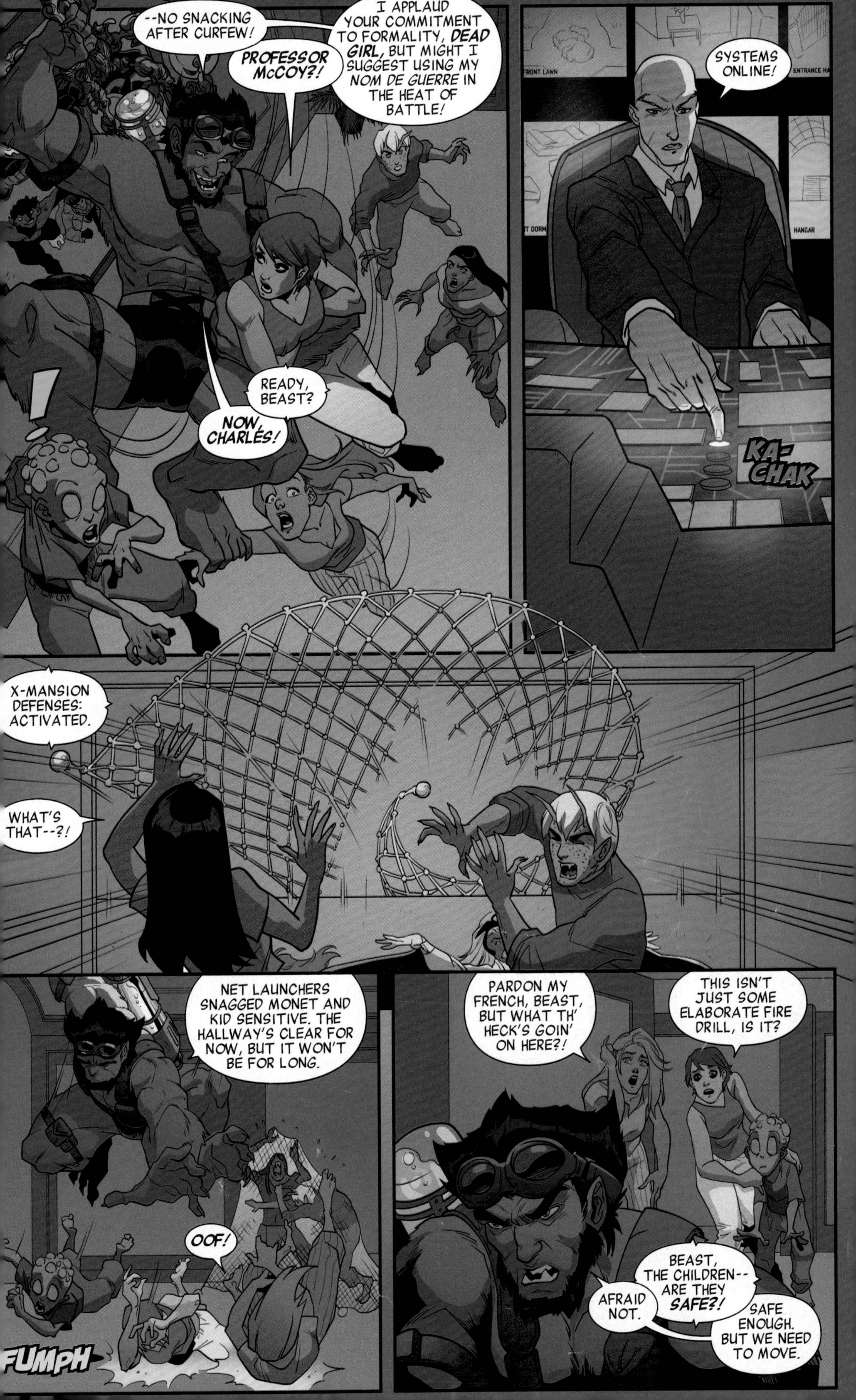

--NO SNACKING AFTER CURFEW!
PROFESSOR McCOY?!
I APPLAUD YOUR COMMITMENT TO FORMALITY, DEAD GIRL, BUT MIGHT I SUGGEST USING MY NOM DE GUERRE IN THE HEAT OF BATTLE!
READY, BEAST?
NOW, CHARLES!
FRONT LAWN
ENTRANCE HA
HANGAR
SYSTEMS ONLINE!
KA-CHAK
X-MANSION DEFENSES: ACTIVATED.
WHAT'S THAT--?!
NET LAUNCHERS SNAGGED MONET AND KID SENSITIVE. THE HALLWAY'S CLEAR FOR NOW, BUT IT WON'T BE FOR LONG.
OOF!
FUMPH
PARDON MY FRENCH, BEAST, BUT WHAT TH' HECK'S GOIN' ON HERE?!
THIS ISN'T JUST SOME ELABORATE FIRE DRILL, IS IT?
AFRAID NOT.
BEAST, THE CHILDREN--ARE THEY SAFE?!
SAFE ENOUGH. BUT WE NEED TO MOVE.

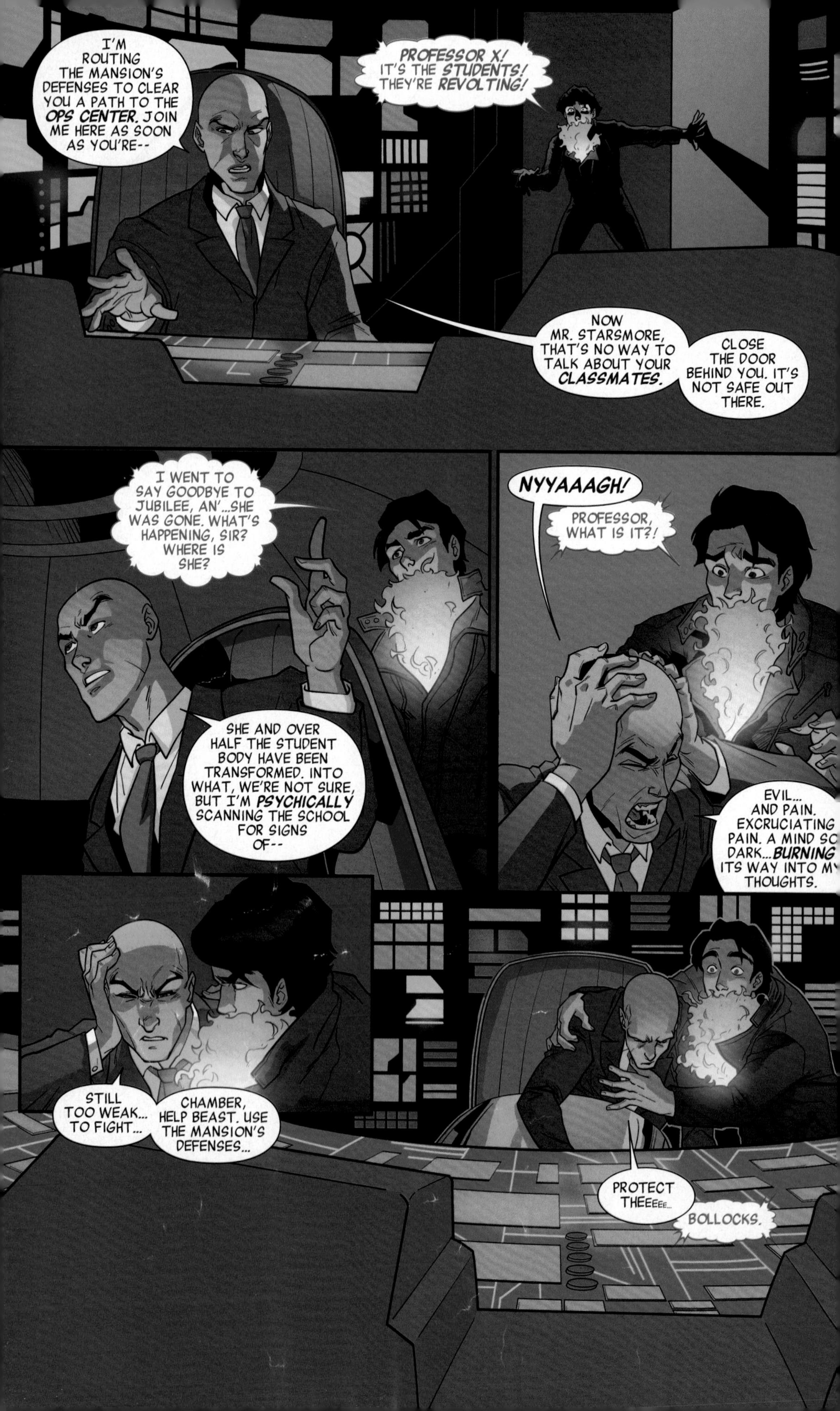
I'M ROUTING THE MANSION'S DEFENSES TO CLEAR YOU A PATH TO THE OPS CENTER. JOIN ME HERE AS SOON AS YOU'RE--
PROFESSOR X! IT'S THE STUDENTS! THEY'RE REVOLTING!
NOW MR. STARSMORE, THAT'S NO WAY TO TALK ABOUT YOUR CLASSMATES.
CLOSE THE DOOR BEHIND YOU. IT'S NOT SAFE OUT THERE.
I WENT TO SAY GOODBYE TO JUBILEE, AN'...SHE WAS GONE. WHAT'S HAPPENING, SIR? WHERE IS SHE?
SHE AND OVER HALF THE STUDENT BODY HAVE BEEN TRANSFORMED. INTO WHAT, WE'RE NOT SURE, BUT I'M PSYCHICALLY SCANNING THE SCHOOL FOR SIGNS OF--
NYYAAAGH!
PROFESSOR, WHAT IS IT?!
EVIL... AND PAIN. EXCRUCIATING PAIN. A MIND SO DARK...BURNING ITS WAY INTO MY THOUGHTS.
STILL TOO WEAK... TO FIGHT...
CHAMBER, HELP BEAST. USE THE MANSION'S DEFENSES...
PROTECT THEEEEE...
BOLLOCKS.

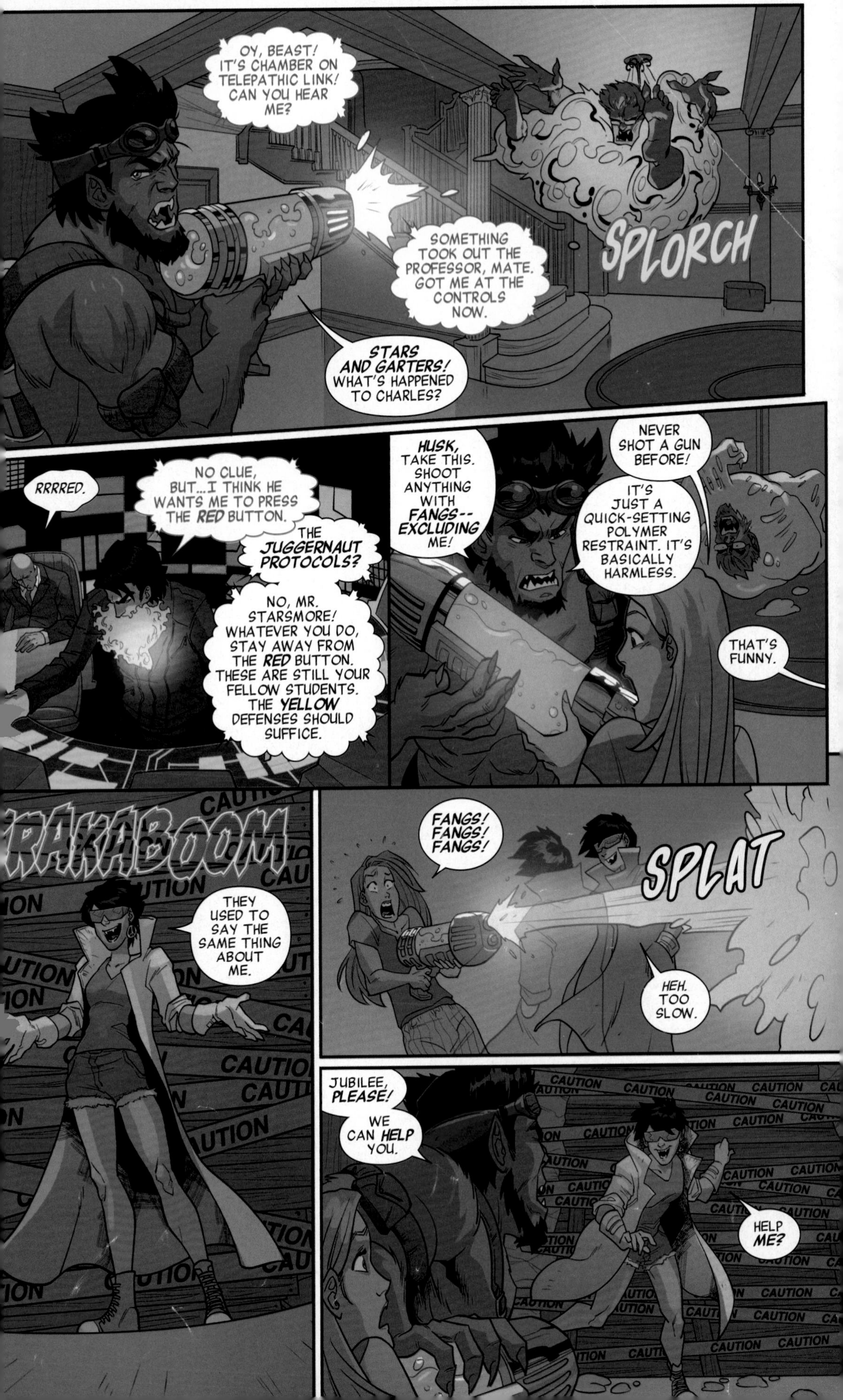
OY, BEAST! IT'S CHAMBER ON TELEPATHIC LINK! CAN YOU HEAR ME?
SOMETHING TOOK OUT THE PROFESSOR, MATE. GOT ME AT THE CONTROLS NOW.
SPLORCH
STARS AND GARTERS! WHAT'S HAPPENED TO CHARLES?
RRRRED.
NO CLUE, BUT...I THINK HE WANTS ME TO PRESS THE RED BUTTON.
THE JUGGERNAUT PROTOCOLS?
NO, MR. STARSMORE! WHATEVER YOU DO, STAY AWAY FROM THE RED BUTTON. THESE ARE STILL YOUR FELLOW STUDENTS. THE YELLOW DEFENSES SHOULD SUFFICE.
HUSK, TAKE THIS. SHOOT ANYTHING WITH FANGS-- EXCLUDING ME!
NEVER SHOT A GUN BEFORE!
IT'S JUST A QUICK-SETTING POLYMER RESTRAINT. IT'S BASICALLY HARMLESS.
THAT'S FUNNY.
RAKABOOM
THEY USED TO SAY THE SAME THING ABOUT ME.
FANGS! FANGS! FANGS!
SPLAT
HEH. TOO SLOW.
JUBILEE, PLEASE!
WE CAN HELP YOU.
HELP ME?

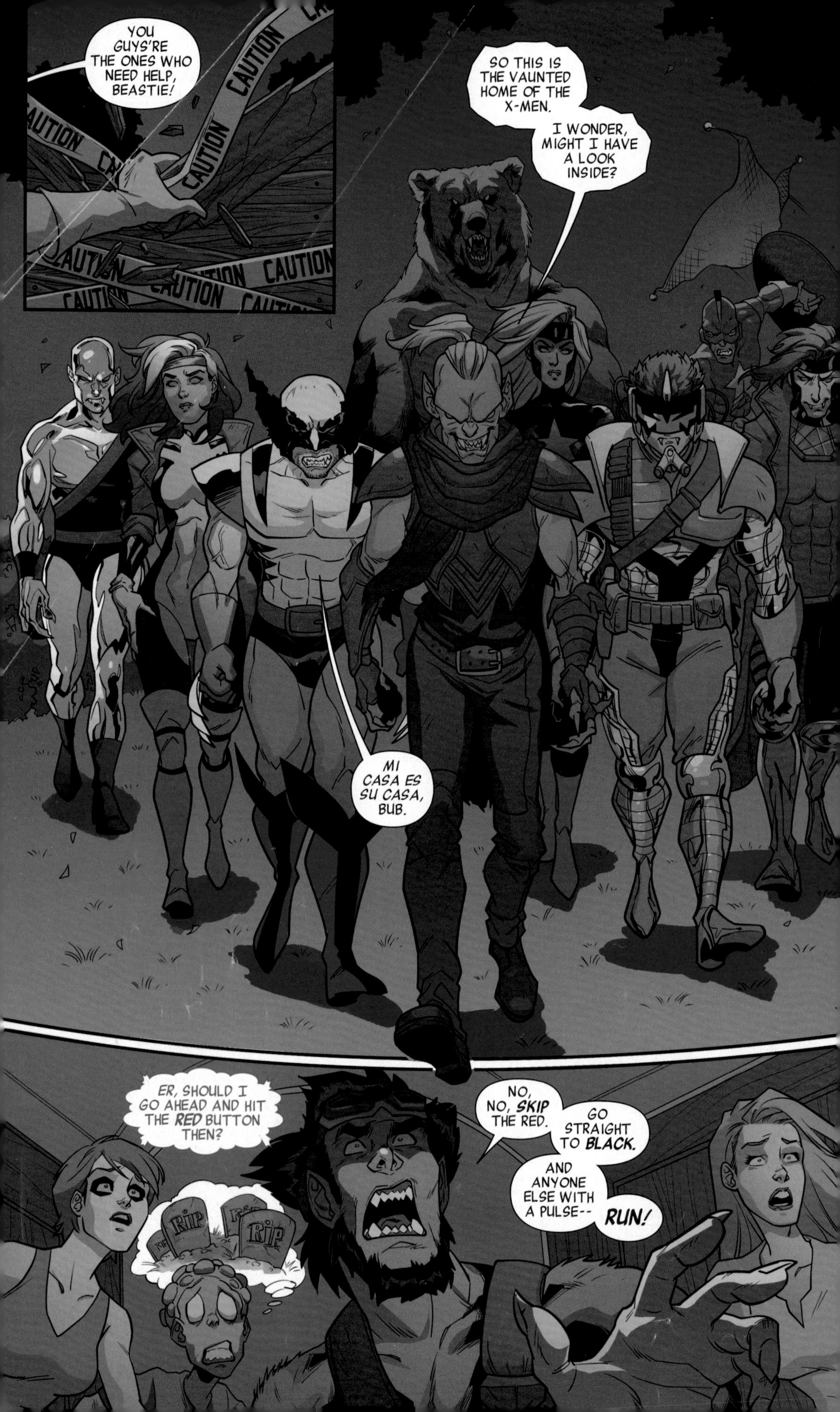

YOU GUY'S'RE THE ONES WHO NEED HELP, BEASTIE!
CAUTION
SO THIS IS THE VAUNTED HOME OF THE X-MEN.
I WONDER, MIGHT I HAVE A LOOK INSIDE?
MI CASA ES SU CASA, BUB.
ER, SHOULD I GO AHEAD AND HIT THE RED BUTTON THEN?
RIP
NO, NO, SKIP THE RED.
GO STRAIGHT TO BLACK.
AND ANYONE ELSE WITH A PULSE--
RUN!

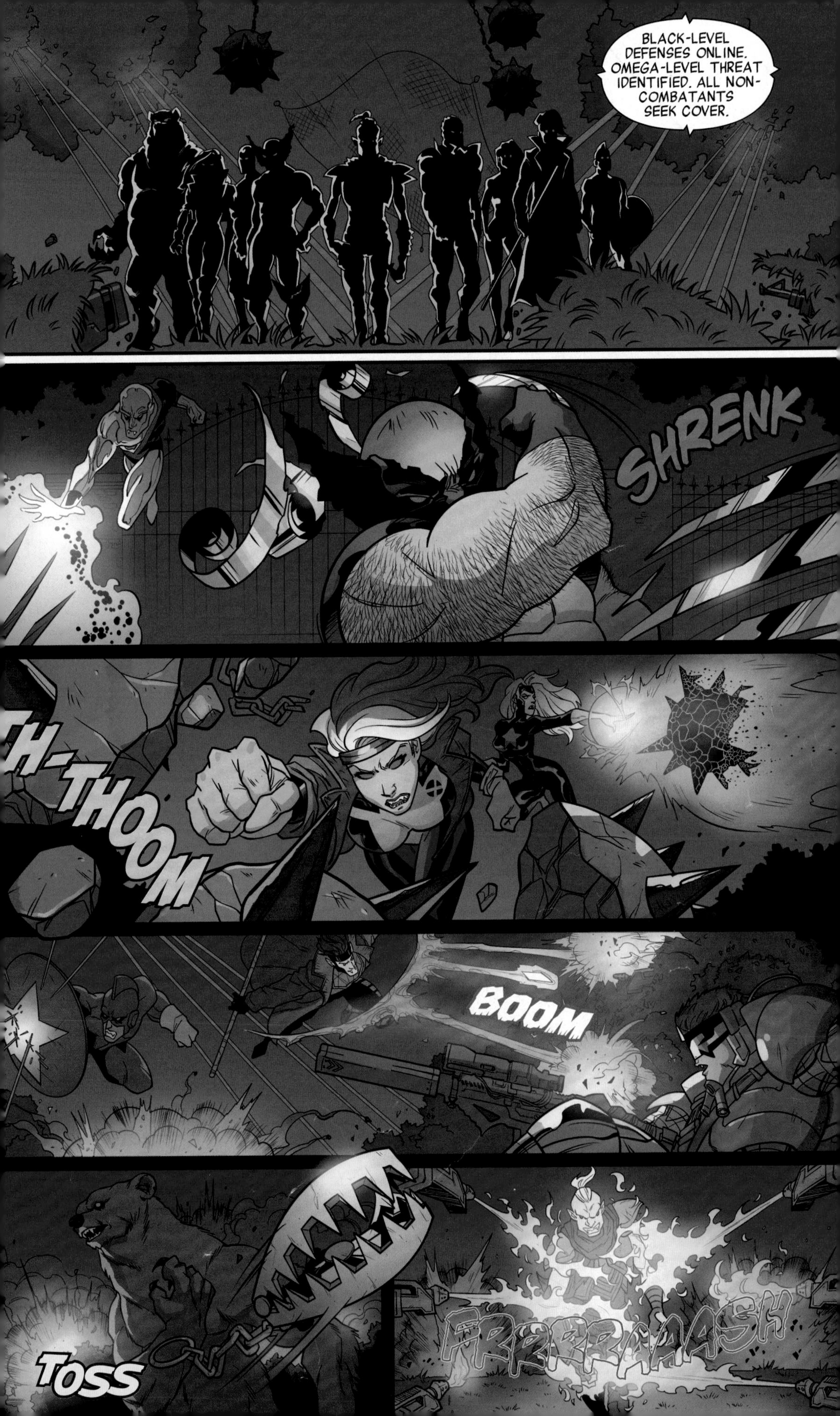
BLACK-LEVEL DEFENSES ONLINE. OMEGA-LEVEL THREAT IDENTIFIED. ALL NON-COMBATANTS SEEK COVER.
SHRENK
H-THOOM
BOOM
TOSS
FRRRRAAASH

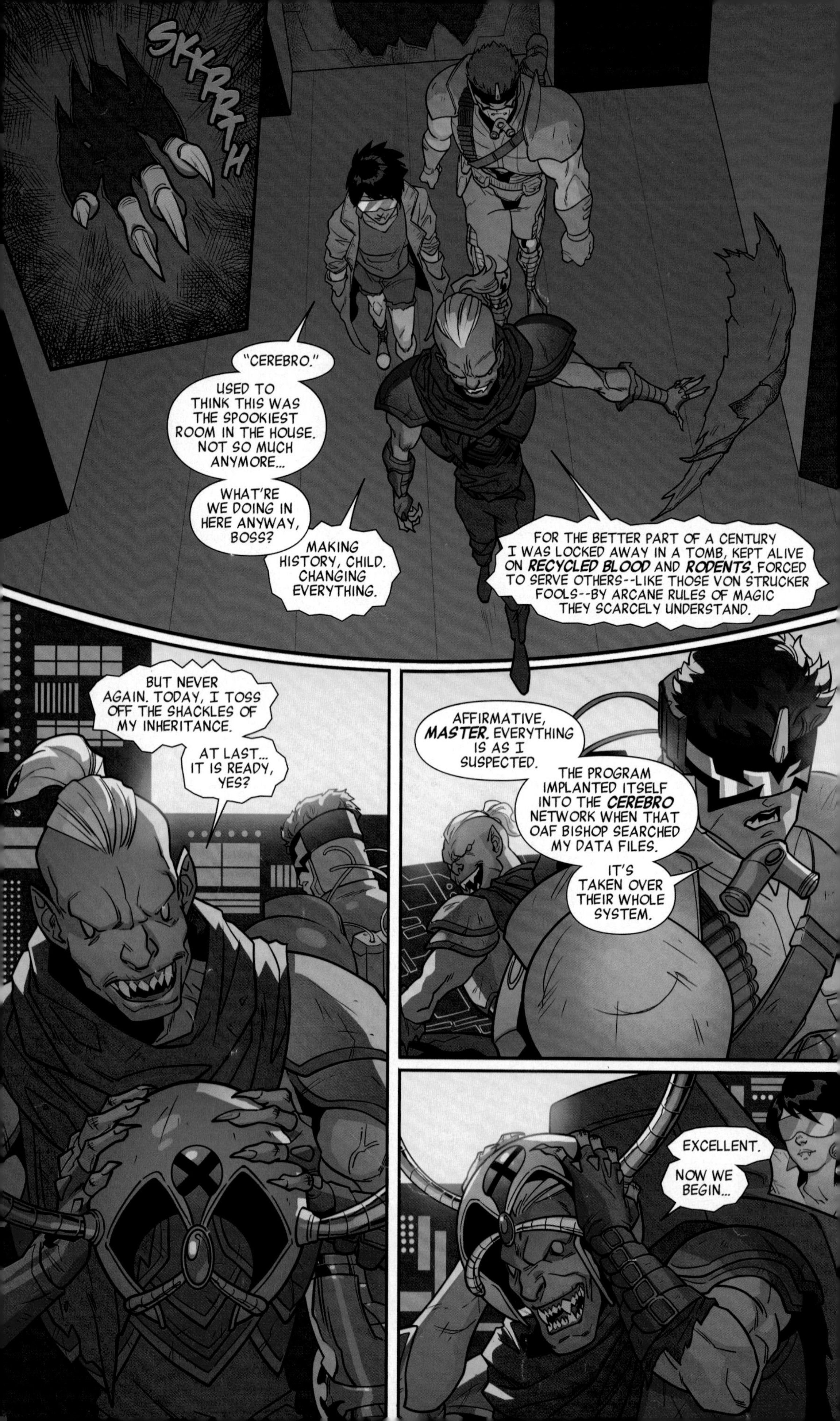
SKKRRRH
"CEREBRO."
USED TO THINK THIS WAS THE SPOOKIEST ROOM IN THE HOUSE. NOT SO MUCH ANYMORE...
WHAT'RE WE DOING IN HERE ANYWAY, BOSS?
MAKING HISTORY, CHILD. CHANGING EVERYTHING.
FOR THE BETTER PART OF A CENTURY I WAS LOCKED AWAY IN A TOMB, KEPT ALIVE ON RECYCLED BLOOD AND RODENTS. FORCED TO SERVE OTHERS--LIKE THOSE VON STRUCKER FOOLS--BY ARCANE RULES OF MAGIC THEY SCARCELY UNDERSTAND.
BUT NEVER AGAIN. TODAY, I TOSS OFF THE SHACKLES OF MY INHERITANCE.
AT LAST... IT IS READY, YES?
AFFIRMATIVE, MASTER. EVERYTHING IS AS I SUSPECTED.
THE PROGRAM IMPLANTED ITSELF INTO THE CEREBRO NETWORK WHEN THAT OAF BISHOP SEARCHED MY DATA FILES.
IT'S TAKEN OVER THEIR WHOLE SYSTEM.
EXCELLENT.
NOW WE BEGIN...

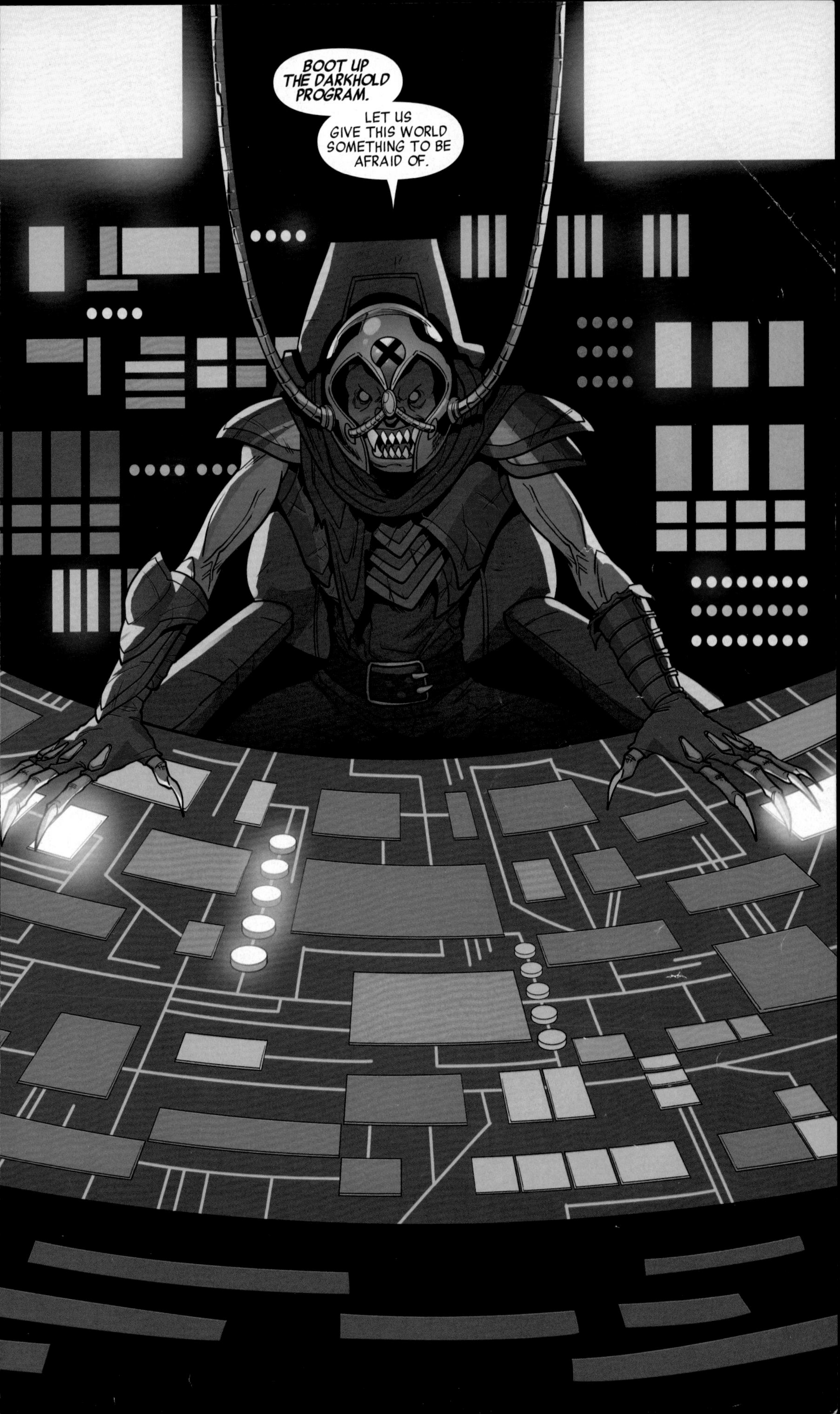

BOOT UP THE DARKHOLD PROGRAM.
LET US GIVE THIS WORLD SOMETHING TO BE AFRAID OF.

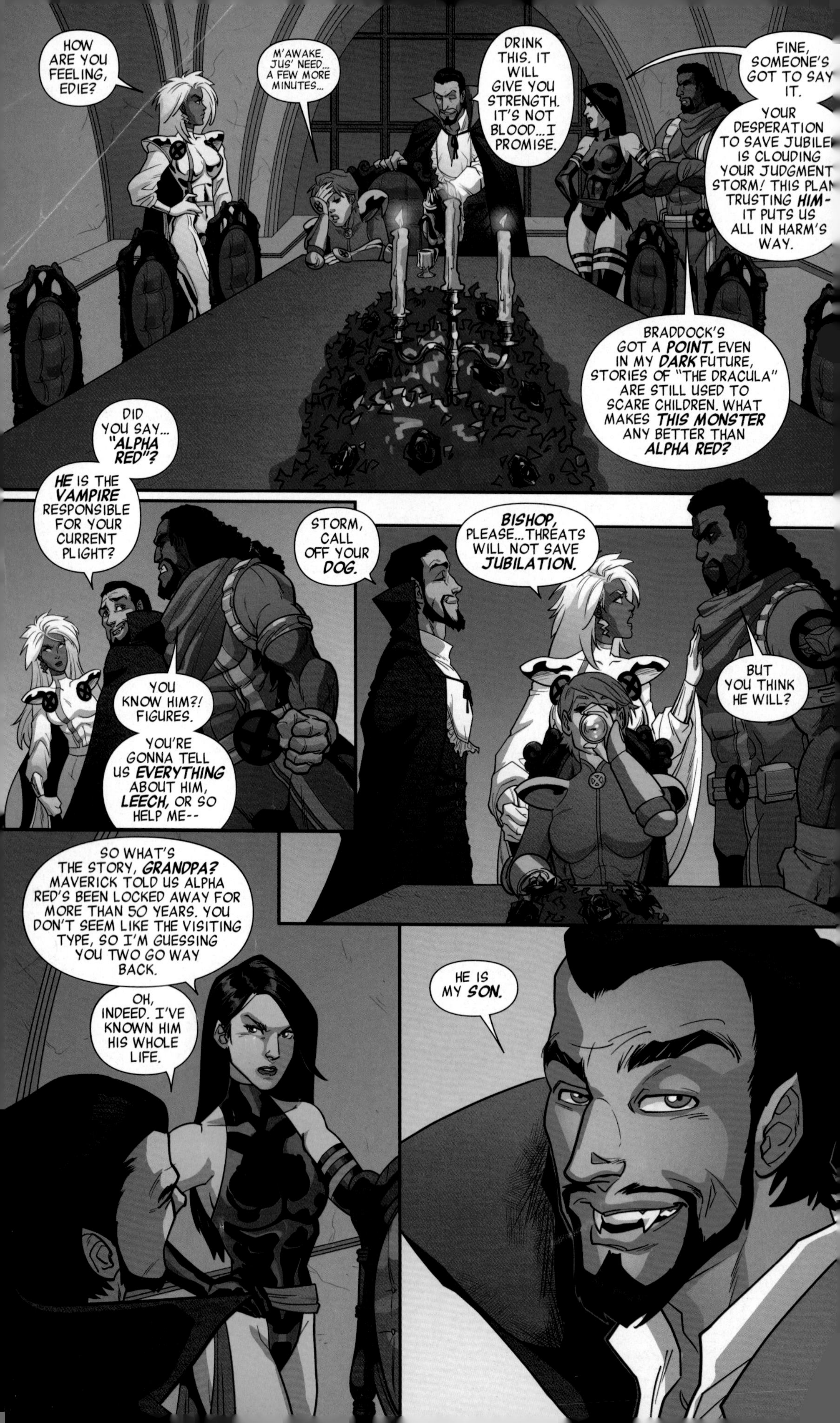
HOW ARE YOU FEELING, EDIE?
M'AWAKE. JUS' NEED... A FEW MORE MINUTES...
DRINK THIS. IT WILL GIVE YOU STRENGTH. IT'S NOT BLOOD...I PROMISE.
FINE, SOMEONE'S GOT TO SAY IT.
YOUR DESPERATION TO SAVE JUBILEE IS CLOUDING YOUR JUDGMENT, STORM! THIS PLAN-- TRUSTING HIM-- IT PUTS US ALL IN HARM'S WAY.
BRADDOCK'S GOT A POINT. EVEN IN MY DARK FUTURE, STORIES OF "THE DRACULA" ARE STILL USED TO SCARE CHILDREN. WHAT MAKES THIS MONSTER ANY BETTER THAN ALPHA RED?
DID YOU SAY... "ALPHA RED"?
HE IS THE VAMPIRE RESPONSIBLE FOR YOUR CURRENT PLIGHT?
YOU KNOW HIM?! FIGURES.
YOU'RE GONNA TELL US EVERYTHING ABOUT HIM, LEECH, OR SO HELP ME--
STORM, CALL OFF YOUR DOG.
BISHOP, PLEASE...THREATS WILL NOT SAVE JUBILATION.
BUT YOU THINK HE WILL?
SO WHAT'S THE STORY, GRANDPA? MAVERICK TOLD US ALPHA RED'S BEEN LOCKED AWAY FOR MORE THAN 50 YEARS. YOU DON'T SEEM LIKE THE VISITING TYPE, SO I'M GUESSING YOU TWO GO WAY BACK.
OH, INDEED. I'VE KNOWN HIM HIS WHOLE LIFE.
HE IS MY SON.

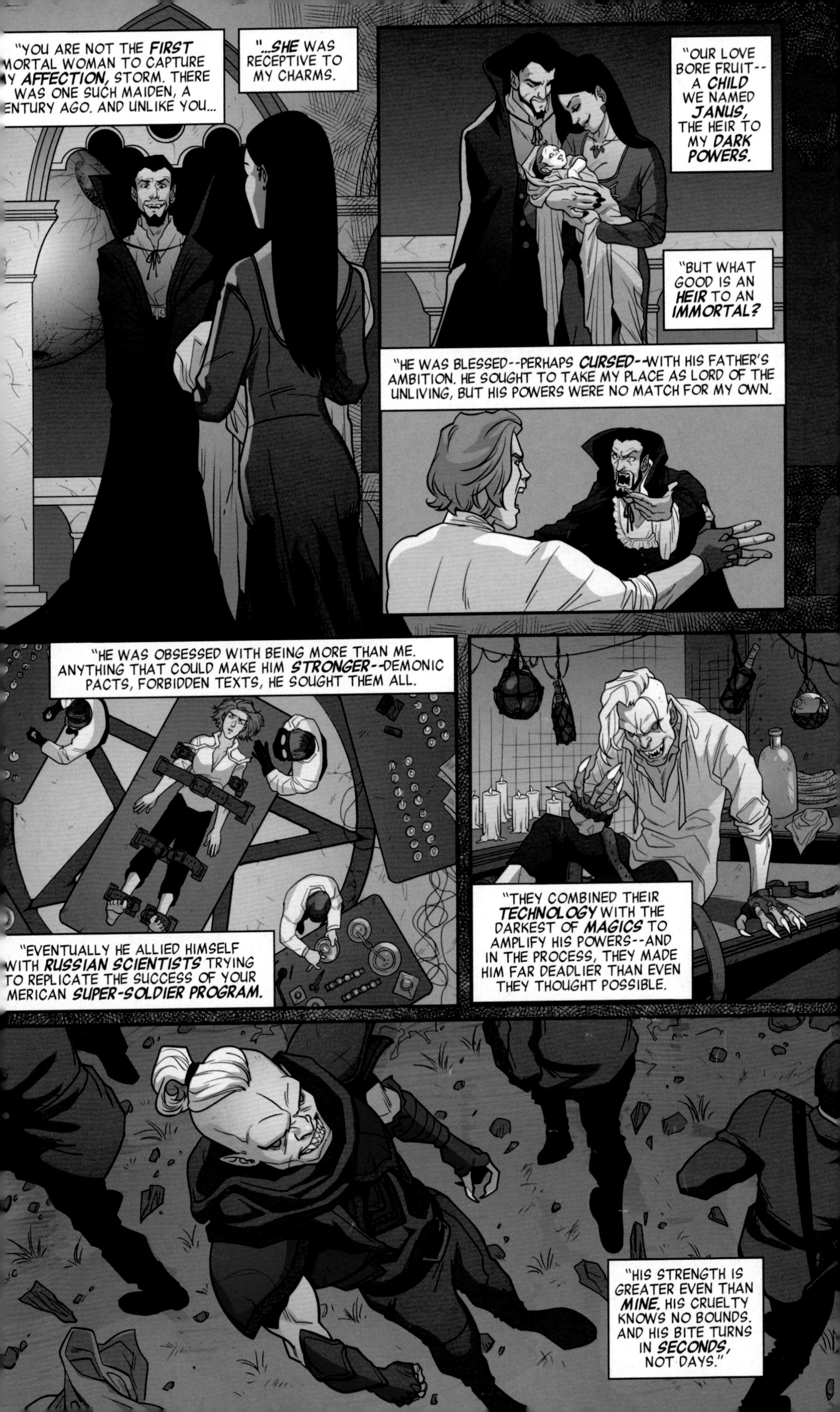
"YOU ARE NOT THE FIRST MORTAL WOMAN TO CAPTURE MY AFFECTION, STORM. THERE WAS ONE SUCH MAIDEN, A CENTURY AGO. AND UNLIKE YOU...
"...SHE WAS RECEPTIVE TO MY CHARMS.
"OUR LOVE BORE FRUIT--A CHILD WE NAMED JANUS, THE HEIR TO MY DARK POWERS.
"BUT WHAT GOOD IS AN HEIR TO AN IMMORTAL?
"HE WAS BLESSED--PERHAPS CURSED--WITH HIS FATHER'S AMBITION. HE SOUGHT TO TAKE MY PLACE AS LORD OF THE UNLIVING, BUT HIS POWERS WERE NO MATCH FOR MY OWN.
"HE WAS OBSESSED WITH BEING MORE THAN ME. ANYTHING THAT COULD MAKE HIM STRONGER--DEMONIC PACTS, FORBIDDEN TEXTS, HE SOUGHT THEM ALL.
"EVENTUALLY HE ALLIED HIMSELF WITH RUSSIAN SCIENTISTS TRYING TO REPLICATE THE SUCCESS OF YOUR AMERICAN SUPER-SOLDIER PROGRAM.
"THEY COMBINED THEIR TECHNOLOGY WITH THE DARKEST OF MAGICS TO AMPLIFY HIS POWERS--AND IN THE PROCESS, THEY MADE HIM FAR DEADLIER THAN EVEN THEY THOUGHT POSSIBLE.
"HIS STRENGTH IS GREATER EVEN THAN MINE. HIS CRUELTY KNOWS NO BOUNDS. AND HIS BITE TURNS IN SECONDS, NOT DAYS."

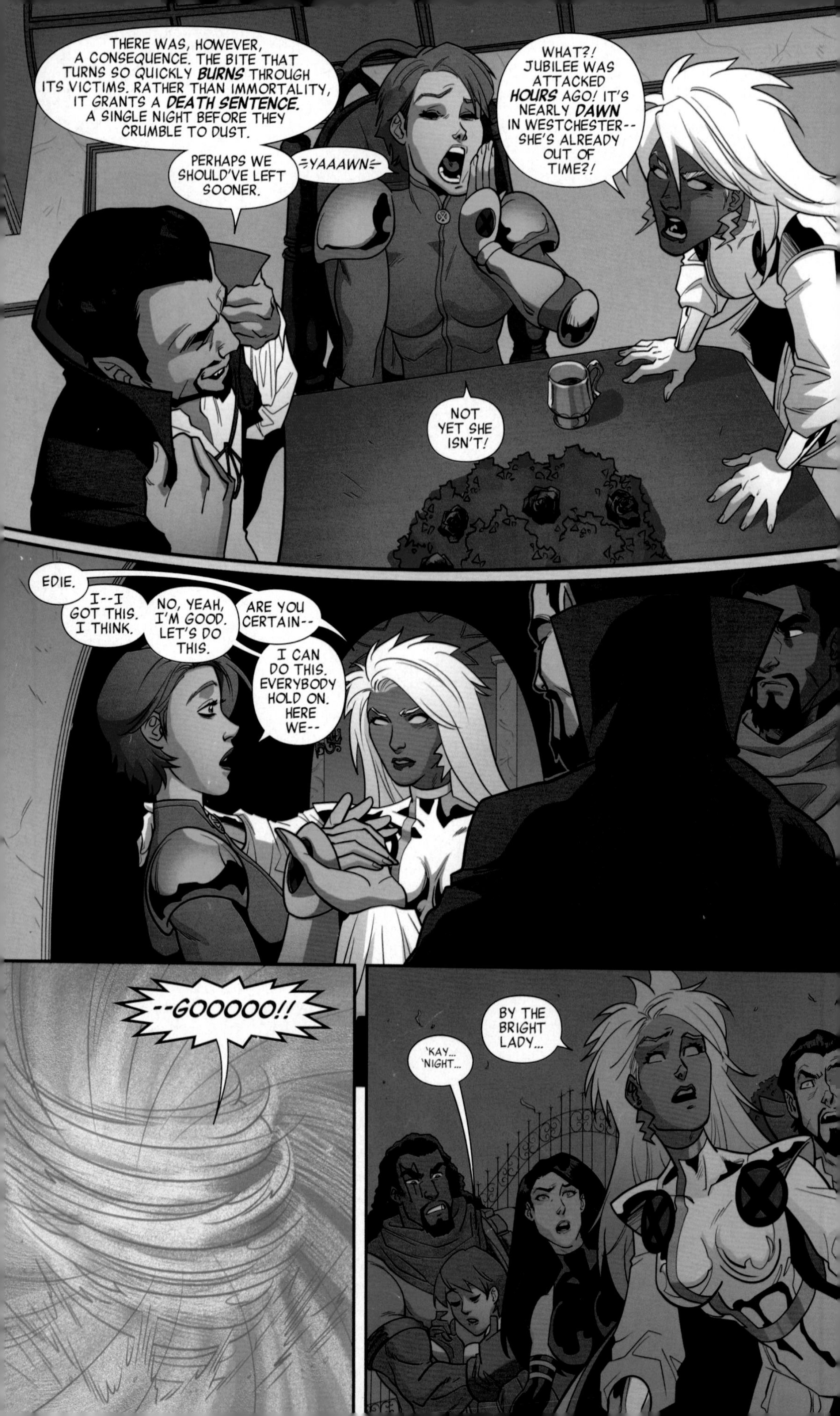
THERE WAS, HOWEVER, A CONSEQUENCE. THE BITE THAT TURNS SO QUICKLY BURNS THROUGH ITS VICTIMS. RATHER THAN IMMORTALITY, IT GRANTS A DEATH SENTENCE. A SINGLE NIGHT BEFORE THEY CRUMBLE TO DUST.
PERHAPS WE SHOULD'VE LEFT SOONER.
YAAAWN
WHAT?! JUBILEE WAS ATTACKED HOURS AGO! IT'S NEARLY DAWN IN WESTCHESTER--SHE'S ALREADY OUT OF TIME?!
NOT YET SHE ISN'T!
EDIE.
I--I GOT THIS. I THINK.
NO, YEAH, I'M GOOD. LET'S DO THIS.
ARE YOU CERTAIN--
I CAN DO THIS. EVERYBODY HOLD ON. HERE WE--
--GOOOOO!!
BY THE BRIGHT LADY...
'KAY... 'NIGHT...

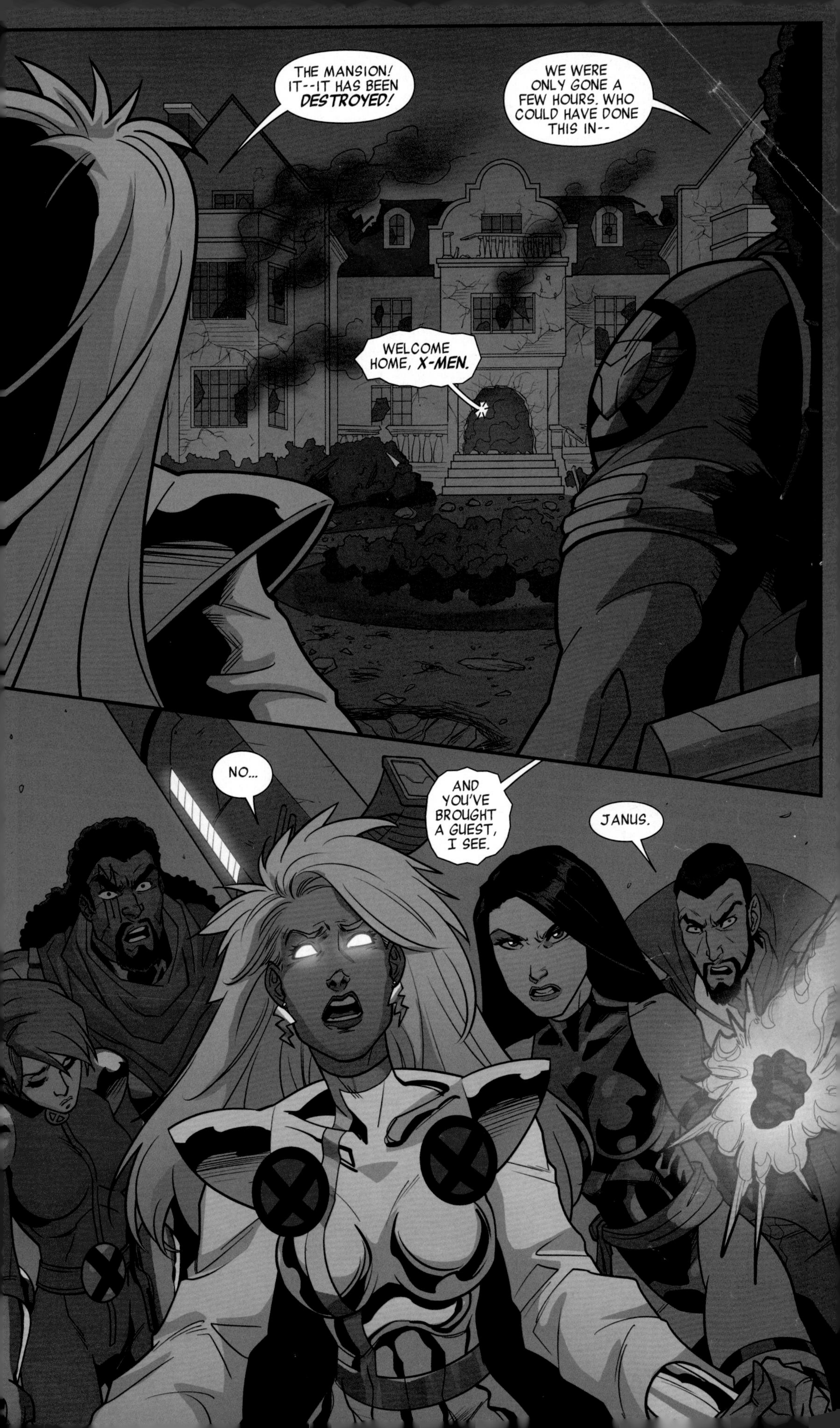
THE MANSION! IT--IT HAS BEEN DESTROYED!
WE WERE ONLY GONE A FEW HOURS. WHO COULD HAVE DONE THIS IN--
WELCOME HOME, X-MEN.
NO...
AND YOU'VE BROUGHT A GUEST, I SEE.
JANUS.

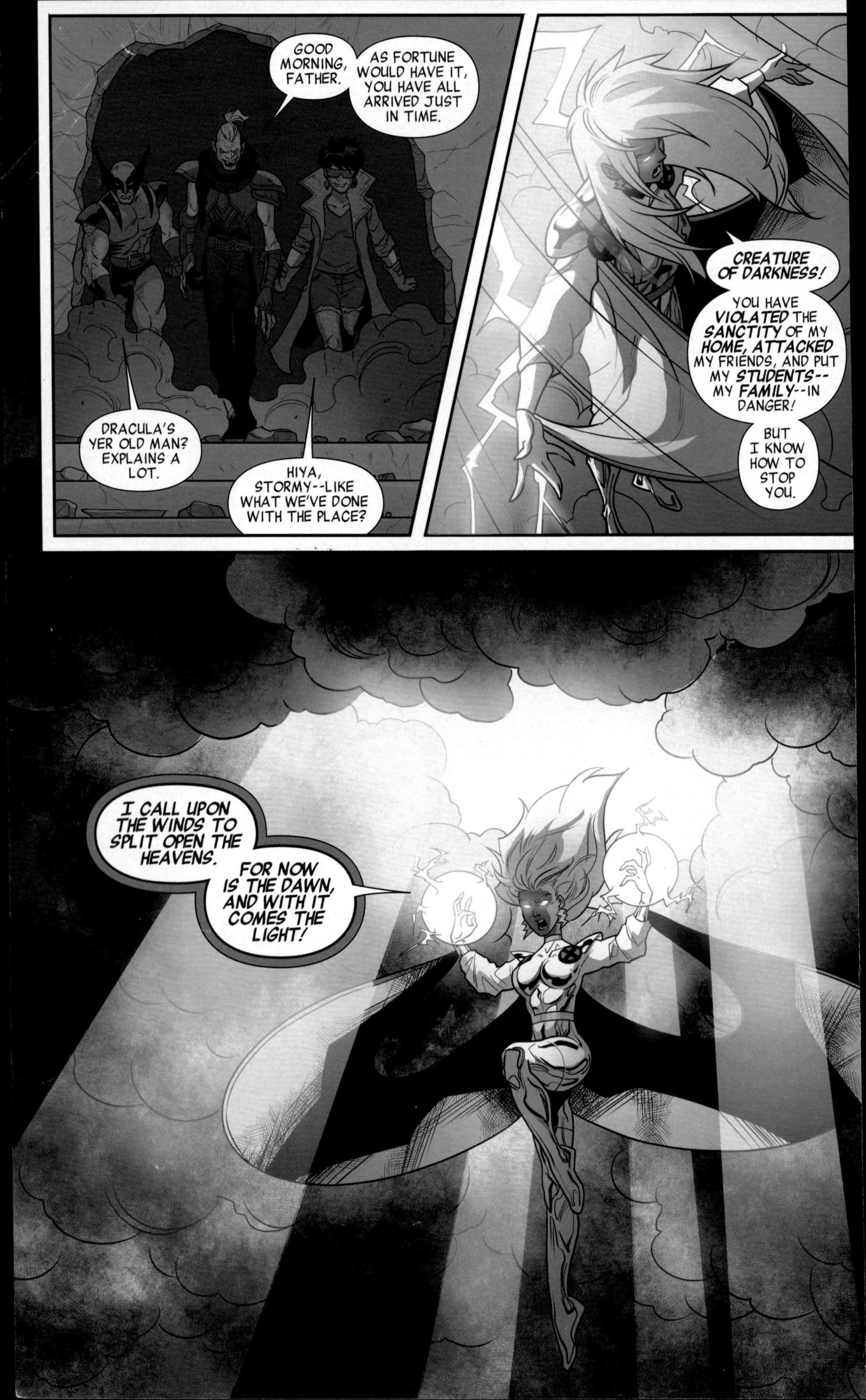
GOOD MORNING, FATHER.
AS FORTUNE WOULD HAVE IT, YOU HAVE ALL ARRIVED JUST IN TIME.
DRACULA'S YER OLD MAN? EXPLAINS A LOT.
HIYA, STORMY--LIKE WHAT WE'VE DONE WITH THE PLACE?
CREATURE OF DARKNESS!
YOU HAVE VIOLATED THE SANCTITY OF MY HOME, ATTACKED MY FRIENDS, AND PUT MY STUDENTS--MY FAMILY--IN DANGER!
BUT I KNOW HOW TO STOP YOU.
I CALL UPON THE WINDS TO SPLIT OPEN THE HEAVENS.
FOR NOW IS THE DAWN, AND WITH IT COMES THE LIGHT!

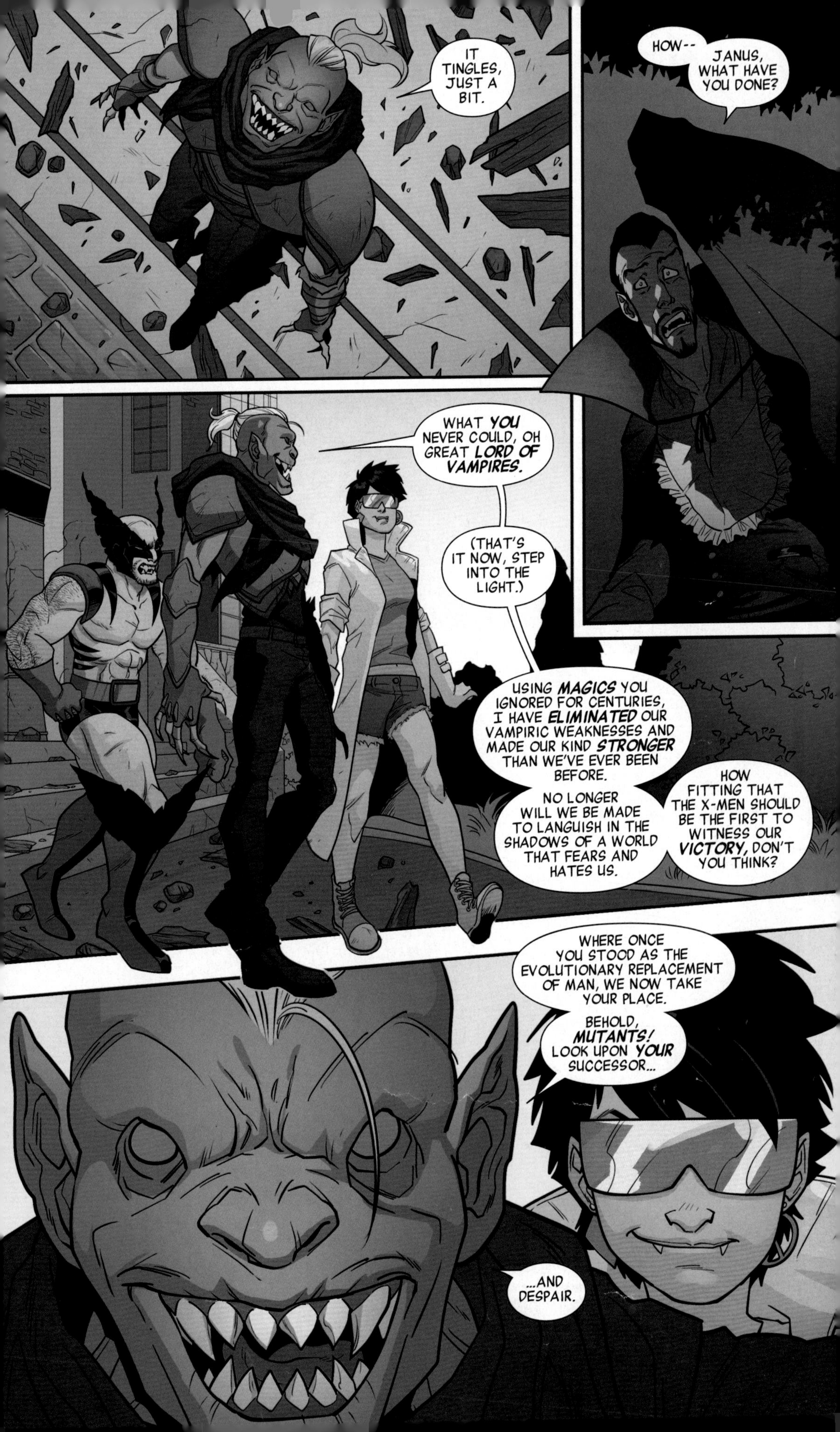
IT TINGLES, JUST A BIT.
HOW--
JANUS, WHAT HAVE YOU DONE?
WHAT YOU NEVER COULD, OH GREAT LORD OF VAMPIRES.
(THAT'S IT NOW, STEP INTO THE LIGHT.)
USING MAGICS YOU IGNORED FOR CENTURIES, I HAVE ELIMINATED OUR VAMPIRIC WEAKNESSES AND MADE OUR KIND STRONGER THAN WE'VE EVER BEEN BEFORE.
NO LONGER WILL WE BE MADE TO LANGUISH IN THE SHADOWS OF A WORLD THAT FEARS AND HATES US.
HOW FITTING THAT THE X-MEN SHOULD BE THE FIRST TO WITNESS OUR VICTORY, DON'T YOU THINK?
WHERE ONCE YOU STOOD AS THE EVOLUTIONARY REPLACEMENT OF MAN, WE NOW TAKE YOUR PLACE.
BEHOLD, MUTANTS! LOOK UPON YOUR SUCCESSOR...
...AND DESPAIR.

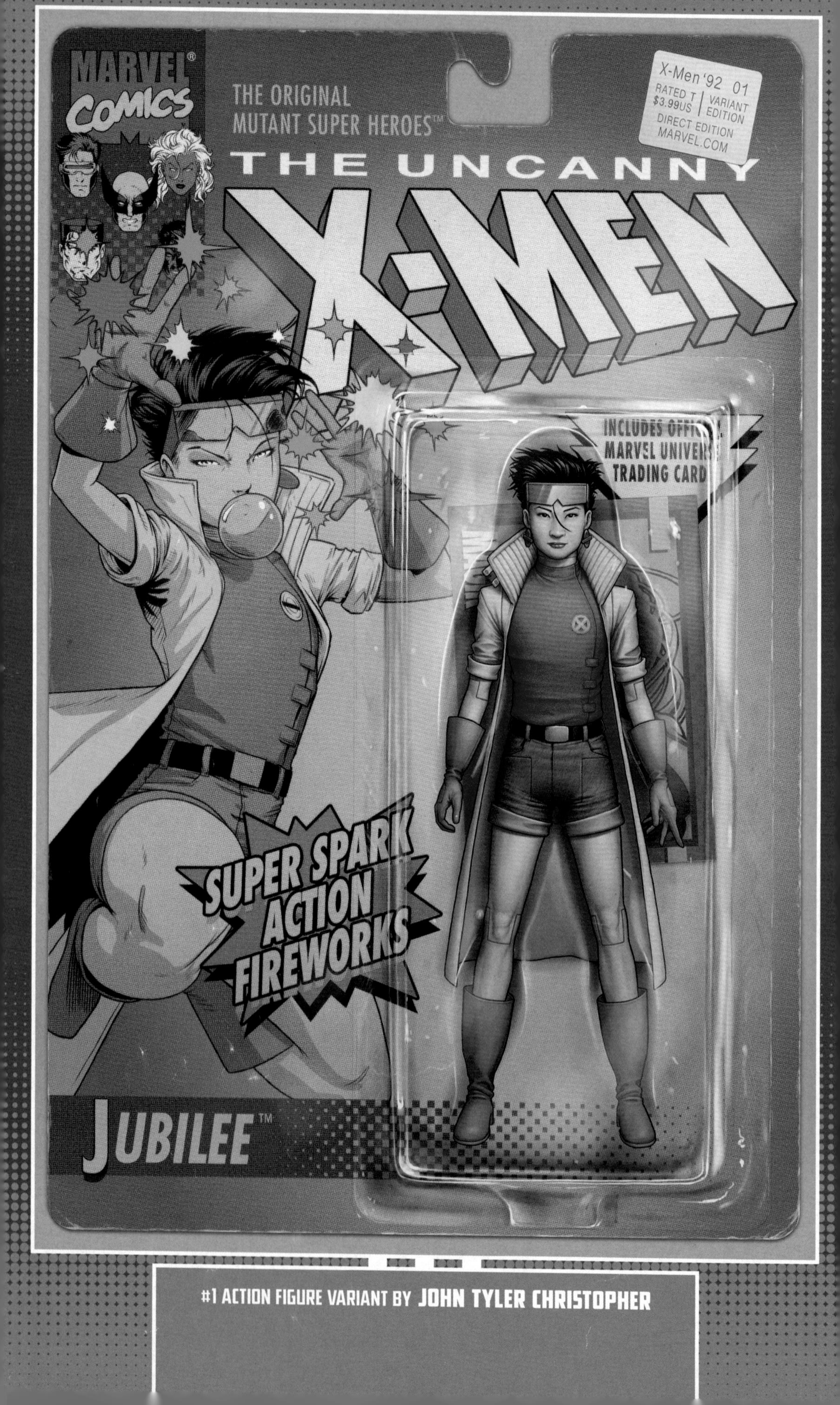
MARVEL® COMICS
THE ORIGINAL
MUTANT SUPER HEROES™
X-Men '92 01
RATED T
$3.99US
VARIANT EDITION
DIRECT EDITION
MARVEL.COM
THE UNCANNY
X-MEN
INCLUDES OFFICIAL
MARVEL UNIVERSE
TRADING CARD
SUPER SPARK
ACTION
FIREWORKS
JUBILEE™

#1 ACTION FIGURE VARIANT BY JOHN TYLER CHRISTOPHER

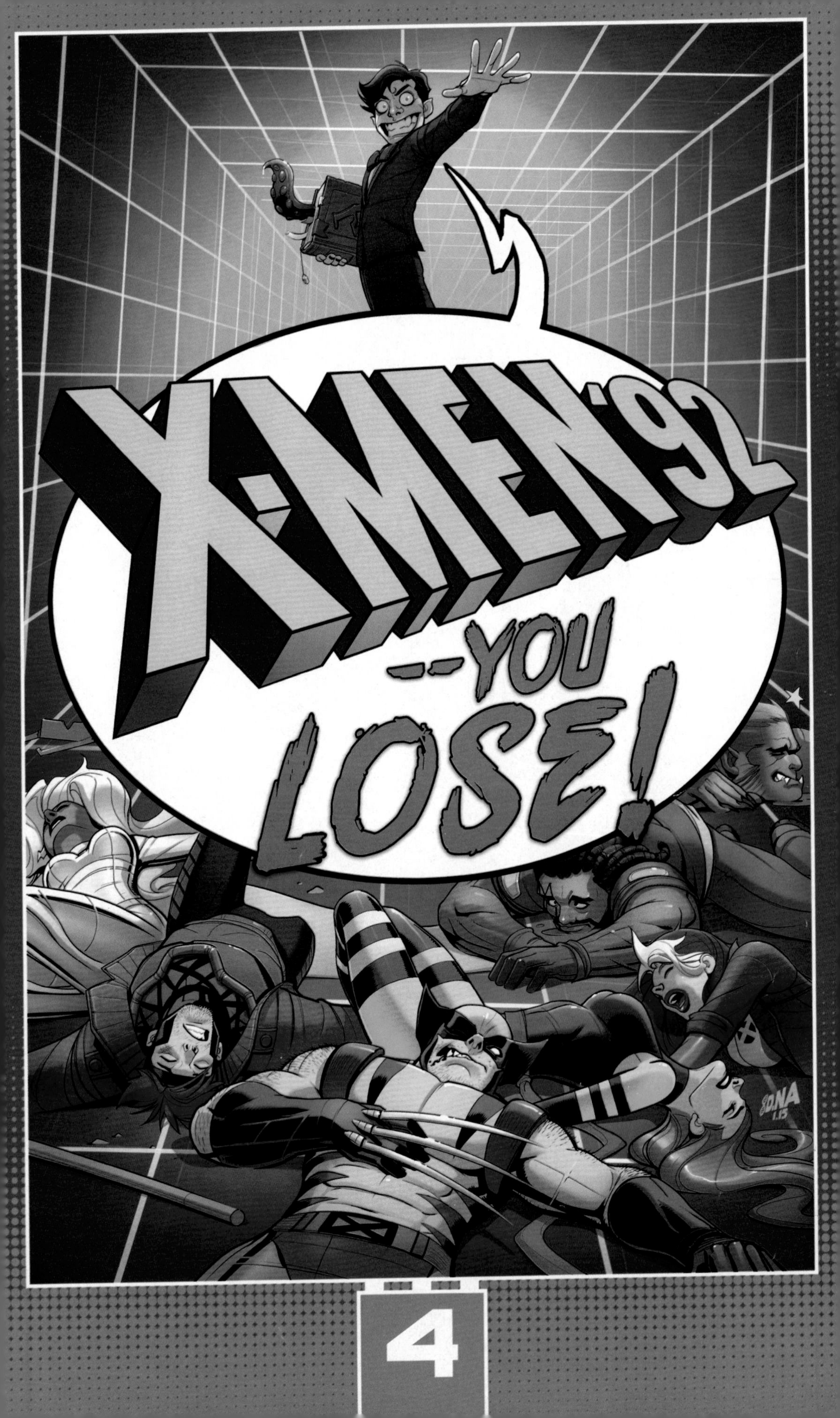
X-MEN '92
--YOU LOSE!
4

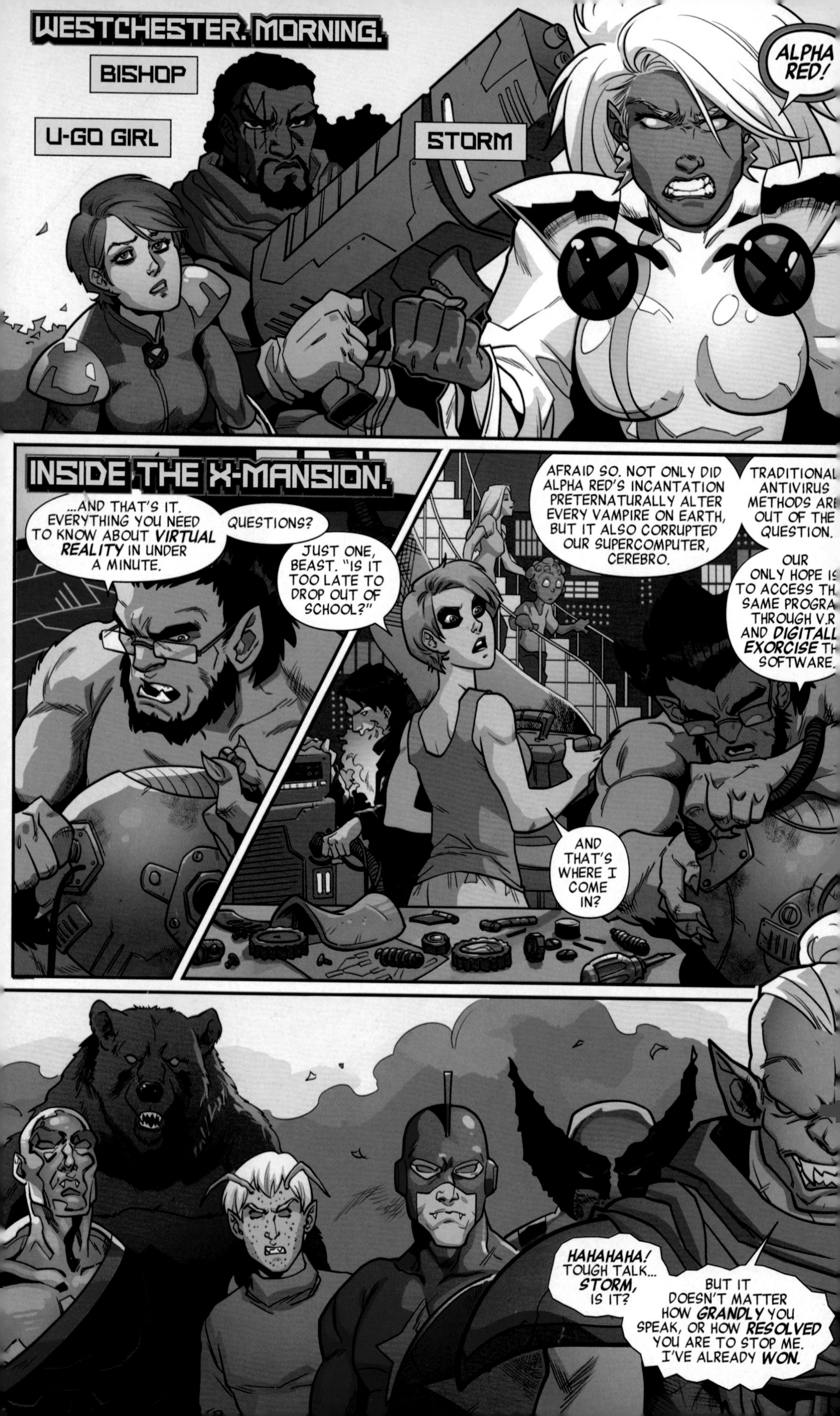
WESTCHESTER. MORNING.
BISHOP
U-GO GIRL
STORM
ALPHA RED!
INSIDE THE X-MANSION.
...AND THAT'S IT. EVERYTHING YOU NEED TO KNOW ABOUT VIRTUAL REALITY IN UNDER A MINUTE.
QUESTIONS?
JUST ONE, BEAST. "IS IT TOO LATE TO DROP OUT OF SCHOOL?"
AFRAID SO. NOT ONLY DID ALPHA RED'S INCANTATION PRETERNATURALLY ALTER EVERY VAMPIRE ON EARTH, BUT IT ALSO CORRUPTED OUR SUPERCOMPUTER, CEREBRO.
TRADITIONAL ANTIVIRUS METHODS ARE OUT OF THE QUESTION.
OUR ONLY HOPE IS TO ACCESS TH SAME PROGRA THROUGH V.R AND DIGITALL EXORCISE TH SOFTWARE.
AND THAT'S WHERE I COME IN?
HAHAHAHA! TOUGH TALK... STORM, IS IT?
BUT IT DOESN'T MATTER HOW GRANDLY YOU SPEAK, OR HOW RESOLVED YOU ARE TO STOP ME. I'VE ALREADY WON.

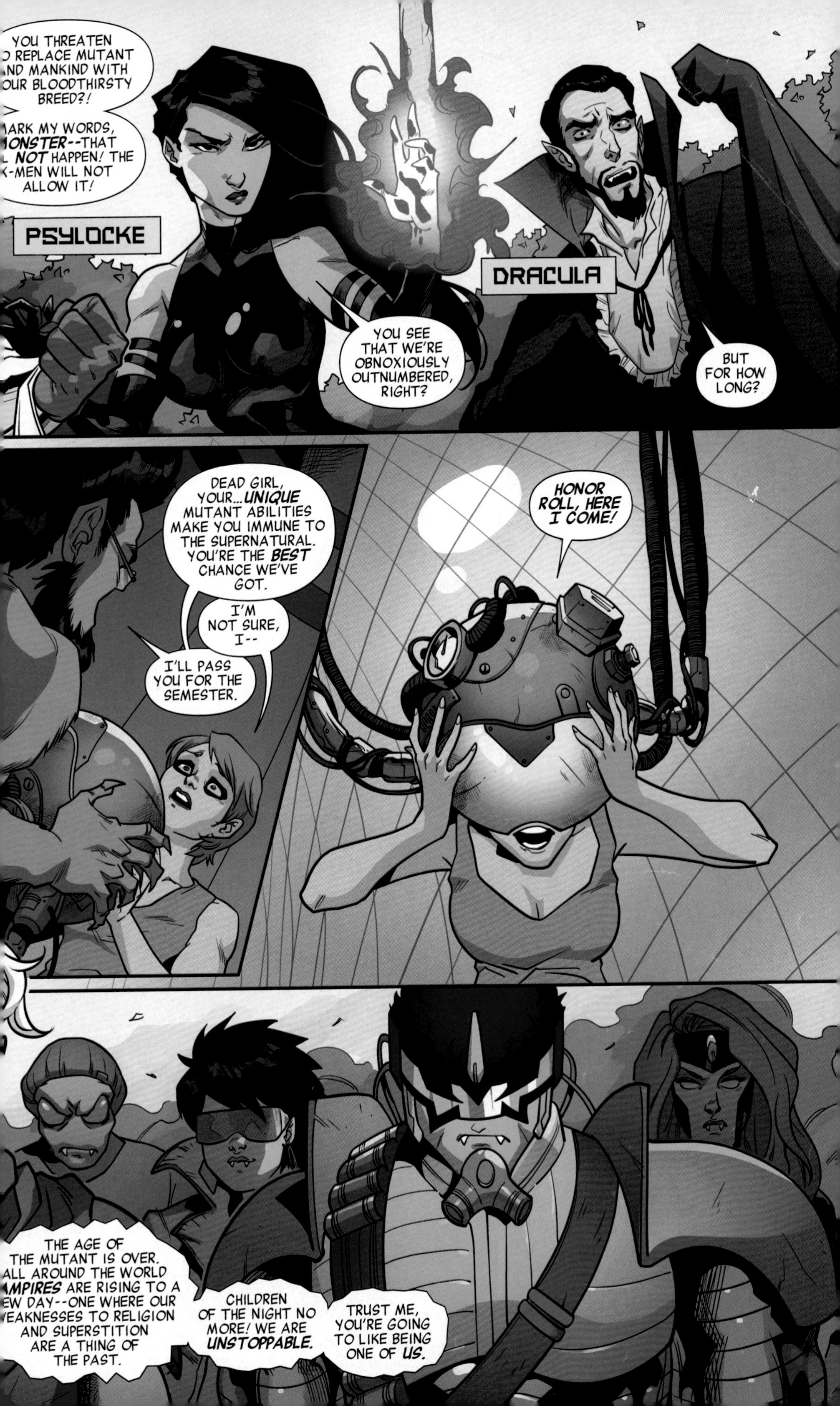
YOU THREATEN
O REPLACE MUTANT
ND MANKIND WITH
OUR BLOODTHIRSTY
BREED?!
ARK MY WORDS, ONSTER--THAT
L NOT HAPPEN! THE
-MEN WILL NOT
ALLOW IT!
PSYLOCKE
DRACULA
YOU SEE THAT WE'RE OBNOXIOUSLY OUTNUMBERED, RIGHT?
BUT FOR HOW LONG?
DEAD GIRL, YOUR... UNIQUE MUTANT ABILITIES MAKE YOU IMMUNE TO THE SUPERNATURAL. YOU'RE THE BEST CHANCE WE'VE GOT.
I'M NOT SURE, I--
I'LL PASS YOU FOR THE SEMESTER.
HONOR ROLL, HERE I COME!
THE AGE OF THE MUTANT IS OVER. ALL AROUND THE WORLD AMPIRES ARE RISING TO A EW DAY--ONE WHERE OUR EAKNESSES TO RELIGION AND SUPERSTITION ARE A THING OF THE PAST.
CHILDREN OF THE NIGHT NO MORE! WE ARE UNSTOPPABLE.
TRUST ME, YOU'RE GOING TO LIKE BEING ONE OF US.

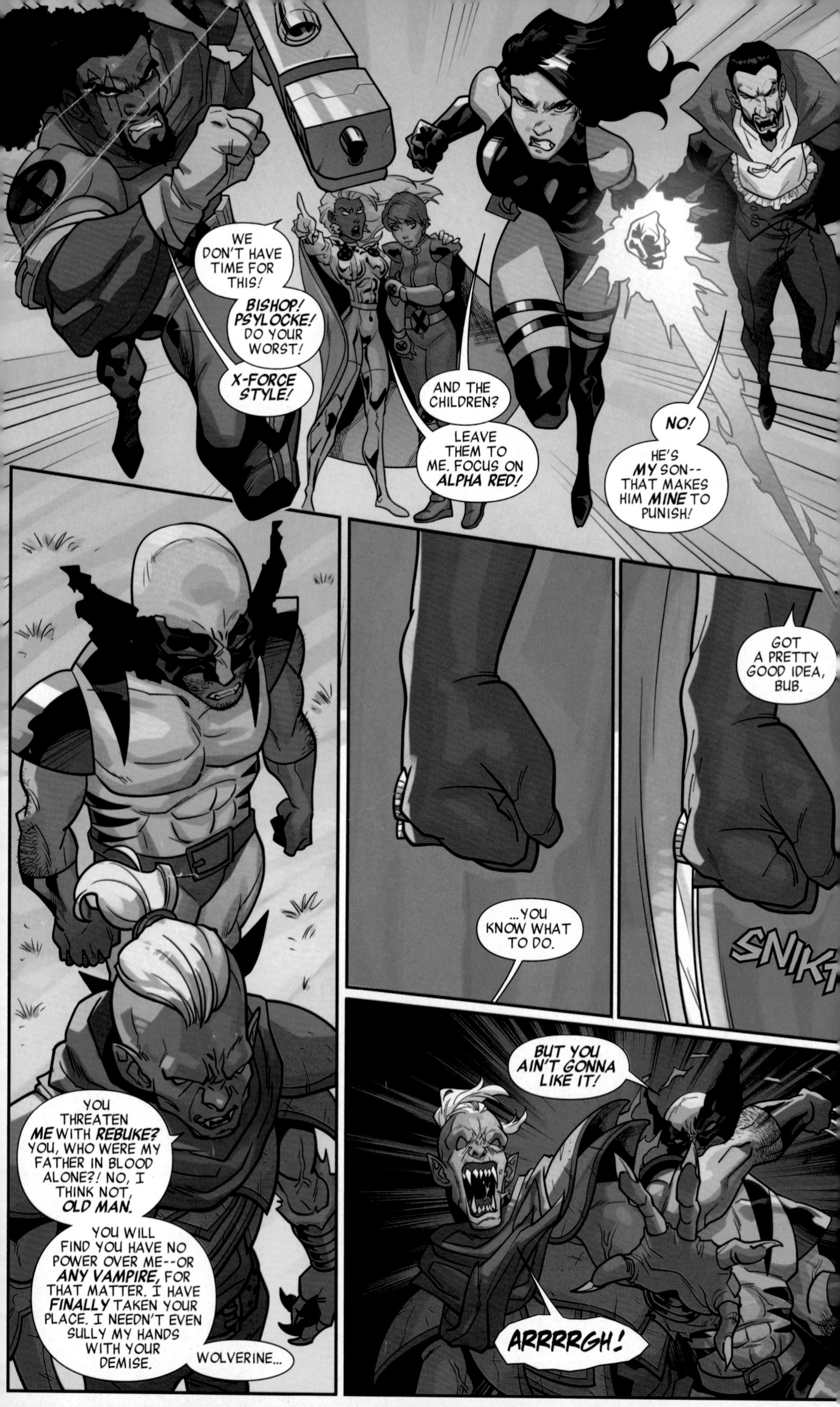

WE DON'T HAVE TIME FOR THIS!
BISHOP! PSYLOCKE! DO YOUR WORST!
X-FORCE STYLE!
AND THE CHILDREN?
LEAVE THEM TO ME. FOCUS ON ALPHA RED!
NO!
HE'S MY SON-- THAT MAKES HIM MINE TO PUNISH!
YOU THREATEN ME WITH REBUKE? YOU, WHO WERE MY FATHER IN BLOOD ALONE?! NO, I THINK NOT, OLD MAN.
YOU WILL FIND YOU HAVE NO POWER OVER ME--OR ANY VAMPIRE, FOR THAT MATTER. I HAVE FINALLY TAKEN YOUR PLACE. I NEEDN'T EVEN SULLY MY HANDS WITH YOUR DEMISE.
WOLVERINE...
...YOU KNOW WHAT TO DO.
GOT A PRETTY GOOD IDEA, BUB.
SNIKT
BUT YOU AIN'T GONNA LIKE IT!
ARRRRGH!

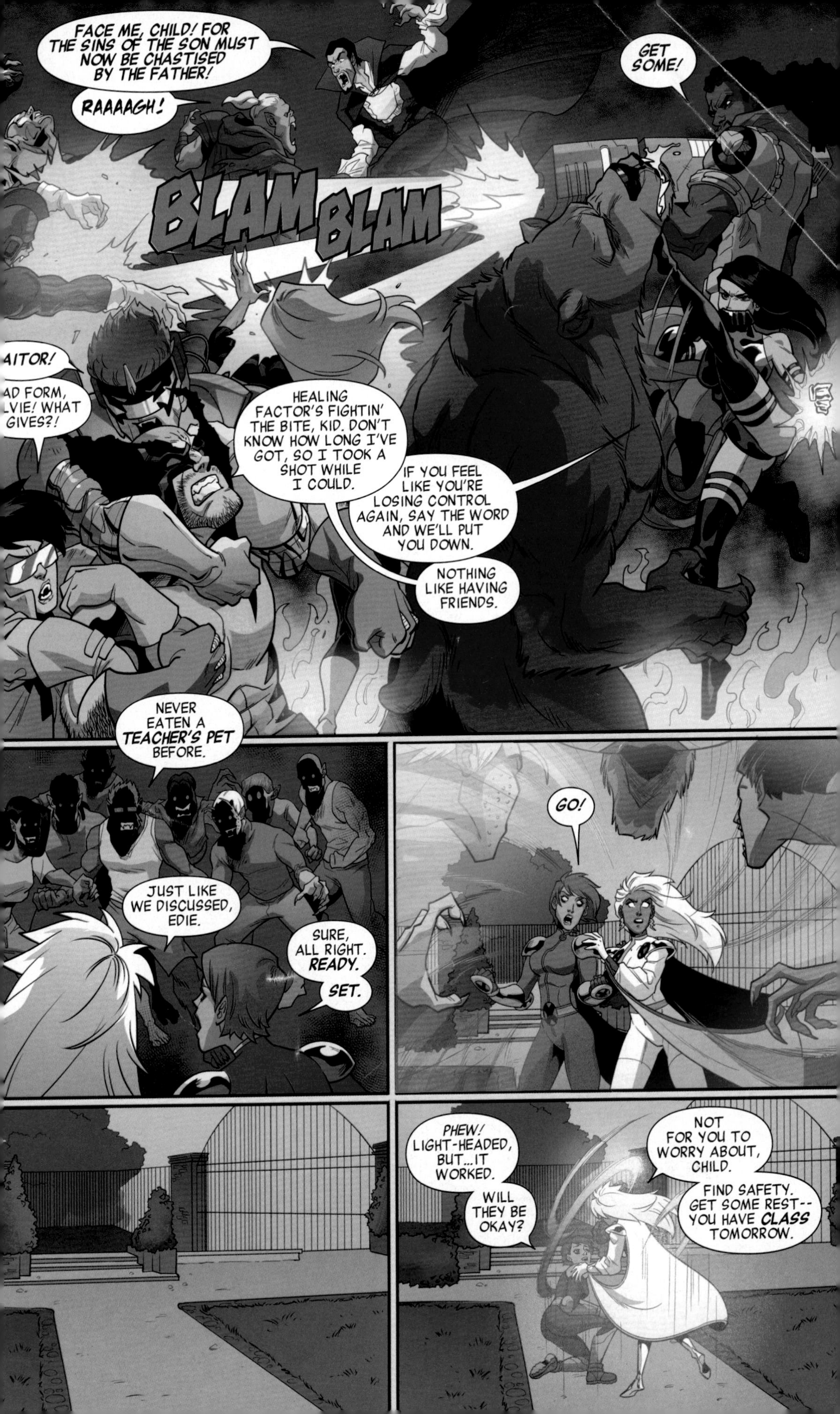
FACE ME, CHILD! FOR THE SINS OF THE SON MUST NOW BE CHASTISED BY THE FATHER!
RAAAAGH!
GET SOME!
BLAM BLAM
AITOR!
AD FORM, LVIE! WHAT GIVES?!
HEALING FACTOR'S FIGHTIN' THE BITE, KID. DON'T KNOW HOW LONG I'VE GOT, SO I TOOK A SHOT WHILE I COULD.
IF YOU FEEL LIKE YOU'RE LOSING CONTROL AGAIN, SAY THE WORD AND WE'LL PUT YOU DOWN.
NOTHING LIKE HAVING FRIENDS.
NEVER EATEN A TEACHER'S PET BEFORE.
JUST LIKE WE DISCUSSED, EDIE.
SURE, ALL RIGHT. READY.
SET.
GO!
PHEW! LIGHT-HEADED, BUT...IT WORKED.
WILL THEY BE OKAY?
NOT FOR YOU TO WORRY ABOUT, CHILD.
FIND SAFETY. GET SOME REST-- YOU HAVE CLASS TOMORROW.

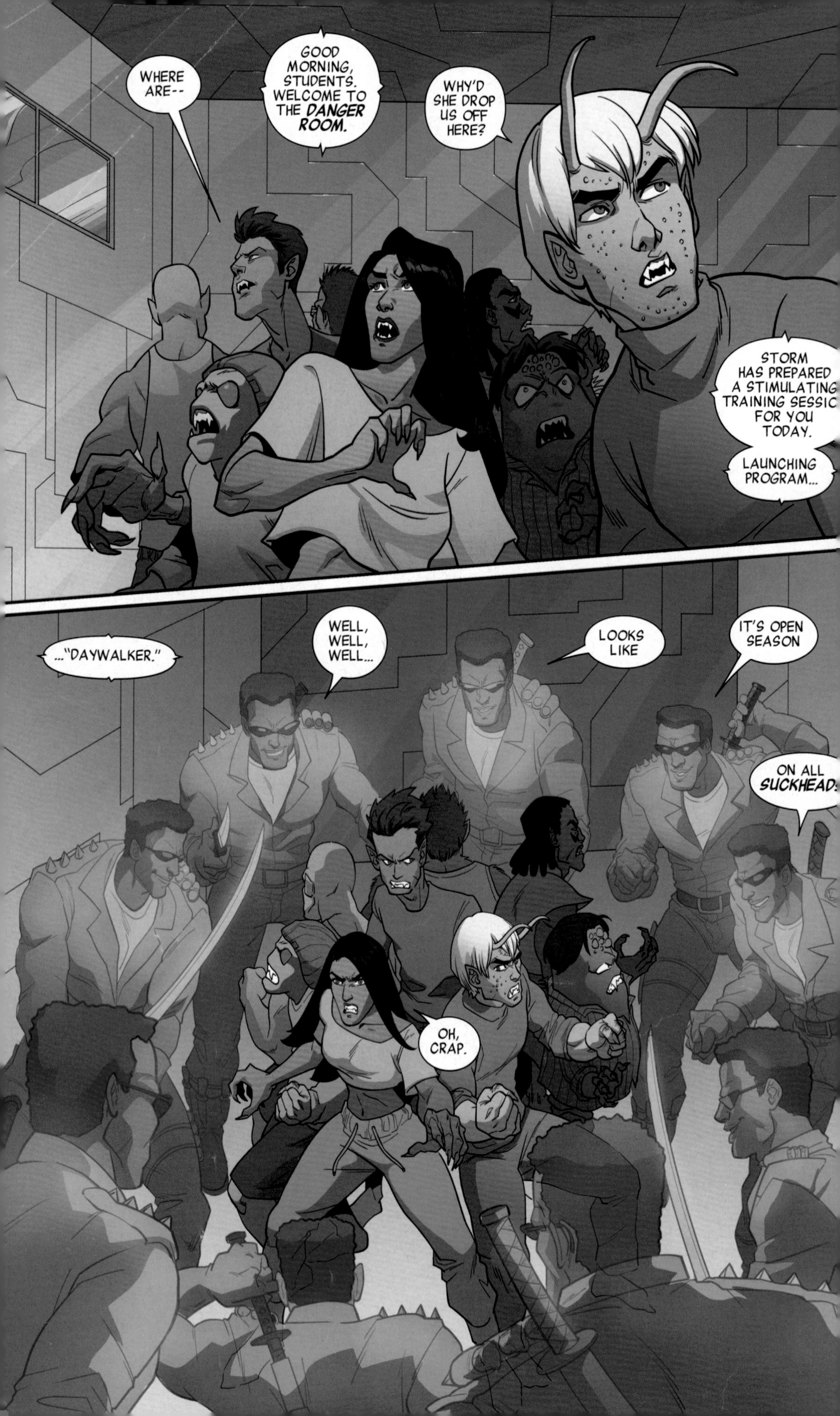
WHERE ARE--
GOOD MORNING, STUDENTS. WELCOME TO THE DANGER ROOM.
WHY'D SHE DROP US OFF HERE?
STORM HAS PREPARED A STIMULATING TRAINING SESSIC FOR YOU TODAY.
LAUNCHING PROGRAM...
..."DAYWALKER."
WELL, WELL, WELL...
LOOKS LIKE
IT'S OPEN SEASON
ON ALL SUCKHEAD
OH, CRAP.

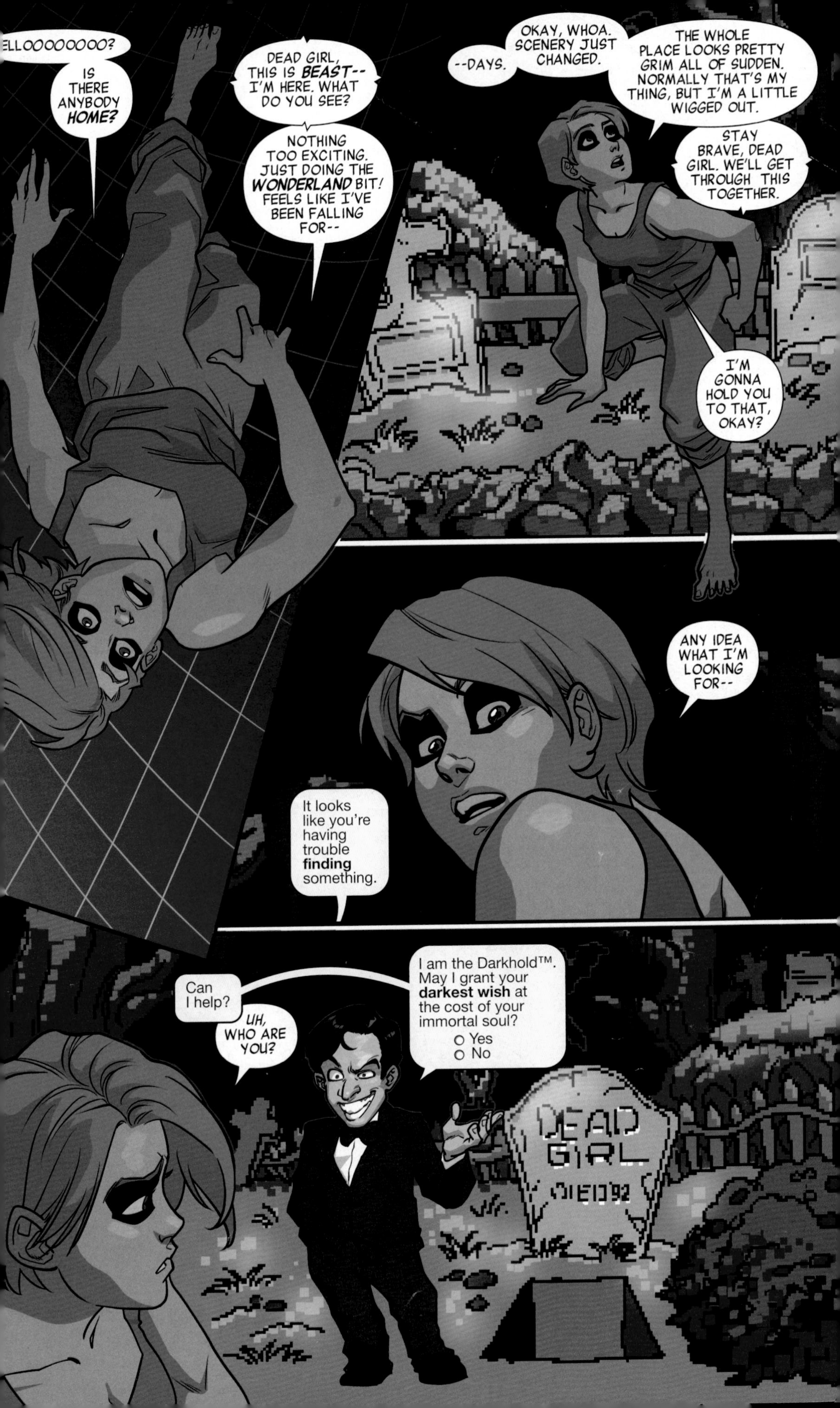

ELLOOOOOOOO?
IS THERE ANYBODY HOME?
DEAD GIRL, THIS IS BEAST-- I'M HERE. WHAT DO YOU SEE?
NOTHING TOO EXCITING. JUST DOING THE WONDERLAND BIT! FEELS LIKE I'VE BEEN FALLING FOR--
--DAYS.
OKAY, WHOA. SCENERY JUST CHANGED.
THE WHOLE PLACE LOOKS PRETTY GRIM ALL OF SUDDEN. NORMALLY THAT'S MY THING, BUT I'M A LITTLE WIGGED OUT.
STAY BRAVE, DEAD GIRL. WE'LL GET THROUGH THIS TOGETHER.
I'M GONNA HOLD YOU TO THAT, OKAY?
ANY IDEA WHAT I'M LOOKING FOR--
It looks like you're having trouble finding something.
Can I help?
UH, WHO ARE YOU?
I am the Darkhold™. May I grant your darkest wish at the cost of your immortal soul?
o Yes
o No
DEAD GIRL

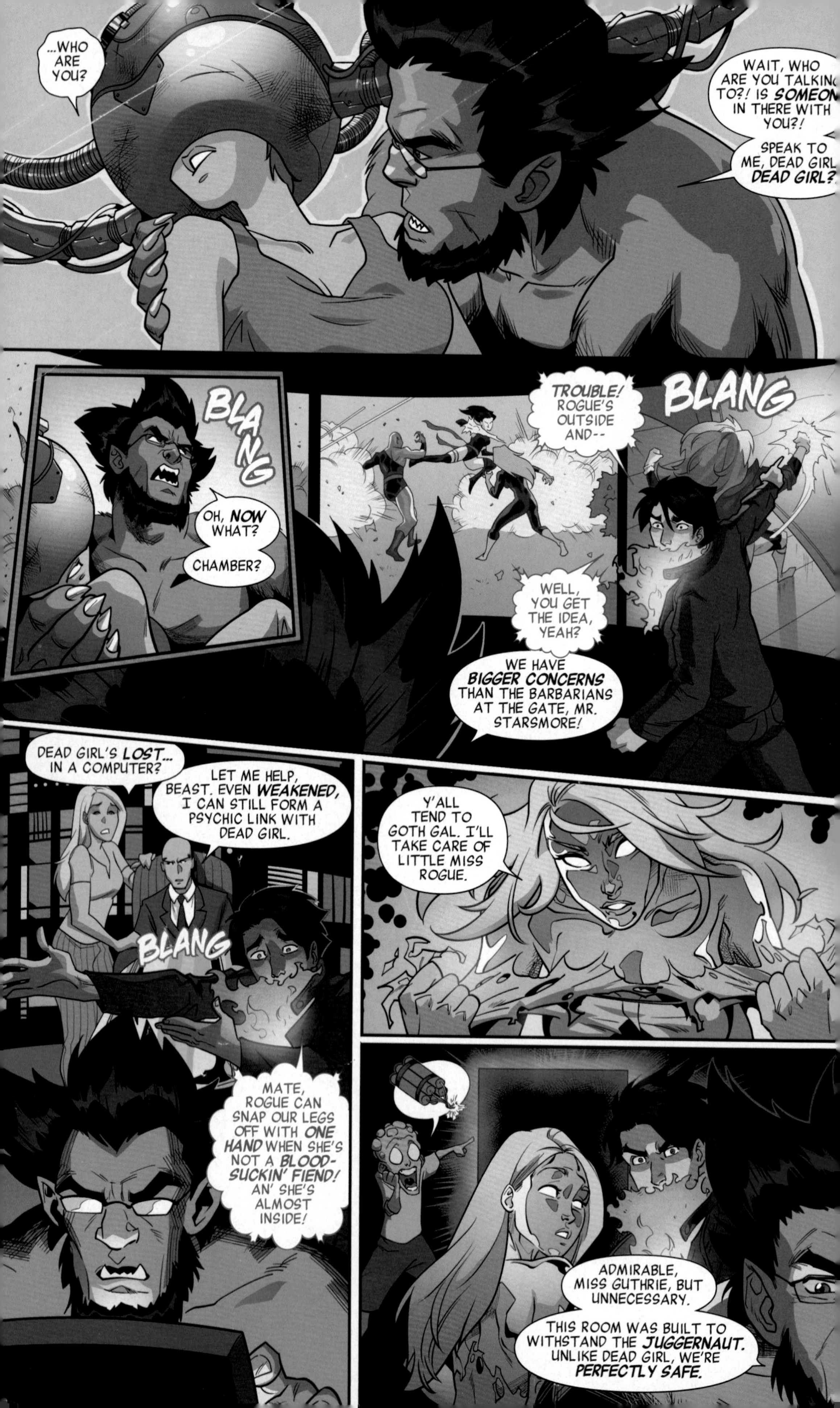
...WHO ARE YOU?
WAIT, WHO ARE YOU TALKIN TO?! IS SOMEON IN THERE WITH YOU?!
SPEAK TO ME, DEAD GIRL DEAD GIRL?
BLANG
OH, NOW WHAT?
CHAMBER?
TROUBLE! ROGUE'S OUTSIDE AND--
BLANG
WELL, YOU GET THE IDEA, YEAH?
WE HAVE BIGGER CONCERNS THAN THE BARBARIANS AT THE GATE, MR. STARSMORE!
DEAD GIRL'S LOST... IN A COMPUTER?
LET ME HELP, BEAST. EVEN WEAKENED, I CAN STILL FORM A PSYCHIC LINK WITH DEAD GIRL.
BLANG
Y'ALL TEND TO GOTH GAL. I'LL TAKE CARE OF LITTLE MISS ROGUE.
MATE, ROGUE CAN SNAP OUR LEGS OFF WITH ONE HAND WHEN SHE'S NOT A BLOOD-SUCKIN' FIEND! AN' SHE'S ALMOST INSIDE!
ADMIRABLE, MISS GUTHRIE, BUT UNNECESSARY.
THIS ROOM WAS BUILT TO WITHSTAND THE JUGGERNAUT. UNLIKE DEAD GIRL, WE'RE PERFECTLY SAFE.

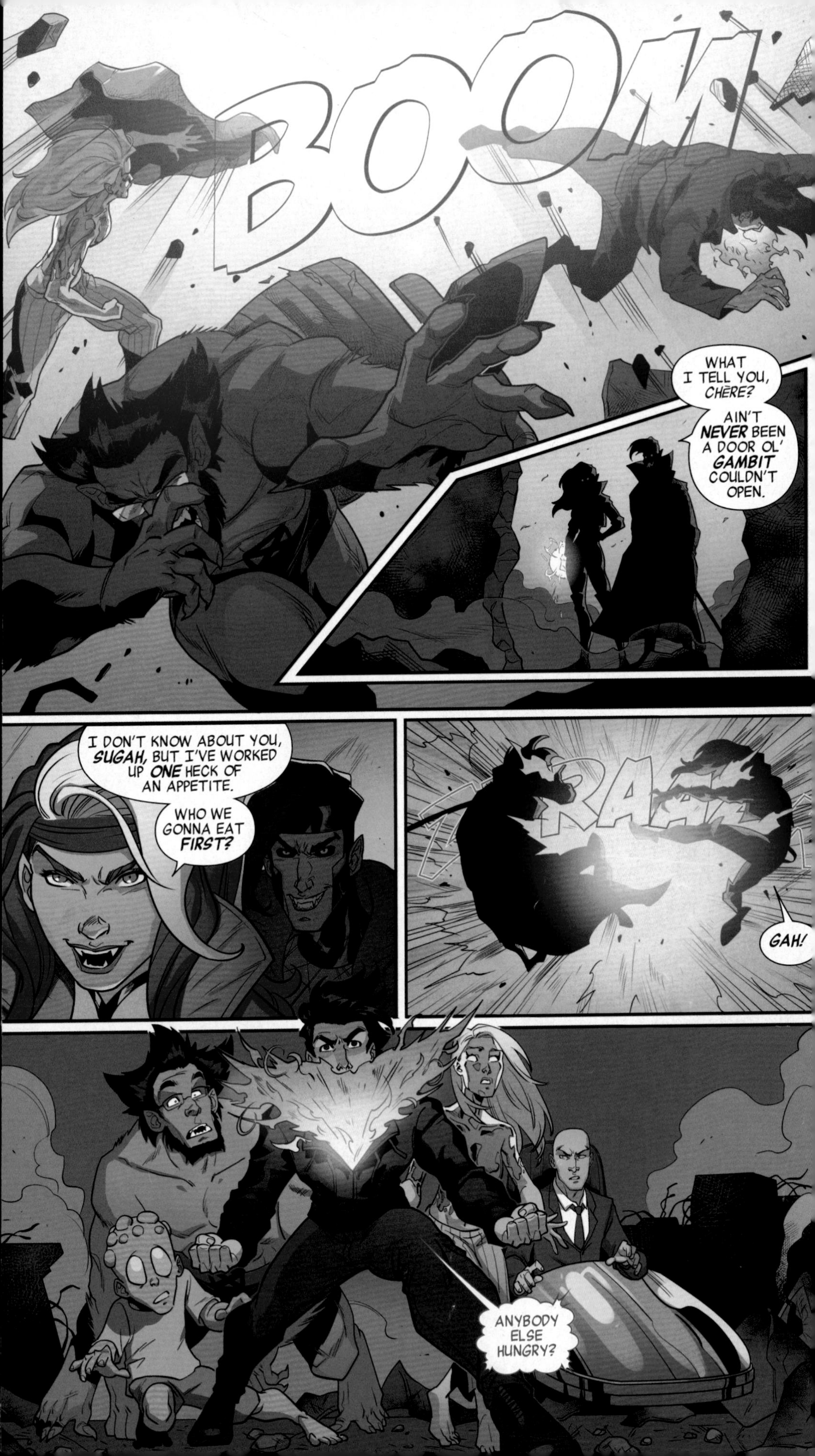

BOOM!
WHAT I TELL YOU, CHÈRE?
AIN'T NEVER BEEN A DOOR OL' GAMBIT COULDN'T OPEN.
I DON'T KNOW ABOUT YOU, SUGAH, BUT I'VE WORKED UP ONE HECK OF AN APPETITE.
WHO WE GONNA EAT FIRST?
GAH!
ANYBODY ELSE HUNGRY?

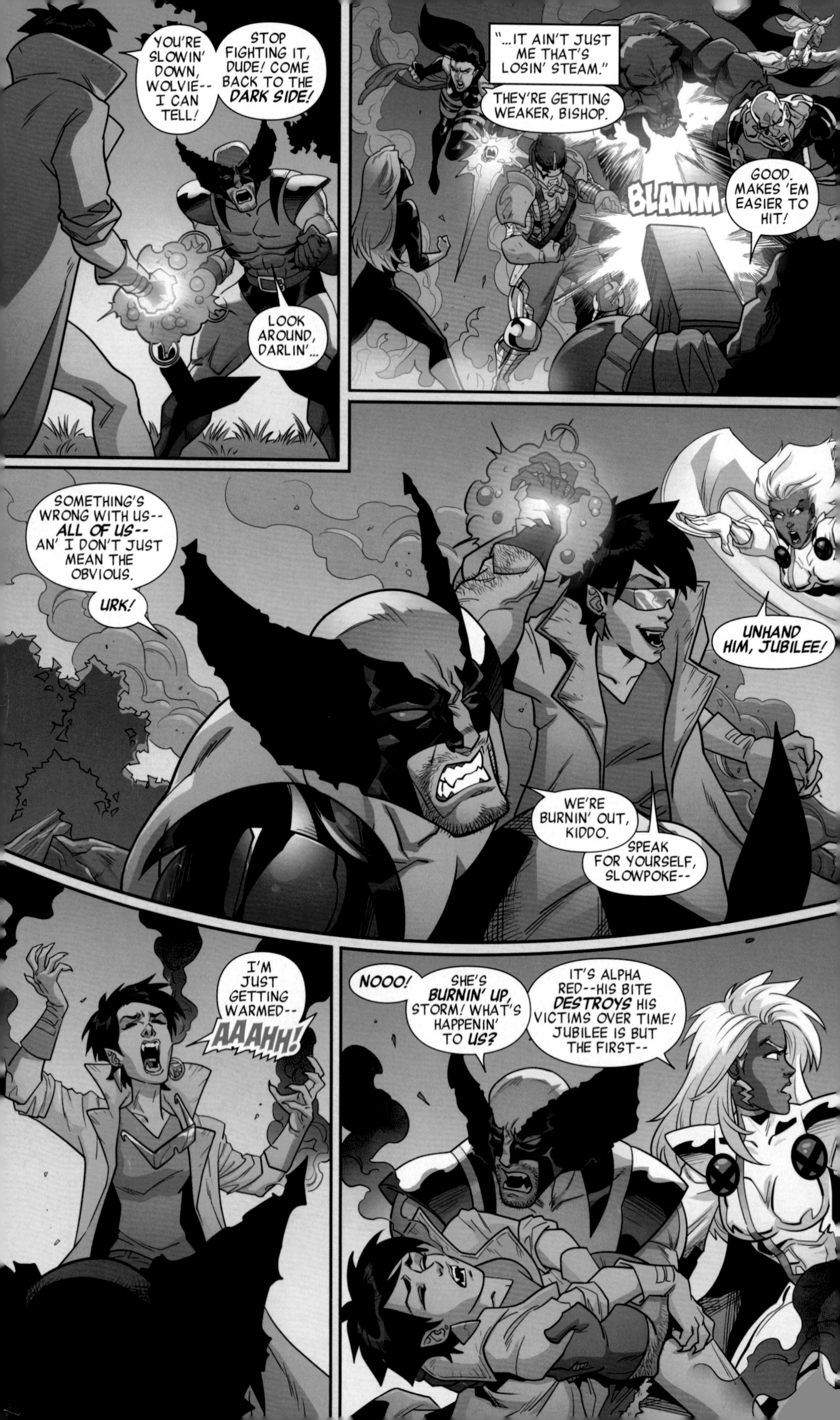
YOU'RE SLOWIN' DOWN, WOLVIE-- I CAN TELL!
STOP FIGHTING IT, DUDE! COME BACK TO THE DARK SIDE!
LOOK AROUND, DARLIN'...
"...IT AIN'T JUST ME THAT'S LOSIN' STEAM."
THEY'RE GETTING WEAKER, BISHOP.
BLAMM
GOOD. MAKES 'EM EASIER TO HIT!
SOMETHING'S WRONG WITH US-- ALL OF US-- AN' I DON'T JUST MEAN THE OBVIOUS.
URK!
UNHAND HIM, JUBILEE!
WE'RE BURNIN' OUT, KIDDO.
SPEAK FOR YOURSELF, SLOWPOKE--
I'M JUST GETTING WARMED--
AAAHH!
NOOO!
SHE'S BURNIN' UP, STORM! WHAT'S HAPPENIN' TO US?
IT'S ALPHA RED--HIS BITE DESTROYS HIS VICTIMS OVER TIME! JUBILEE IS BUT THE FIRST--

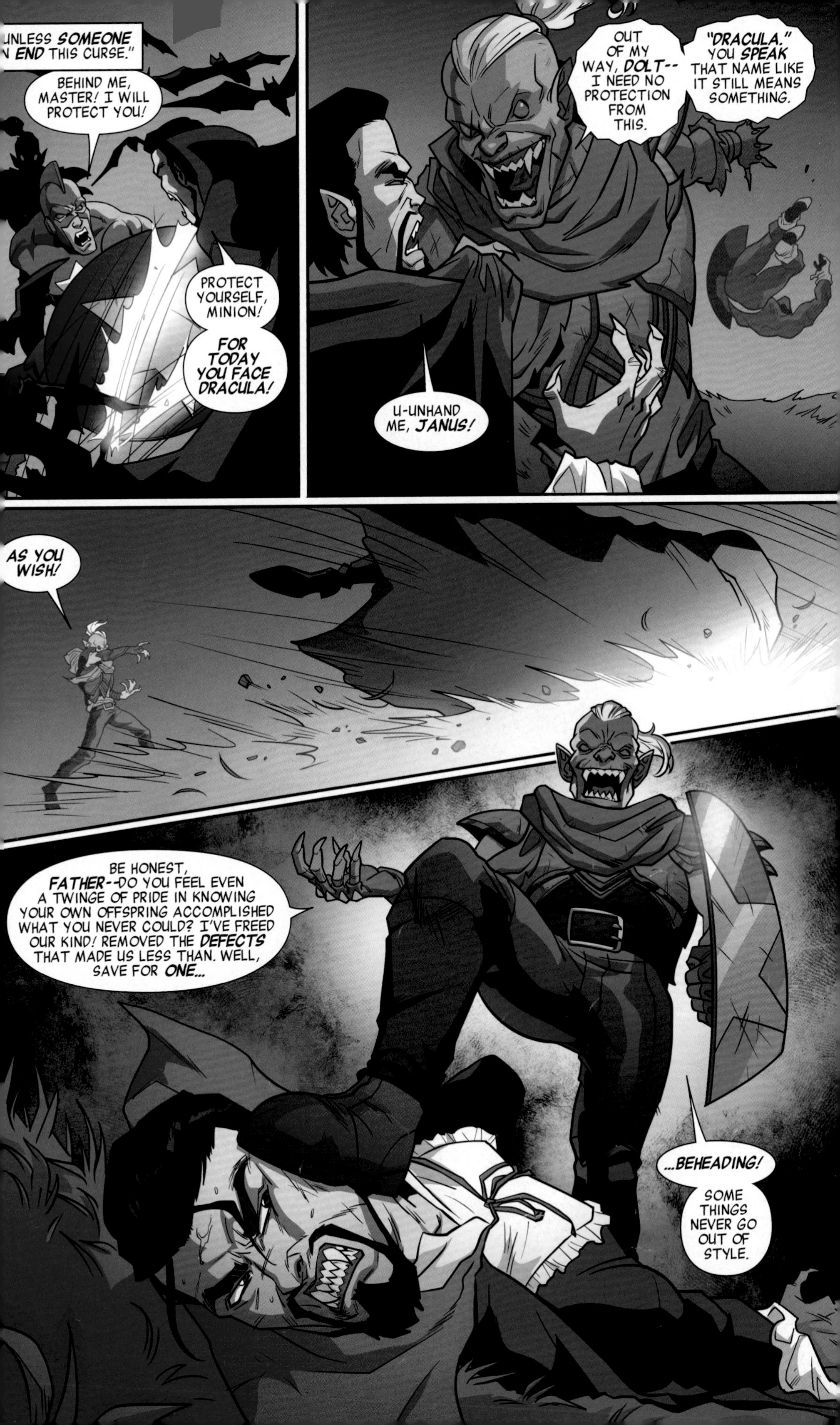

UNLESS SOMEONE
N END THIS CURSE."
BEHIND ME, MASTER! I WILL PROTECT YOU!
PROTECT YOURSELF, MINION!
FOR TODAY YOU FACE DRACULA!
OUT OF MY WAY, DOLT-- I NEED NO PROTECTION FROM THIS.
"DRACULA." YOU SPEAK THAT NAME LIKE IT STILL MEANS SOMETHING.
U-UNHAND ME, JANUS!
AS YOU WISH!
BE HONEST, FATHER--DO YOU FEEL EVEN A TWINGE OF PRIDE IN KNOWING YOUR OWN OFFSPRING ACCOMPLISHED WHAT YOU NEVER COULD? I'VE FREED OUR KIND! REMOVED THE DEFECTS THAT MADE US LESS THAN. WELL, SAVE FOR ONE...
...BEHEADING!
SOME THINGS NEVER GO OUT OF STYLE.

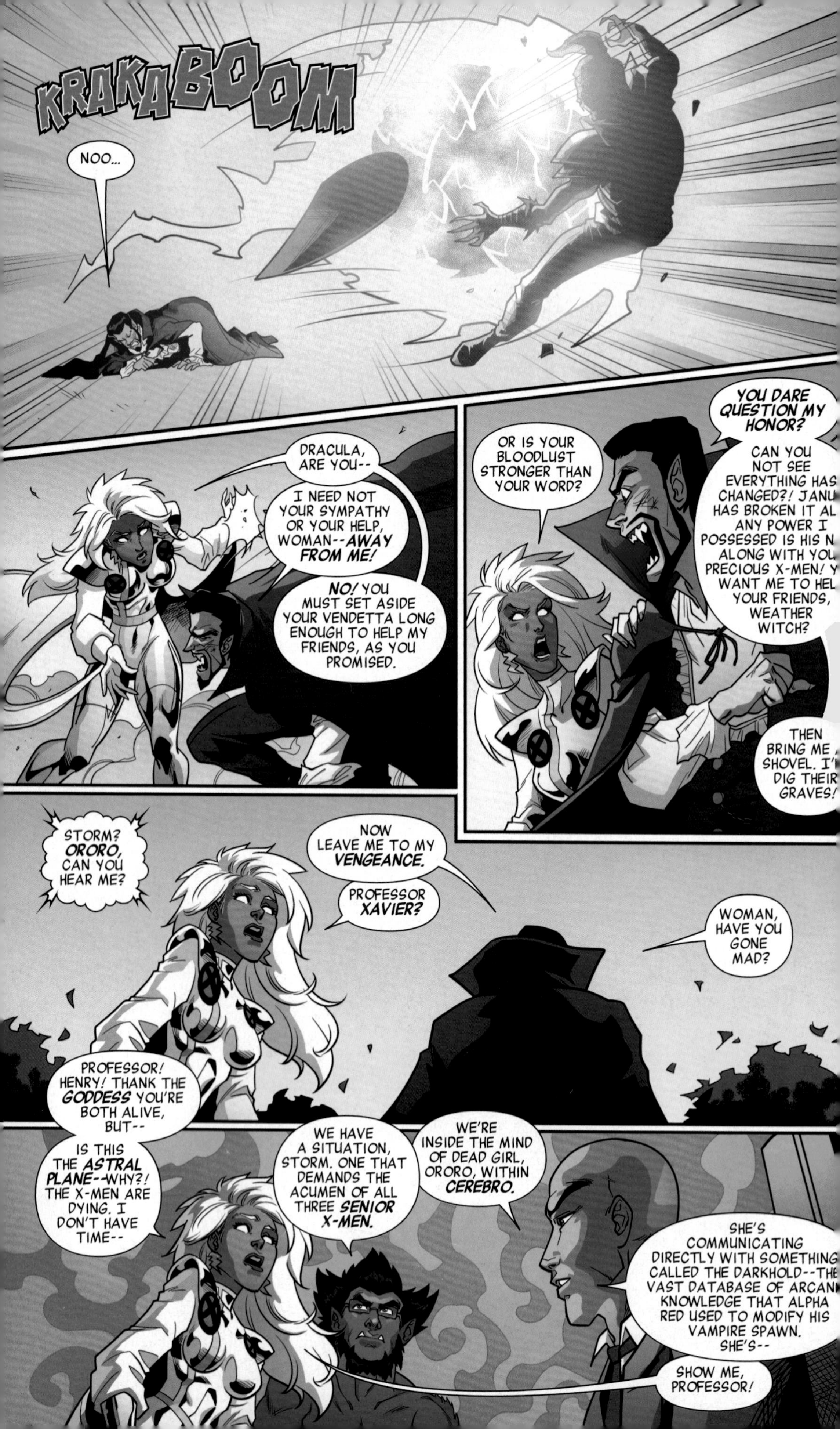
KRAKABOOM
NOO...
DRACULA, ARE YOU--
I NEED NOT YOUR SYMPATHY OR YOUR HELP, WOMAN--AWAY FROM ME!
NO! YOU MUST SET ASIDE YOUR VENDETTA LONG ENOUGH TO HELP MY FRIENDS, AS YOU PROMISED.
OR IS YOUR BLOODLUST STRONGER THAN YOUR WORD?
YOU DARE QUESTION MY HONOR?
CAN YOU NOT SEE EVERYTHING HAS CHANGED?! JANU HAS BROKEN IT AL ANY POWER I POSSESSED IS HIS N ALONG WITH YOU PRECIOUS X-MEN! Y WANT ME TO HEL YOUR FRIENDS, WEATHER WITCH?
THEN BRING ME SHOVEL. I' DIG THEIR GRAVES!
STORM? ORORO, CAN YOU HEAR ME?
NOW LEAVE ME TO MY VENGEANCE.
PROFESSOR XAVIER?
WOMAN, HAVE YOU GONE MAD?
PROFESSOR! HENRY! THANK THE GODDESS YOU'RE BOTH ALIVE, BUT--
IS THIS THE ASTRAL PLANE--WHY?! THE X-MEN ARE DYING. I DON'T HAVE TIME--
WE HAVE A SITUATION, STORM. ONE THAT DEMANDS THE ACUMEN OF ALL THREE SENIOR X-MEN.
WE'RE INSIDE THE MIND OF DEAD GIRL, ORORO, WITHIN CEREBRO.
SHE'S COMMUNICATING DIRECTLY WITH SOMETHING CALLED THE DARKHOLD--THE VAST DATABASE OF ARCAN KNOWLEDGE THAT ALPHA RED USED TO MODIFY HIS VAMPIRE SPAWN. SHE'S--
SHOW ME, PROFESSOR!

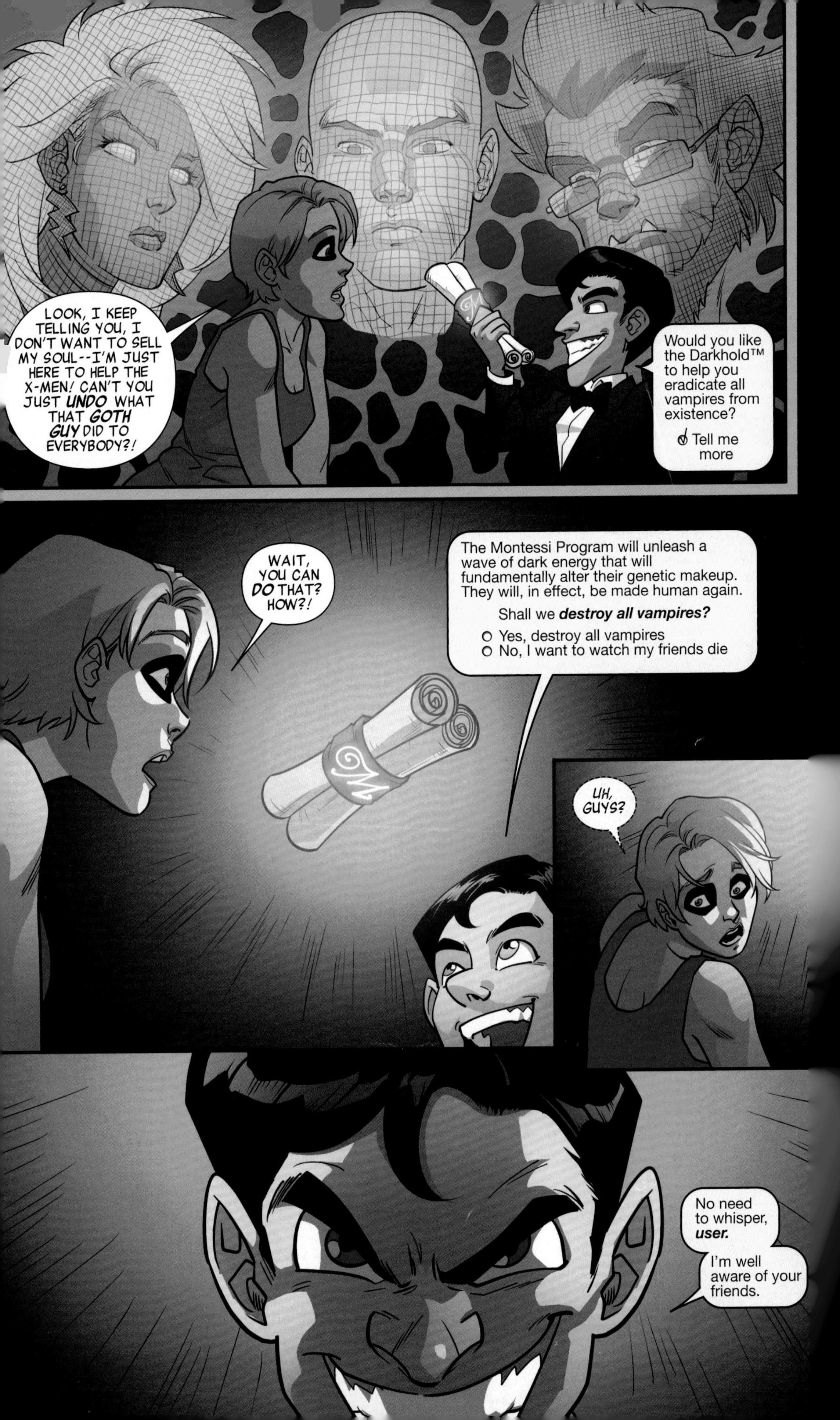
LOOK, I KEEP TELLING YOU, I DON'T WANT TO SELL MY SOUL--I'M JUST HERE TO HELP THE X-MEN! CAN'T YOU JUST **UNDO** WHAT THAT **GOTH GUY** DID TO EVERYBODY?!
Would you like the Darkhold™ to help you eradicate all vampires from existence?
Tell me more
WAIT, YOU CAN **DO** THAT? HOW?!
The Montessi Program will unleash a wave of dark energy that will fundamentally alter their genetic makeup. They will, in effect, be made human again.
Shall we ***destroy all vampires?***
Yes, destroy all vampires
No, I want to watch my friends die
UH, GUYS?
No need to whisper, ***user.***
I'm well aware of your friends.

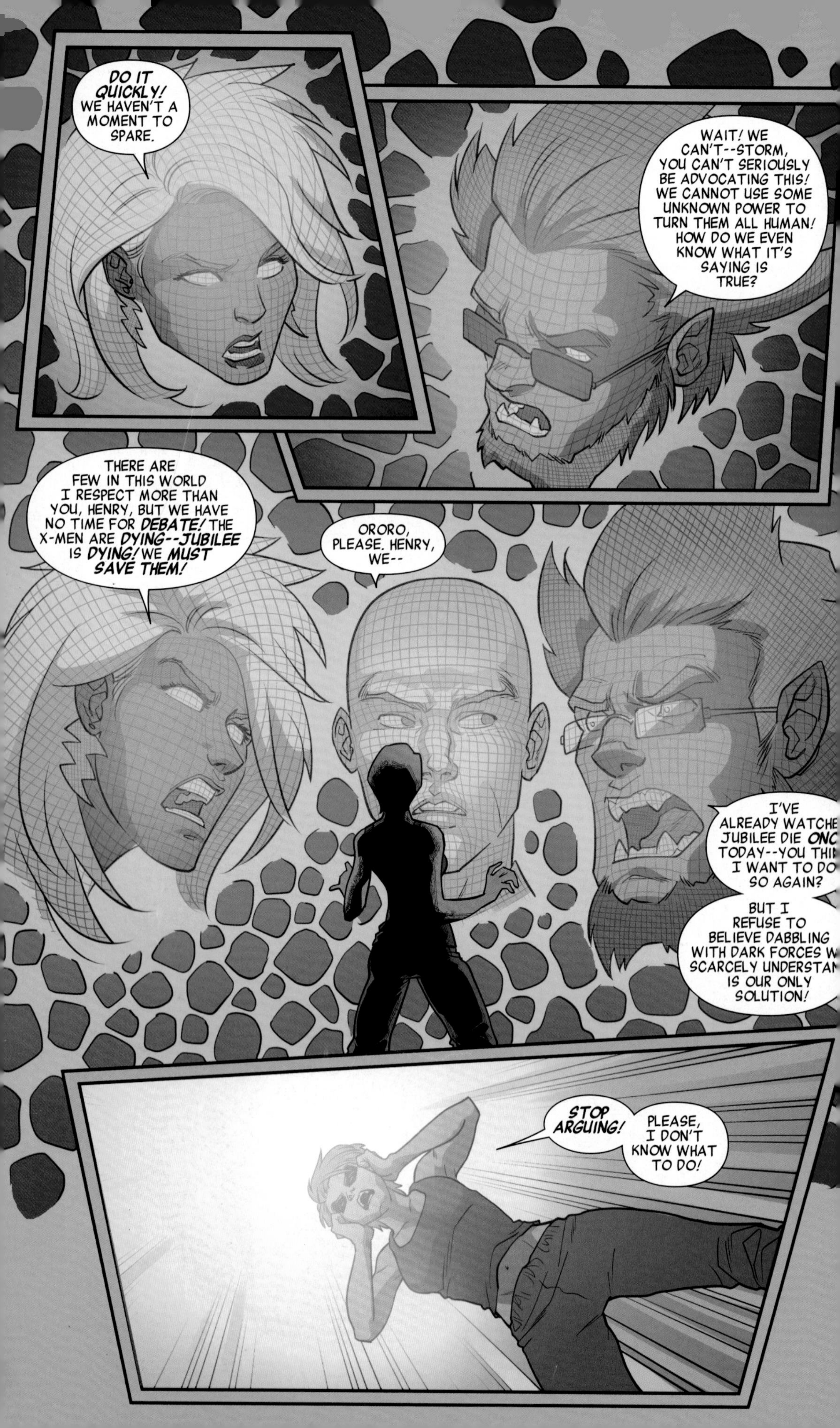
DO IT QUICKLY! WE HAVEN'T A MOMENT TO SPARE.
WAIT! WE CAN'T--STORM, YOU CAN'T SERIOUSLY BE ADVOCATING THIS! WE CANNOT USE SOME UNKNOWN POWER TO TURN THEM ALL HUMAN! HOW DO WE EVEN KNOW WHAT IT'S SAYING IS TRUE?
THERE ARE FEW IN THIS WORLD I RESPECT MORE THAN YOU, HENRY, BUT WE HAVE NO TIME FOR DEBATE! THE X-MEN ARE DYING--JUBILEE IS DYING! WE MUST SAVE THEM!
ORORO, PLEASE. HENRY, WE--
I'VE ALREADY WATCHE JUBILEE DIE ONC TODAY--YOU THI I WANT TO DO SO AGAIN?
BUT I REFUSE TO BELIEVE DABBLING WITH DARK FORCES W SCARCELY UNDERSTA IS OUR ONLY SOLUTION!
STOP ARGUING!
PLEASE, I DON'T KNOW WHAT TO DO!

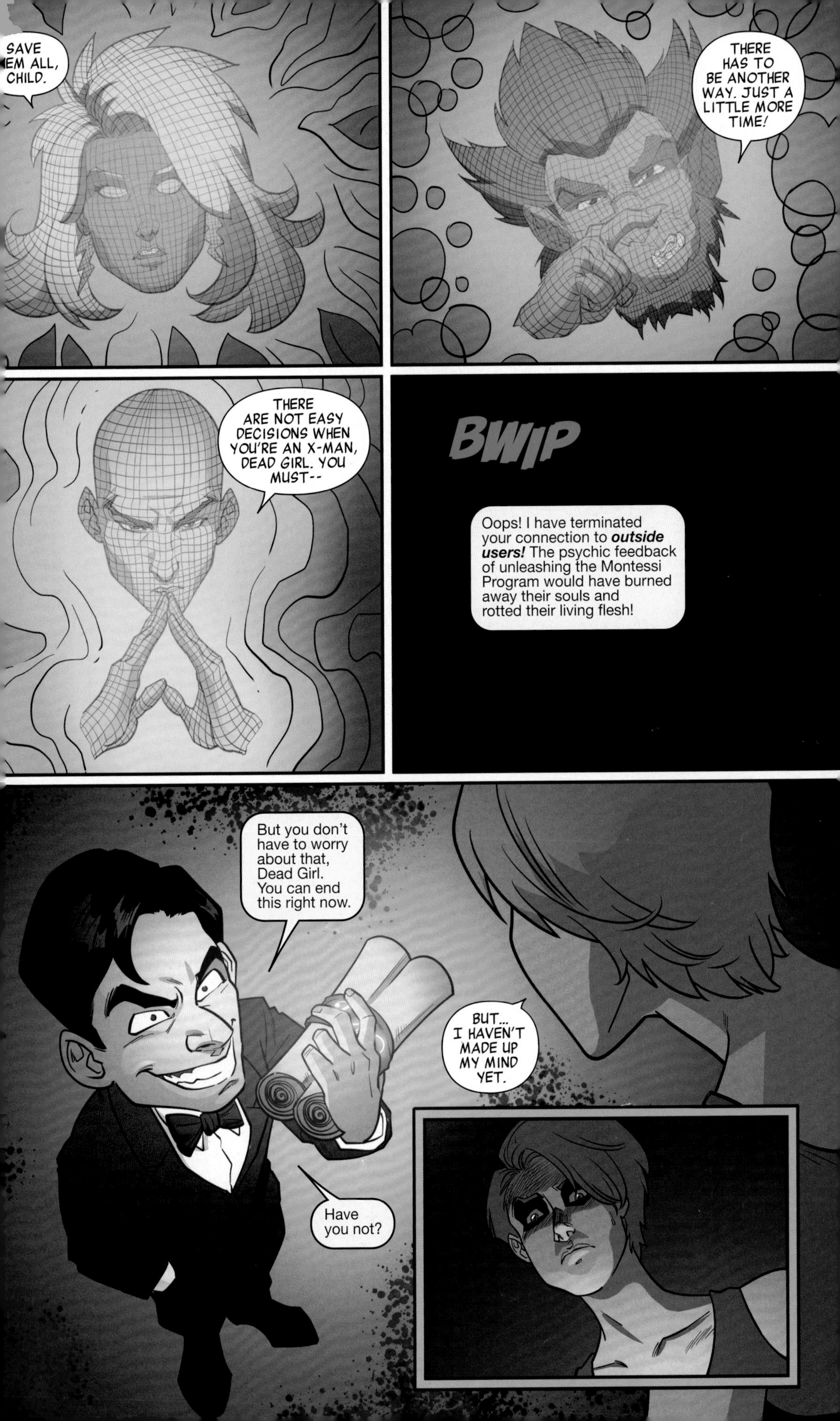
SAVE 'EM ALL, CHILD.
THERE HAS TO BE ANOTHER WAY. JUST A LITTLE MORE TIME!
THERE ARE NOT EASY DECISIONS WHEN YOU'RE AN X-MAN, DEAD GIRL. YOU MUST--
BWIP
Oops! I have terminated your connection to ***outside users!*** The psychic feedback of unleashing the Montessi Program would have burned away their souls and rotted their living flesh!
But you don't have to worry about that, Dead Girl. You can end this right now.
BUT... I HAVEN'T MADE UP MY MIND YET.
Have you not?

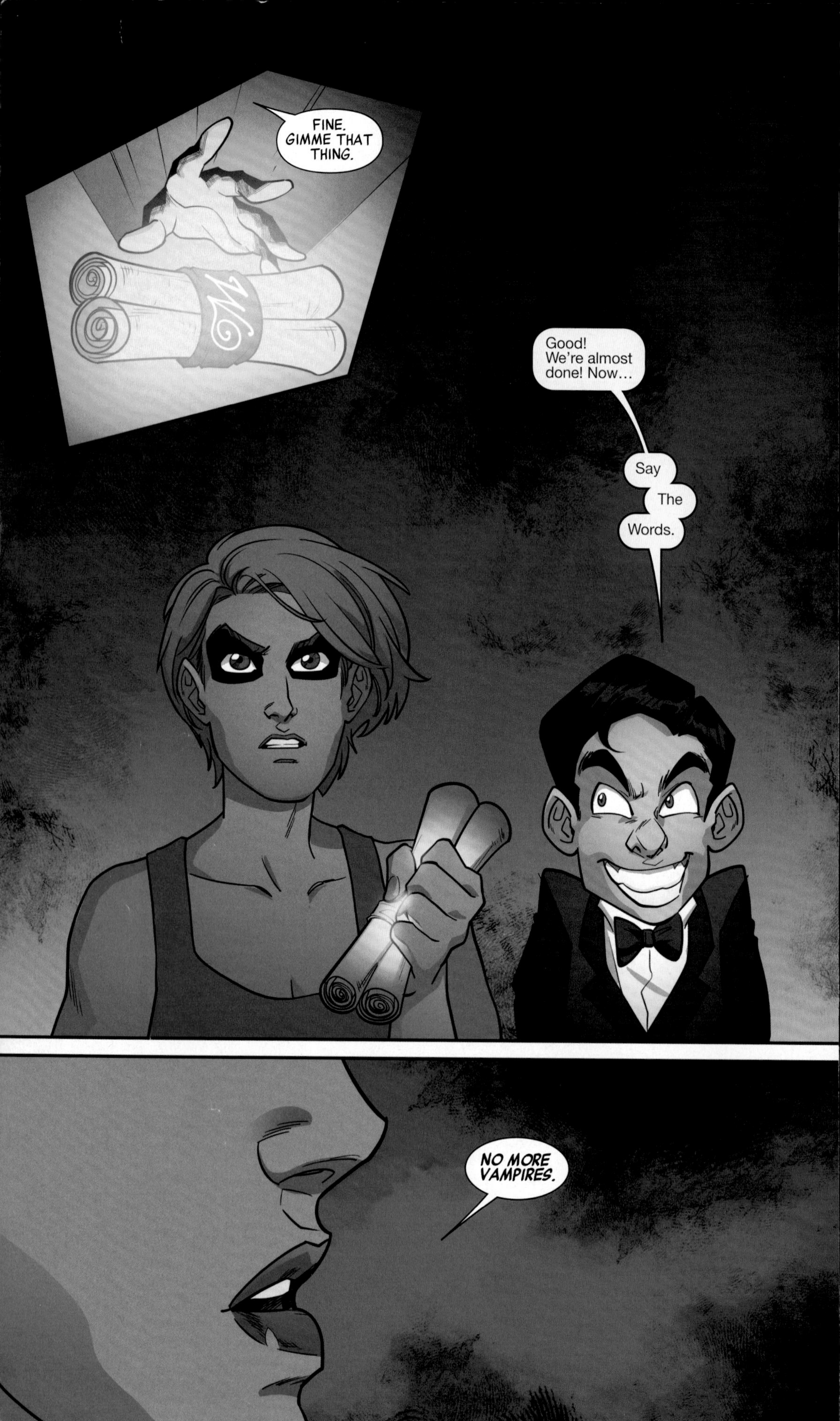

FINE. GIMME THAT THING.
Good! We're almost done! Now...
Say
The
Words.
NO MORE VAMPIRES.

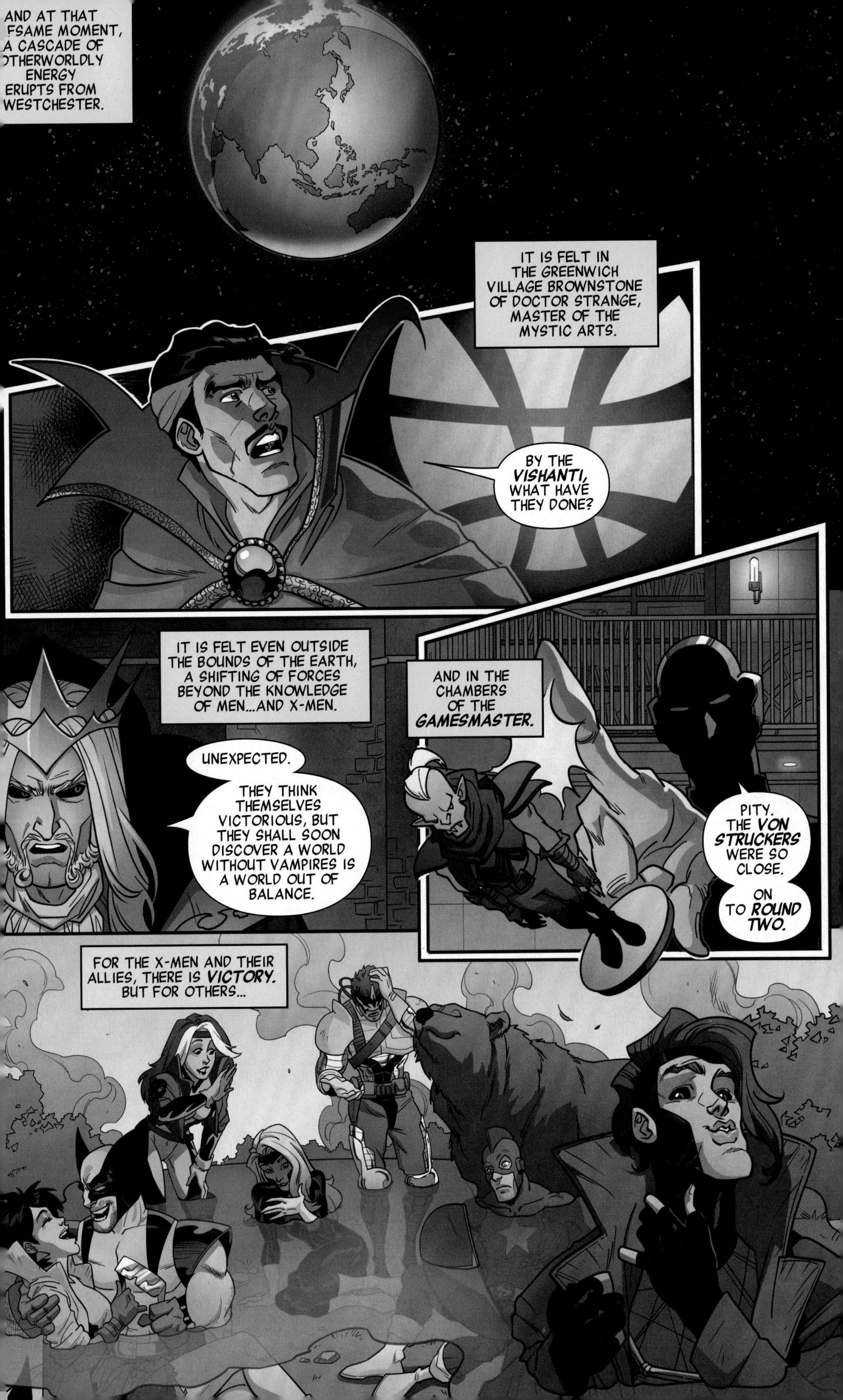

AND AT THAT SAME MOMENT, A CASCADE OF OTHERWORLDLY ENERGY ERUPTS FROM WESTCHESTER.
IT IS FELT IN THE GREENWICH VILLAGE BROWNSTONE OF DOCTOR STRANGE, MASTER OF THE MYSTIC ARTS.
BY THE VISHANTI, WHAT HAVE THEY DONE?
IT IS FELT EVEN OUTSIDE THE BOUNDS OF THE EARTH, A SHIFTING OF FORCES BEYOND THE KNOWLEDGE OF MEN...AND X-MEN.
UNEXPECTED.
THEY THINK THEMSELVES VICTORIOUS, BUT THEY SHALL SOON DISCOVER A WORLD WITHOUT VAMPIRES IS A WORLD OUT OF BALANCE.
AND IN THE CHAMBERS OF THE GAMESMASTER.
PITY. THE VON STRUCKERS WERE SO CLOSE.
ON TO ROUND TWO.
FOR THE X-MEN AND THEIR ALLIES, THERE IS VICTORY. BUT FOR OTHERS...

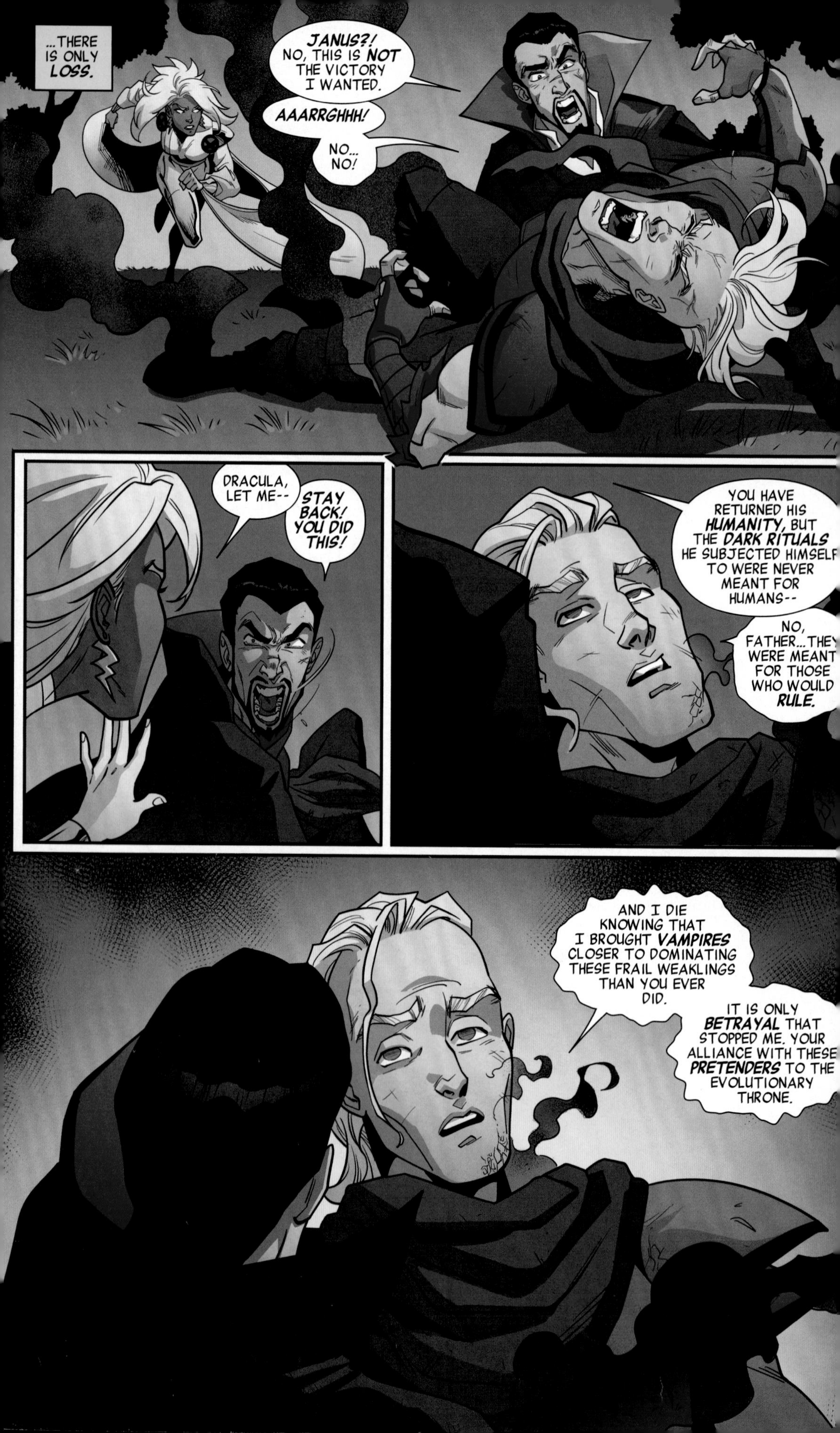
...THERE IS ONLY LOSS.
JANUS?! NO, THIS IS NOT THE VICTORY I WANTED.
AAARRGHHH!
NO... NO!
DRACULA, LET ME--
STAY BACK! YOU DID THIS!
YOU HAVE RETURNED HIS HUMANITY, BUT THE DARK RITUALS HE SUBJECTED HIMSELF TO WERE NEVER MEANT FOR HUMANS--
NO, FATHER...THEY WERE MEANT FOR THOSE WHO WOULD RULE.
AND I DIE KNOWING THAT I BROUGHT VAMPIRES CLOSER TO DOMINATING THESE FRAIL WEAKLINGS THAN YOU EVER DID.
IT IS ONLY BETRAYAL THAT STOPPED ME. YOUR ALLIANCE WITH THESE PRETENDERS TO THE EVOLUTIONARY THRONE.

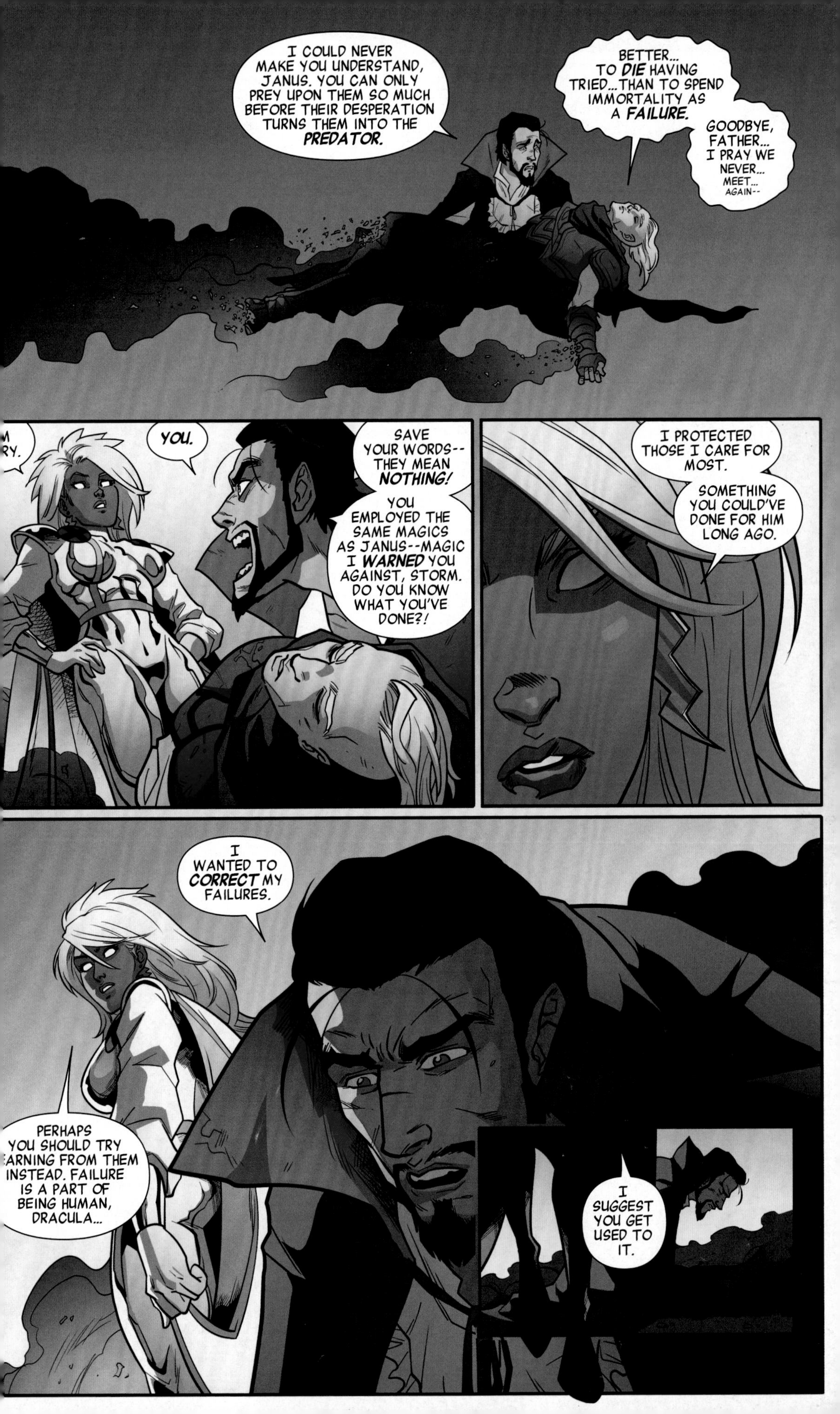
I COULD NEVER MAKE YOU UNDERSTAND, JANUS. YOU CAN ONLY PREY UPON THEM SO MUCH BEFORE THEIR DESPERATION TURNS THEM INTO THE PREDATOR.
BETTER... TO DIE HAVING TRIED...THAN TO SPEND IMMORTALITY AS A FAILURE.
GOODBYE, FATHER... I PRAY WE NEVER... MEET... AGAIN--
YOU.
SAVE YOUR WORDS-- THEY MEAN NOTHING!
YOU EMPLOYED THE SAME MAGICS AS JANUS--MAGIC I WARNED YOU AGAINST, STORM. DO YOU KNOW WHAT YOU'VE DONE?!
I PROTECTED THOSE I CARE FOR MOST.
SOMETHING YOU COULD'VE DONE FOR HIM LONG AGO.
I WANTED TO CORRECT MY FAILURES.
PERHAPS YOU SHOULD TRY EARNING FROM THEM INSTEAD. FAILURE IS A PART OF BEING HUMAN, DRACULA...
I SUGGEST YOU GET USED TO IT.

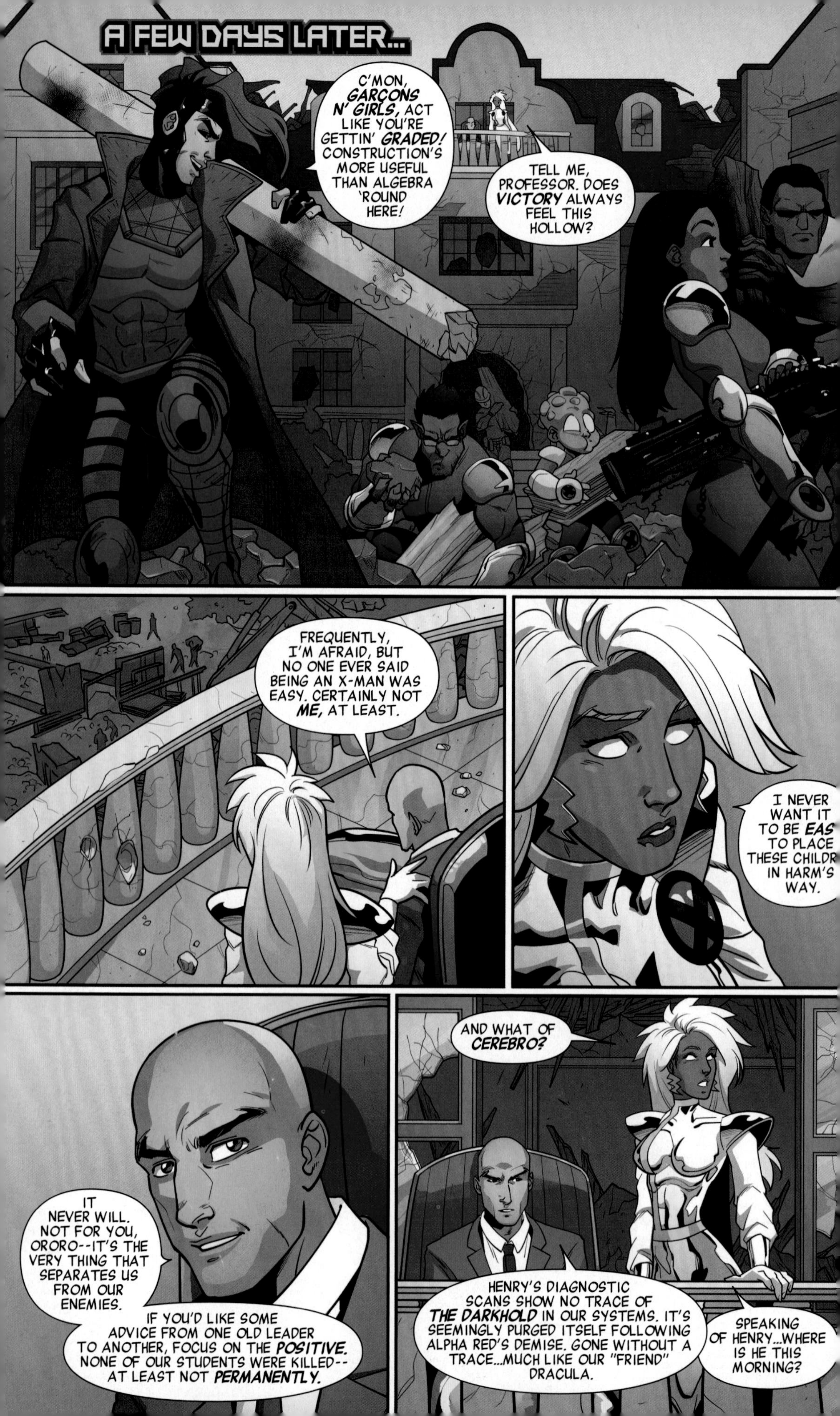
A FEW DAYS LATER...
C'MON, GARÇONS N' GIRLS, ACT LIKE YOU'RE GETTIN' GRADED! CONSTRUCTION'S MORE USEFUL THAN ALGEBRA 'ROUND HERE!
TELL ME, PROFESSOR. DOES VICTORY ALWAYS FEEL THIS HOLLOW?
FREQUENTLY, I'M AFRAID, BUT NO ONE EVER SAID BEING AN X-MAN WAS EASY. CERTAINLY NOT ME, AT LEAST.
I NEVER WANT IT TO BE EAS TO PLACE THESE CHILDR IN HARM'S WAY.
IT NEVER WILL. NOT FOR YOU, ORORO--IT'S THE VERY THING THAT SEPARATES US FROM OUR ENEMIES.
IF YOU'D LIKE SOME ADVICE FROM ONE OLD LEADER TO ANOTHER, FOCUS ON THE POSITIVE. NONE OF OUR STUDENTS WERE KILLED-- AT LEAST NOT PERMANENTLY.
AND WHAT OF CEREBRO?
HENRY'S DIAGNOSTIC SCANS SHOW NO TRACE OF THE DARKHOLD IN OUR SYSTEMS. IT'S SEEMINGLY PURGED ITSELF FOLLOWING ALPHA RED'S DEMISE. GONE WITHOUT A TRACE...MUCH LIKE OUR "FRIEND" DRACULA.
SPEAKING OF HENRY...WHERE IS HE THIS MORNING?

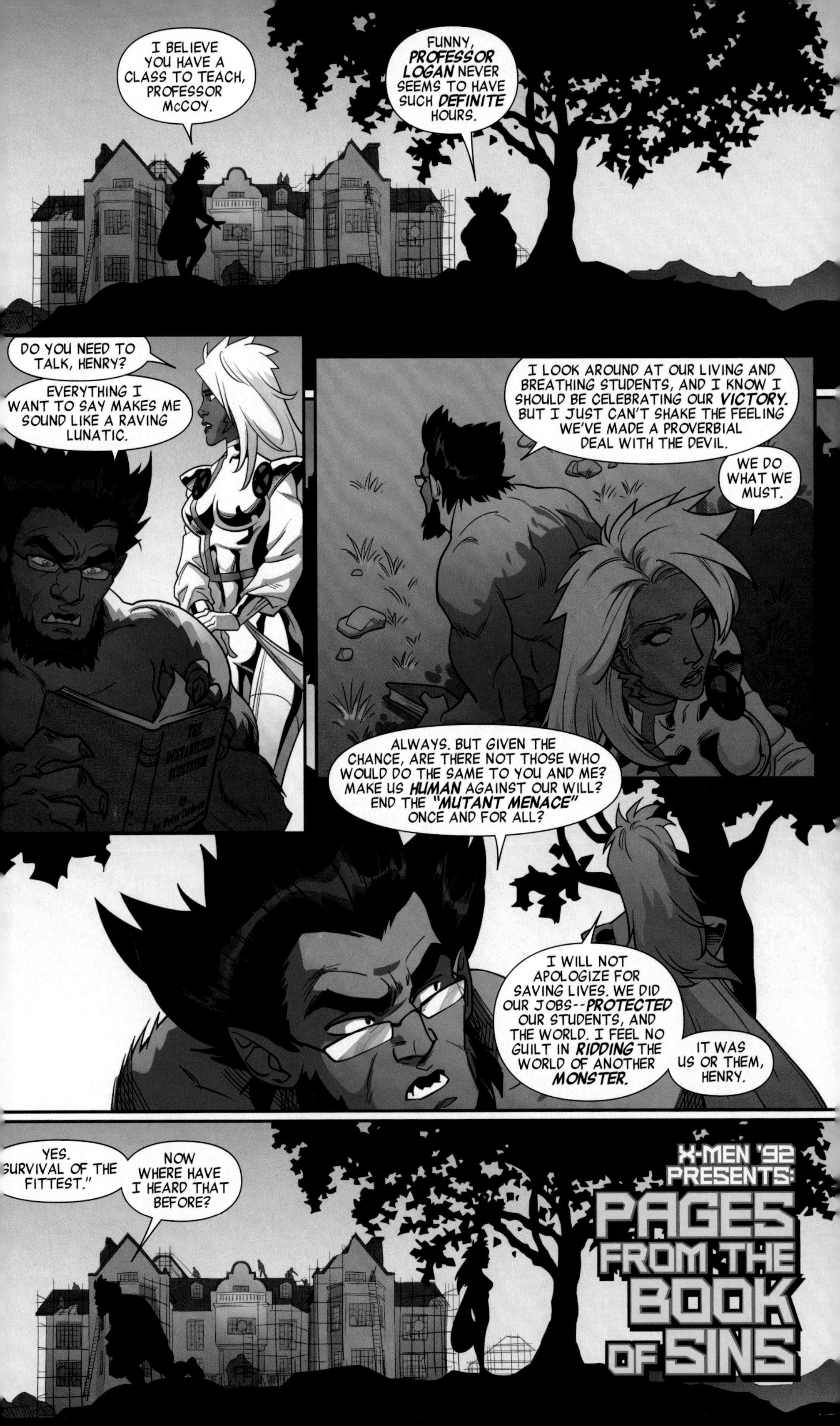
I BELIEVE YOU HAVE A CLASS TO TEACH, PROFESSOR McCOY.
FUNNY, PROFESSOR LOGAN NEVER SEEMS TO HAVE SUCH DEFINITE HOURS.
DO YOU NEED TO TALK, HENRY?
EVERYTHING I WANT TO SAY MAKES ME SOUND LIKE A RAVING LUNATIC.
I LOOK AROUND AT OUR LIVING AND BREATHING STUDENTS, AND I KNOW I SHOULD BE CELEBRATING OUR VICTORY. BUT I JUST CAN'T SHAKE THE FEELING WE'VE MADE A PROVERBIAL DEAL WITH THE DEVIL.
WE DO WHAT WE MUST.
ALWAYS. BUT GIVEN THE CHANCE, ARE THERE NOT THOSE WHO WOULD DO THE SAME TO YOU AND ME? MAKE US HUMAN AGAINST OUR WILL? END THE "MUTANT MENACE" ONCE AND FOR ALL?
I WILL NOT APOLOGIZE FOR SAVING LIVES. WE DID OUR JOBS--PROTECTED OUR STUDENTS, AND THE WORLD. I FEEL NO GUILT IN RIDDING THE WORLD OF ANOTHER MONSTER.
IT WAS US OR THEM, HENRY.
YES. "SURVIVAL OF THE FITTEST."
NOW WHERE HAVE I HEARD THAT BEFORE?
X-MEN '92 PRESENTS:
PAGES FROM THE BOOK OF SINS

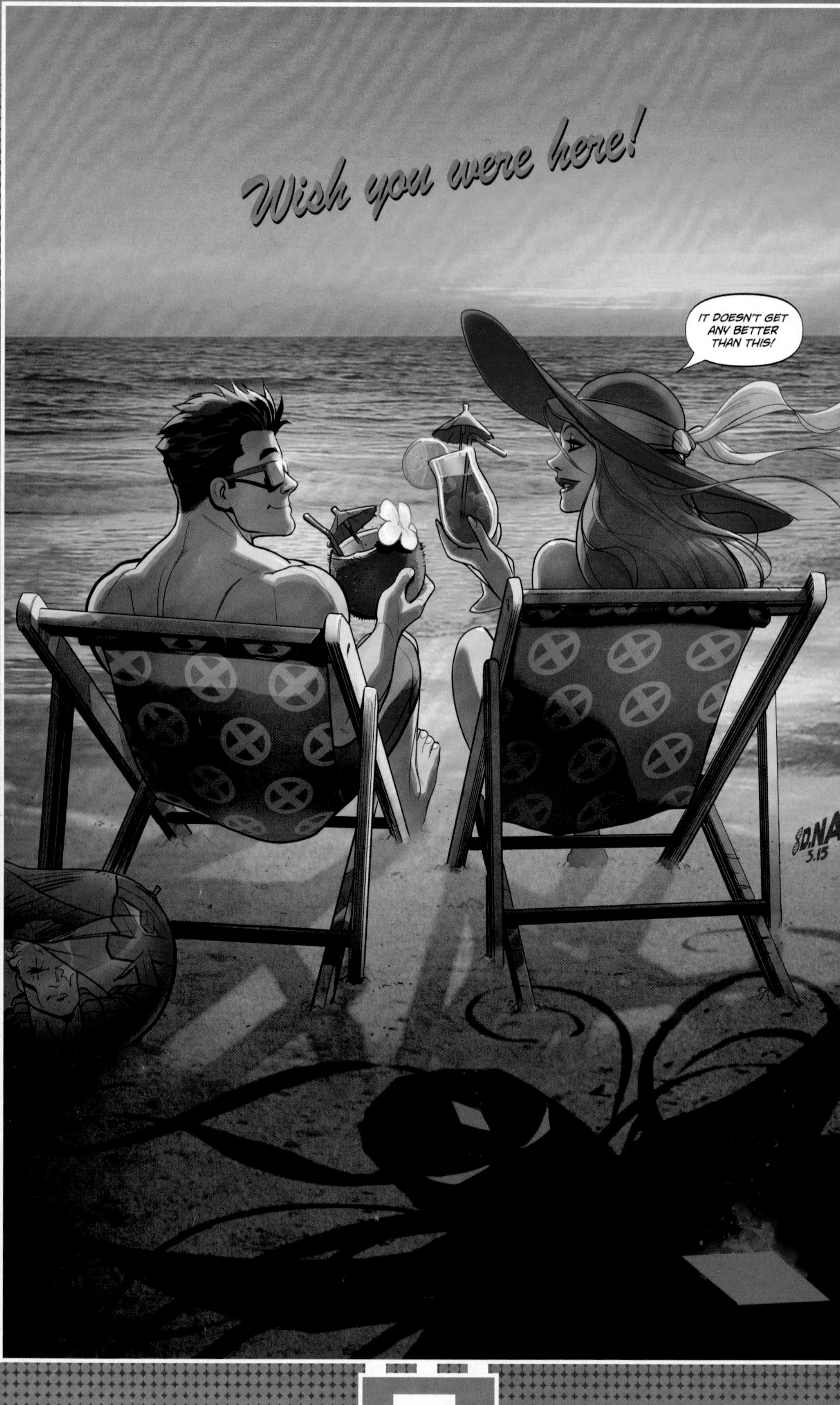
Wish you were here!
IT DOESN'T GET ANY BETTER THAN THIS!
D.NA 3.15

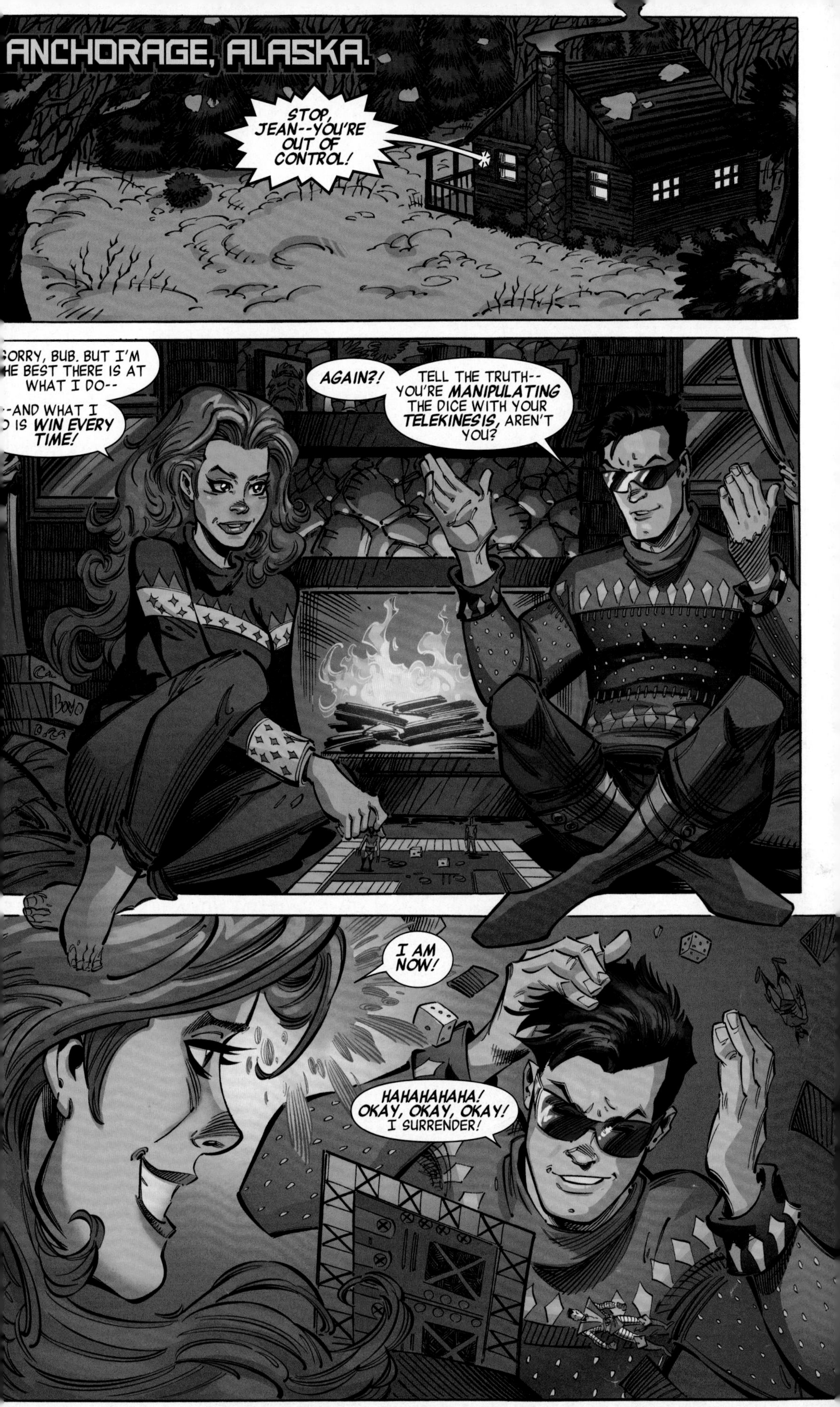
ANCHORAGE, ALASKA.
STOP, JEAN--YOU'RE OUT OF CONTROL!
SORRY, BUB. BUT I'M THE BEST THERE IS AT WHAT I DO--
--AND WHAT I DO IS WIN EVERY TIME!
AGAIN?!
TELL THE TRUTH-- YOU'RE MANIPULATING THE DICE WITH YOUR TELEKINESIS, AREN'T YOU?
I AM NOW!
HAHAHAHAHA! OKAY, OKAY, OKAY! I SURRENDER!

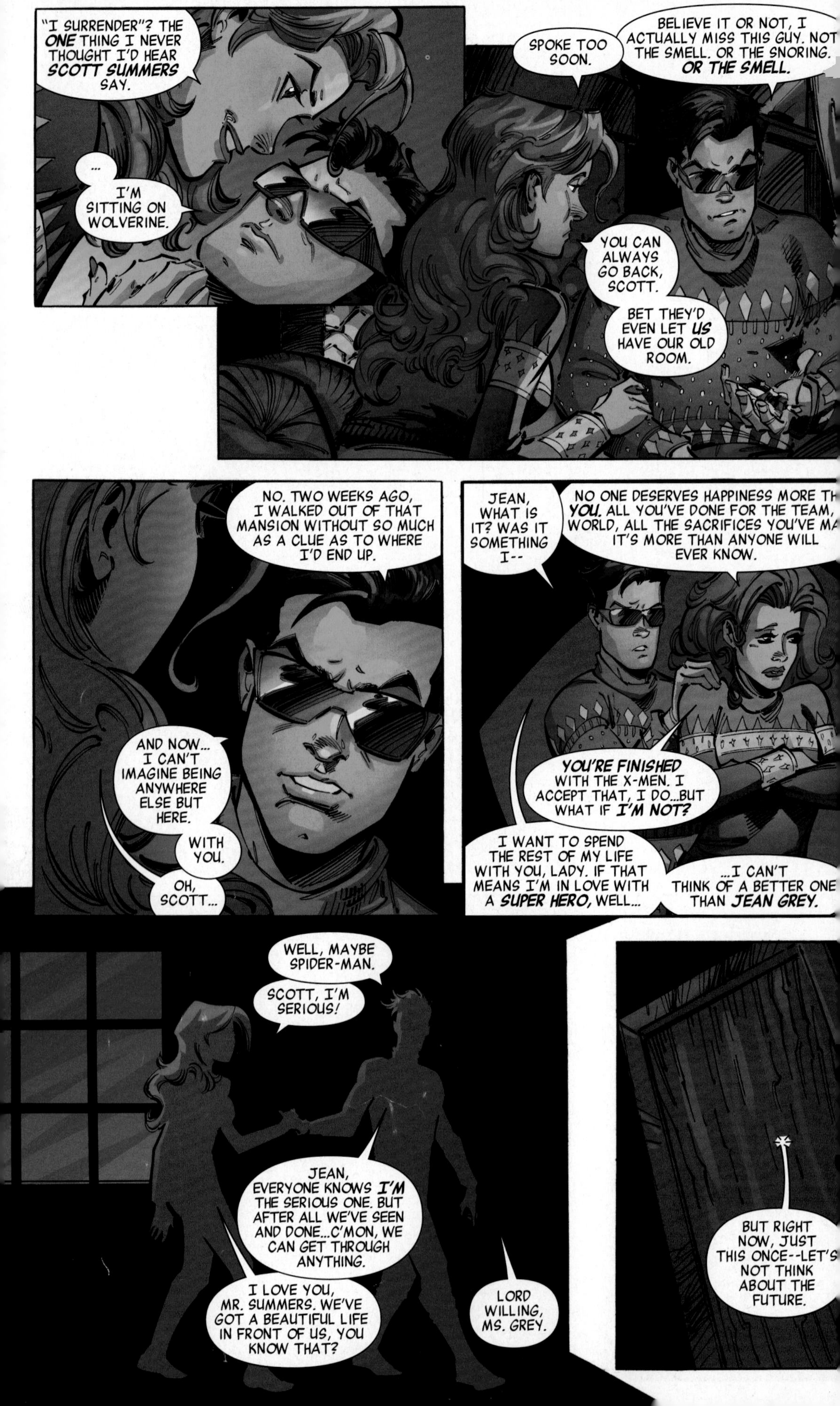
"I SURRENDER"? THE ONE THING I NEVER THOUGHT I'D HEAR SCOTT SUMMERS SAY.
...
I'M SITTING ON WOLVERINE.
SPOKE TOO SOON.
BELIEVE IT OR NOT, I ACTUALLY MISS THIS GUY. NOT THE SMELL. OR THE SNORING. OR THE SMELL.
YOU CAN ALWAYS GO BACK, SCOTT.
BET THEY'D EVEN LET US HAVE OUR OLD ROOM.
NO. TWO WEEKS AGO, I WALKED OUT OF THAT MANSION WITHOUT SO MUCH AS A CLUE AS TO WHERE I'D END UP.
AND NOW... I CAN'T IMAGINE BEING ANYWHERE ELSE BUT HERE.
WITH YOU.
OH, SCOTT...
JEAN, WHAT IS IT? WAS IT SOMETHING I--
NO ONE DESERVES HAPPINESS MORE TH YOU. ALL YOU'VE DONE FOR THE TEAM, WORLD, ALL THE SACRIFICES YOU'VE MA IT'S MORE THAN ANYONE WILL EVER KNOW.
YOU'RE FINISHED WITH THE X-MEN. I ACCEPT THAT, I DO...BUT WHAT IF I'M NOT?
I WANT TO SPEND THE REST OF MY LIFE WITH YOU, LADY. IF THAT MEANS I'M IN LOVE WITH A SUPER HERO, WELL...
...I CAN'T THINK OF A BETTER ONE THAN JEAN GREY.
WELL, MAYBE SPIDER-MAN.
SCOTT, I'M SERIOUS!
JEAN, EVERYONE KNOWS I'M THE SERIOUS ONE. BUT AFTER ALL WE'VE SEEN AND DONE...C'MON, WE CAN GET THROUGH ANYTHING.
I LOVE YOU, MR. SUMMERS. WE'VE GOT A BEAUTIFUL LIFE IN FRONT OF US, YOU KNOW THAT?
LORD WILLING, MS. GREY.
BUT RIGHT NOW, JUST THIS ONCE--LET'S NOT THINK ABOUT THE FUTURE.

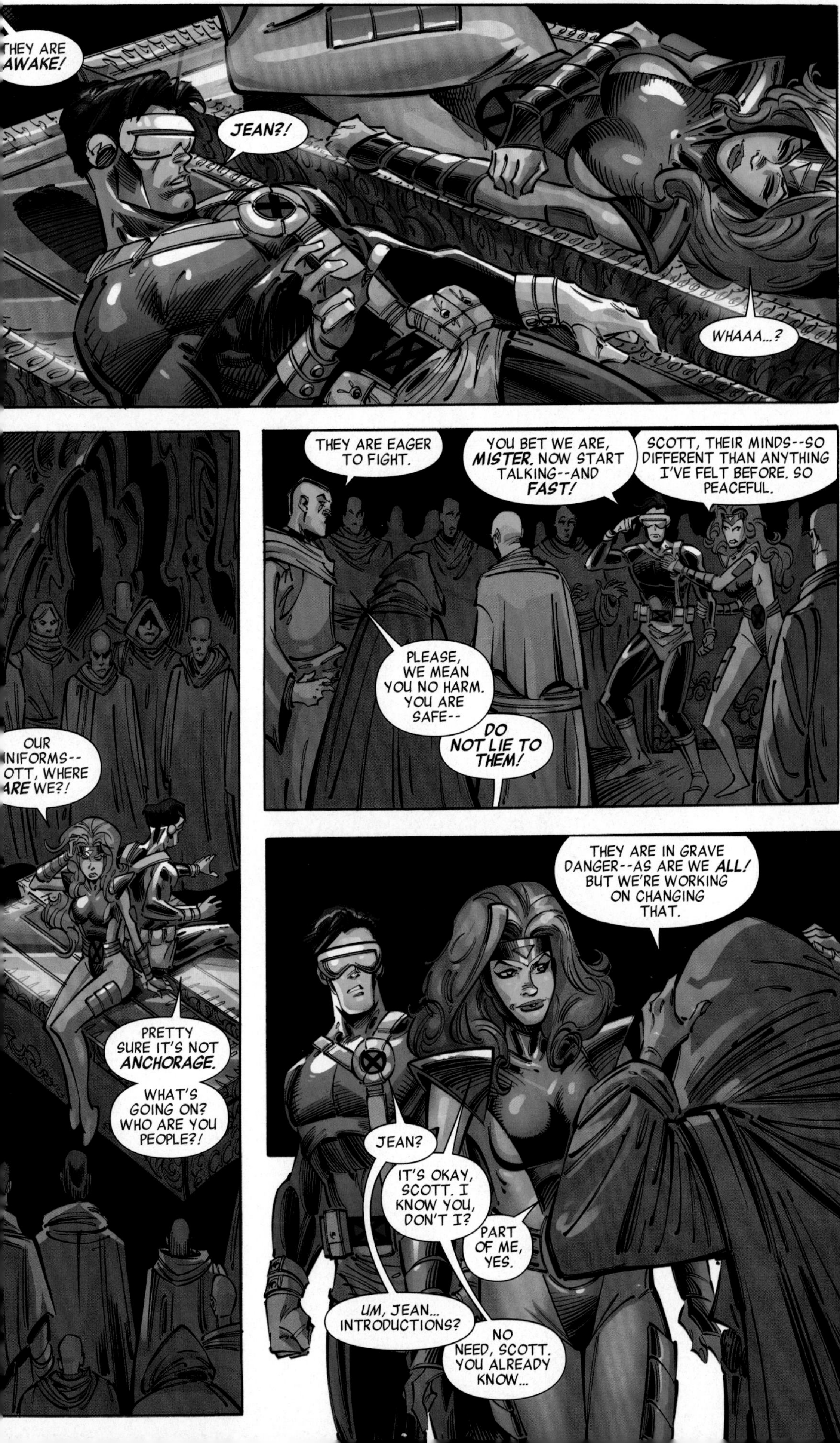
THEY ARE AWAKE!
JEAN?!
WHAAA...?
OUR UNIFORMS-- SCOTT, WHERE ARE WE?!
PRETTY SURE IT'S NOT ANCHORAGE.
WHAT'S GOING ON? WHO ARE YOU PEOPLE?!
THEY ARE EAGER TO FIGHT.
YOU BET WE ARE, MISTER. NOW START TALKING--AND FAST!
SCOTT, THEIR MINDS--SO DIFFERENT THAN ANYTHING I'VE FELT BEFORE. SO PEACEFUL.
PLEASE, WE MEAN YOU NO HARM. YOU ARE SAFE--
DO NOT LIE TO THEM!
THEY ARE IN GRAVE DANGER--AS ARE WE ALL! BUT WE'RE WORKING ON CHANGING THAT.
JEAN?
IT'S OKAY, SCOTT. I KNOW YOU, DON'T I?
PART OF ME, YES.
UM, JEAN... INTRODUCTIONS?
NO NEED, SCOTT. YOU ALREADY KNOW...

...THE. THE PHOENIX.

PLEASE, CALL ME RACHEL.

WELCOME TO THE YEAR 3992.

THE FUTURE? HOW--

THE POWER OF THE PHOENIX IS LIMITLESS.

=COUGH=

OR IT USED TO BE, AT LEAST.

I'M AFRAID PULLING YOU FORWARD THROUGH TIME HAS TAKEN A LOT OUT OF US. NEITHER I NOR THE PHOENIX FORCE PLAN ON BEING AROUND MUCH LONGER.

BUT YOU SPIRIT--I SO BRIG YOU'RE N AFRAID

OF DYING? NOT ANYMORE.

YOU HAVE MY SYMPATHIES, MA'AM. BUT IF YOU BROUGHT US HERE TO HELP SAVE THE PHOENIX OR SOMETHING LIKE THAT, YOU'RE GOING TO BE DISAPPOINTED. THE UNIVERSE IS BETTER OFF WITHOUT IT.

HEH! YOU ARE EXACTLY AS THE LEGENDS DESCRIBE, CYCLOPS.

BUT NO, THE PHOENIX'S TIME HAS COME TO AN END.

FOLLOW ME.

THEY'RE WAITING FOR US BELOW.

"THEY"?

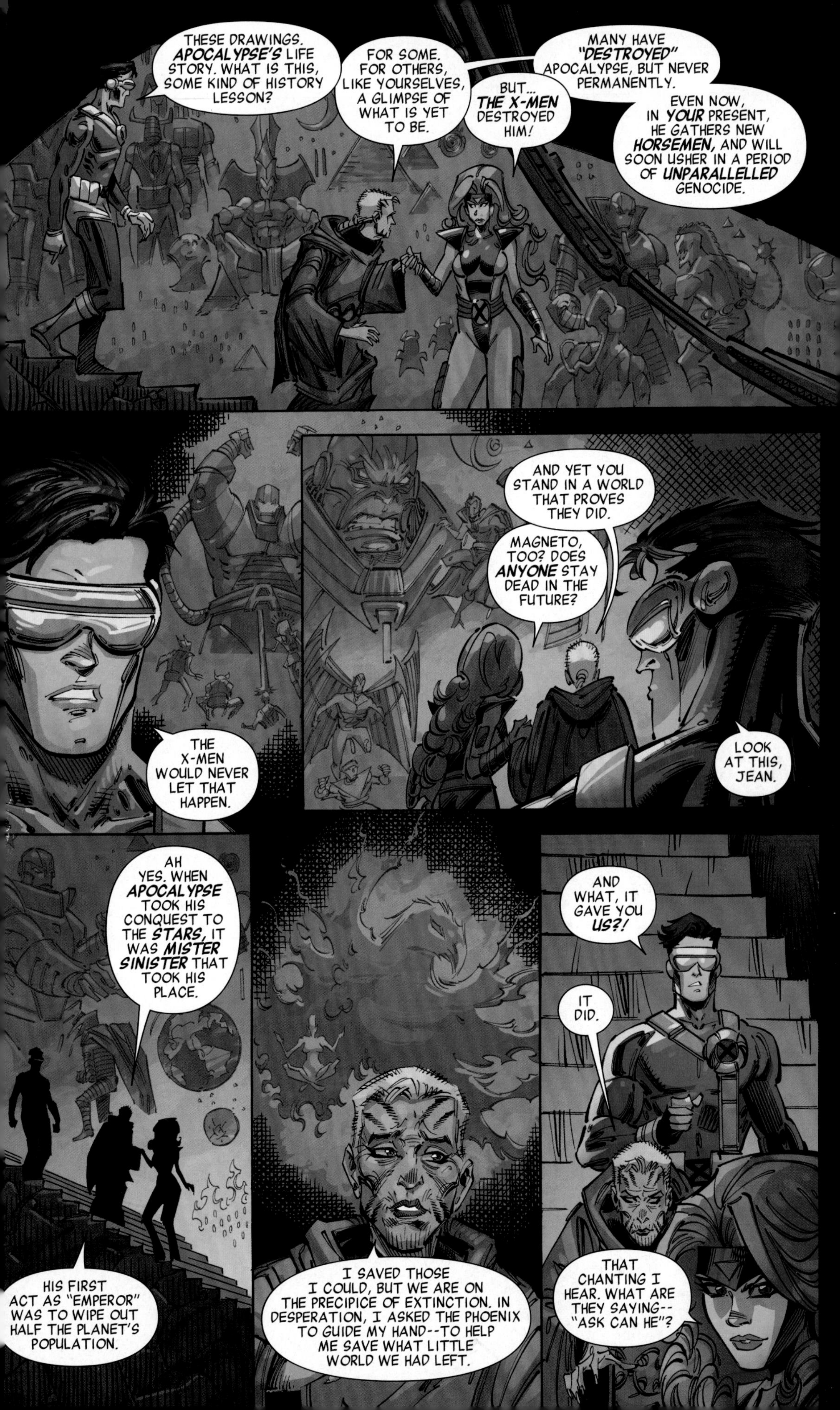

THESE DRAWINGS. APOCALYPSE'S LIFE STORY. WHAT IS THIS, SOME KIND OF HISTORY LESSON?
FOR SOME. FOR OTHERS, LIKE YOURSELVES, A GLIMPSE OF WHAT IS YET TO BE.
BUT... THE X-MEN DESTROYED HIM!
MANY HAVE "DESTROYED" APOCALYPSE, BUT NEVER PERMANENTLY.
EVEN NOW, IN YOUR PRESENT, HE GATHERS NEW HORSEMEN, AND WILL SOON USHER IN A PERIOD OF UNPARALLELLED GENOCIDE.
THE X-MEN WOULD NEVER LET THAT HAPPEN.
AND YET YOU STAND IN A WORLD THAT PROVES THEY DID.
MAGNETO, TOO? DOES ANYONE STAY DEAD IN THE FUTURE?
LOOK AT THIS, JEAN.
AH YES. WHEN APOCALYPSE TOOK HIS CONQUEST TO THE STARS, IT WAS MISTER SINISTER THAT TOOK HIS PLACE.
HIS FIRST ACT AS "EMPEROR" WAS TO WIPE OUT HALF THE PLANET'S POPULATION.
I SAVED THOSE I COULD, BUT WE ARE ON THE PRECIPICE OF EXTINCTION. IN DESPERATION, I ASKED THE PHOENIX TO GUIDE MY HAND--TO HELP ME SAVE WHAT LITTLE WORLD WE HAD LEFT.
AND WHAT, IT GAVE YOU US?!
IT DID.
THAT CHANTING I HEAR. WHAT ARE THEY SAYING-- "ASK CAN HE"?

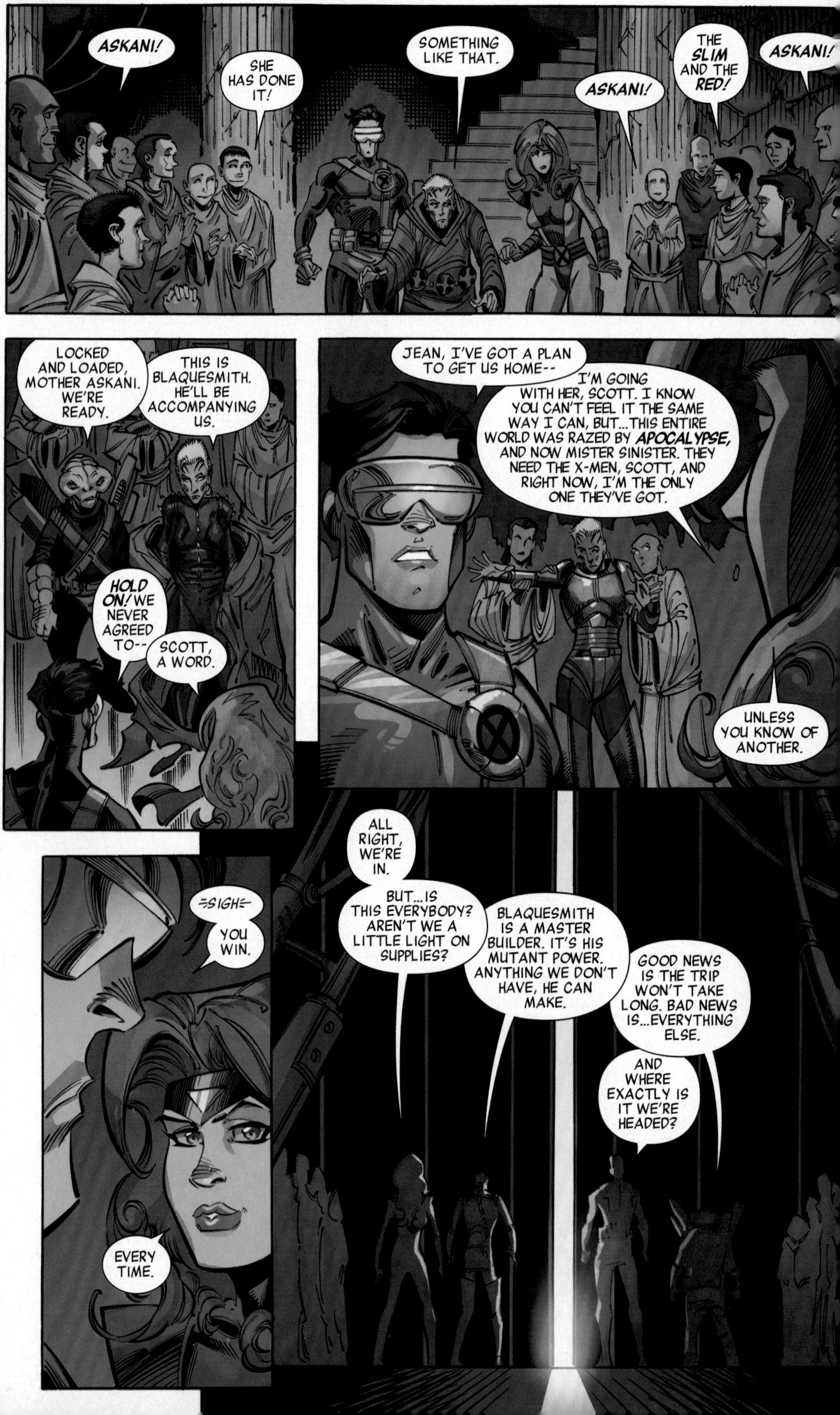
ASKANI!
SHE HAS DONE IT!
SOMETHING LIKE THAT.
ASKANI!
THE SLIM AND THE RED!
ASKANI!
LOCKED AND LOADED, MOTHER ASKANI. WE'RE READY.
THIS IS BLAQUESMITH. HE'LL BE ACCOMPANYING US.
HOLD ON! WE NEVER AGREED TO--
SCOTT, A WORD.
JEAN, I'VE GOT A PLAN TO GET US HOME--
I'M GOING WITH HER, SCOTT. I KNOW YOU CAN'T FEEL IT THE SAME WAY I CAN, BUT...THIS ENTIRE WORLD WAS RAZED BY APOCALYPSE, AND NOW MISTER SINISTER. THEY NEED THE X-MEN, SCOTT, AND RIGHT NOW, I'M THE ONLY ONE THEY'VE GOT.
UNLESS YOU KNOW OF ANOTHER.
=SIGH=
YOU WIN.
EVERY TIME.
ALL RIGHT, WE'RE IN.
BUT...IS THIS EVERYBODY? AREN'T WE A LITTLE LIGHT ON SUPPLIES?
BLAQUESMITH IS A MASTER BUILDER. IT'S HIS MUTANT POWER. ANYTHING WE DON'T HAVE, HE CAN MAKE.
GOOD NEWS IS THE TRIP WON'T TAKE LONG. BAD NEWS IS...EVERYTHING ELSE.
AND WHERE EXACTLY IS IT WE'RE HEADED?

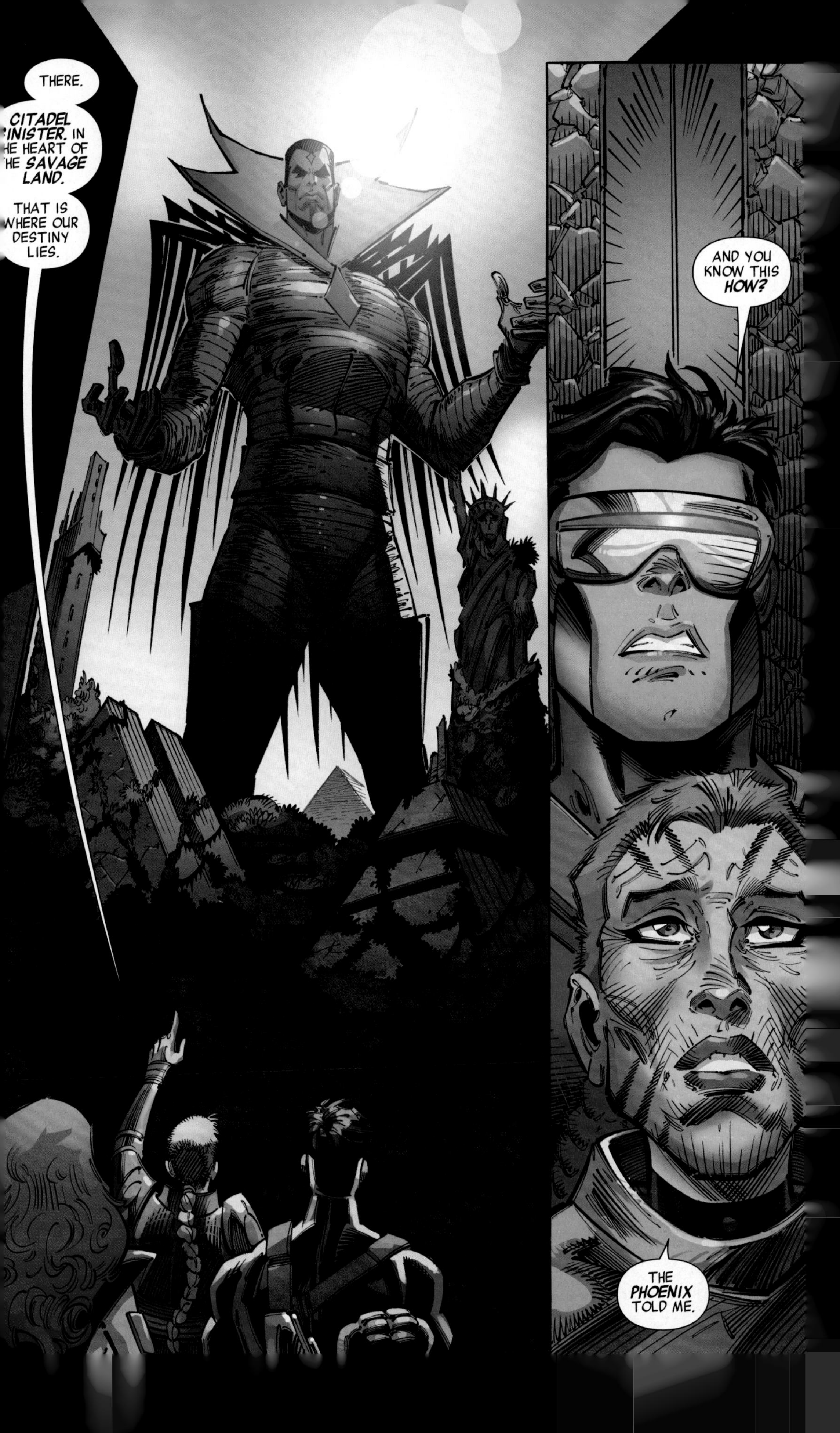
THERE.
CITADEL SINISTER. IN THE HEART OF THE SAVAGE LAND.
THAT IS WHERE OUR DESTINY LIES.
AND YOU KNOW THIS HOW?
THE PHOENIX TOLD ME.

"IN THE *ASKANI SCROLLS*, IT IS WRITTEN THAT A JOURNEY ACROSS THE *SAVAGE LAND* ONCE TOOK MERE MOMENTS.

"AT THE *HEIGHT* OF ITS DECADENCE, THERE WERE *UNDERGROUND TRAINS* AND MYSTERIOUS BEINGS CALLED *TAXIK'AABS* THAT WOULD CARRY THOSE THEY *SWALLOWED* TO THEIR DESTINATION.

"BUT THOSE DAYS ARE *GONE!* IN THIS, THE *SINISTER CENTURY*, YOU'RE MORE LIKELY TO RUN INTO..."

MARAUDERS!

THERE'S A *VOID* WHERE THEIR MINDS SHOULD BE--

QUIT THINKING AT THEM AND *FIGHT*. THIS IS ONLY GONNA GET WORSE!

BREAK HIS JAW, BABY!

DOES THIS COUNT AS A *CAMEO?*

GIMME A BREAK!

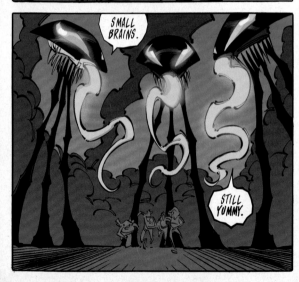

SMALL BRAINS.

STILL *YUMMY.*

WE HAVE TO BE GETTING CLOSE!

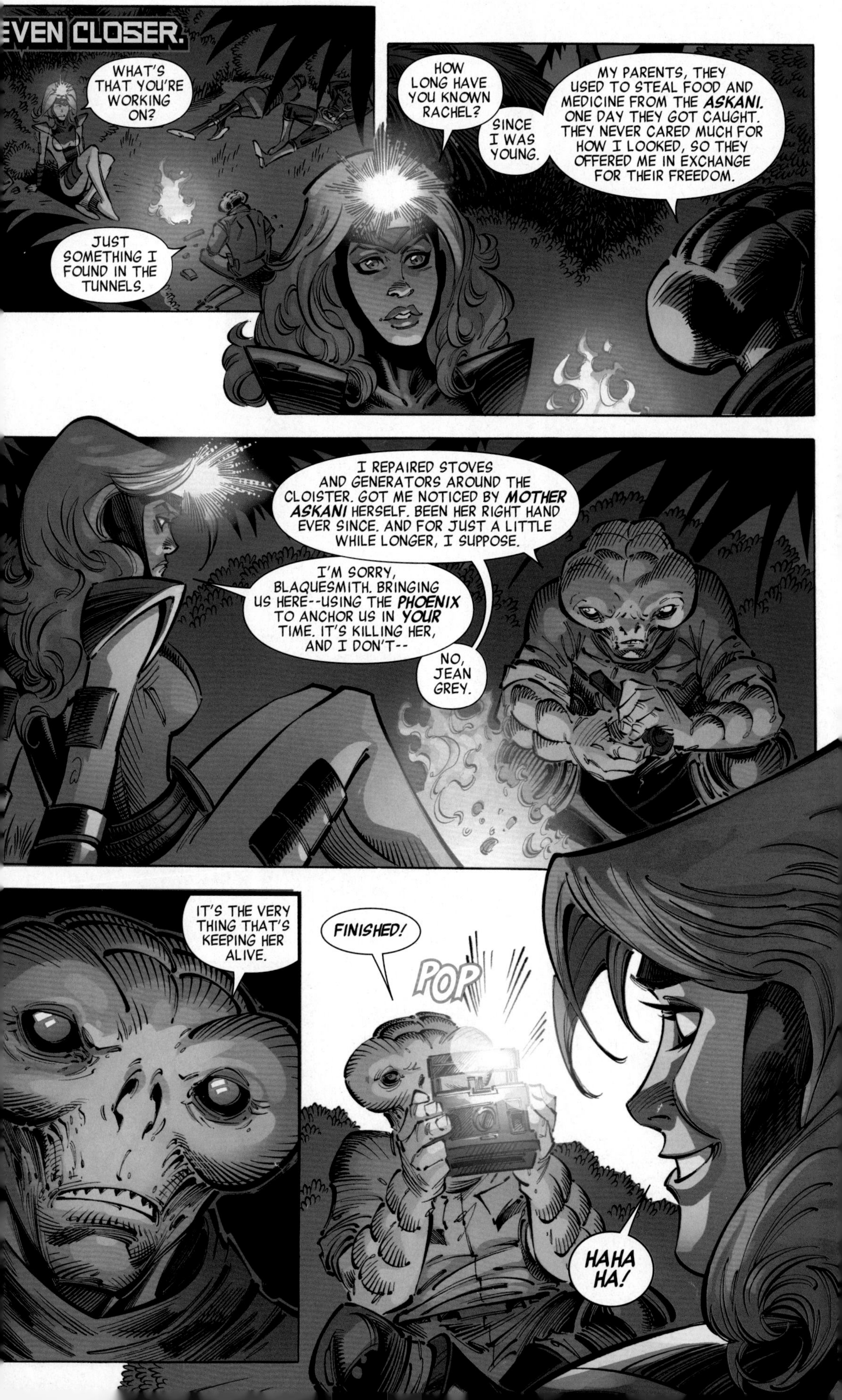
EVEN CLOSER.
WHAT'S THAT YOU'RE WORKING ON?
JUST SOMETHING I FOUND IN THE TUNNELS.
HOW LONG HAVE YOU KNOWN RACHEL?
SINCE I WAS YOUNG.
MY PARENTS, THEY USED TO STEAL FOOD AND MEDICINE FROM THE ASKANI. ONE DAY THEY GOT CAUGHT. THEY NEVER CARED MUCH FOR HOW I LOOKED, SO THEY OFFERED ME IN EXCHANGE FOR THEIR FREEDOM.
I REPAIRED STOVES AND GENERATORS AROUND THE CLOISTER. GOT ME NOTICED BY MOTHER ASKANI HERSELF. BEEN HER RIGHT HAND EVER SINCE. AND FOR JUST A LITTLE WHILE LONGER, I SUPPOSE.
I'M SORRY, BLAQUESMITH. BRINGING US HERE--USING THE PHOENIX TO ANCHOR US IN YOUR TIME. IT'S KILLING HER, AND I DON'T--
NO, JEAN GREY.
IT'S THE VERY THING THAT'S KEEPING HER ALIVE.
FINISHED!
POP
HAHA HA!

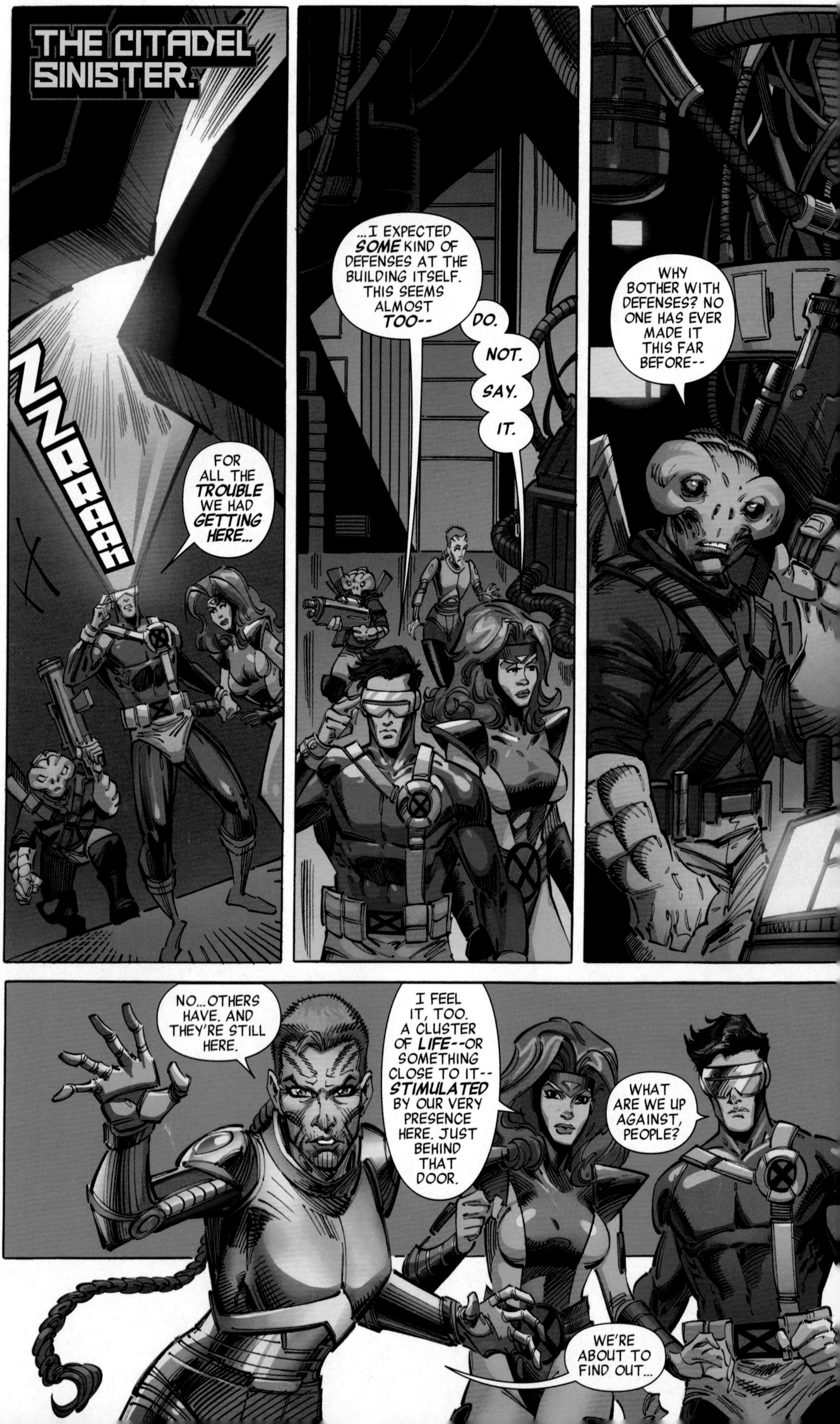
THE CITADEL SINISTER.
NNRRAAN
FOR ALL THE TROUBLE WE HAD GETTING HERE...
...I EXPECTED SOME KIND OF DEFENSES AT THE BUILDING ITSELF. THIS SEEMS ALMOST TOO--
DO.
NOT.
SAY.
IT.
WHY BOTHER WITH DEFENSES? NO ONE HAS EVER MADE IT THIS FAR BEFORE--
NO...OTHERS HAVE. AND THEY'RE STILL HERE.
I FEEL IT, TOO. A CLUSTER OF LIFE--OR SOMETHING CLOSE TO IT--STIMULATED BY OUR VERY PRESENCE HERE. JUST BEHIND THAT DOOR.
WHAT ARE WE UP AGAINST, PEOPLE?
WE'RE ABOUT TO FIND OUT...

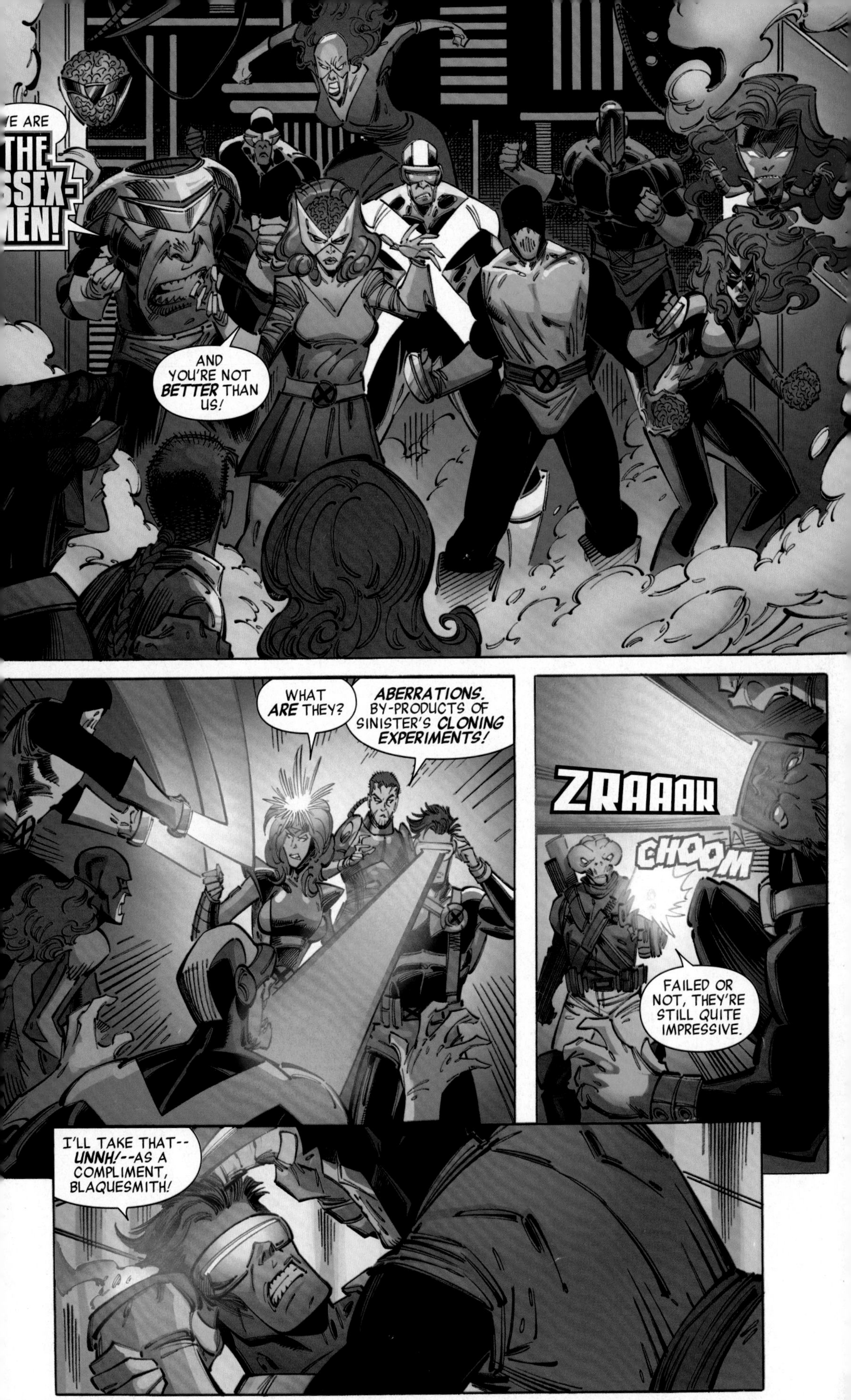

WE ARE THE DESSEX-MEN!
AND YOU'RE NOT BETTER THAN US!
WHAT ARE THEY?
ABERRATIONS. BY-PRODUCTS OF SINISTER'S CLONING EXPERIMENTS!
ZRAAAK
CHOOM
FAILED OR NOT, THEY'RE STILL QUITE IMPRESSIVE.
I'LL TAKE THAT--UNNH!--AS A COMPLIMENT, BLAQUESMITH!

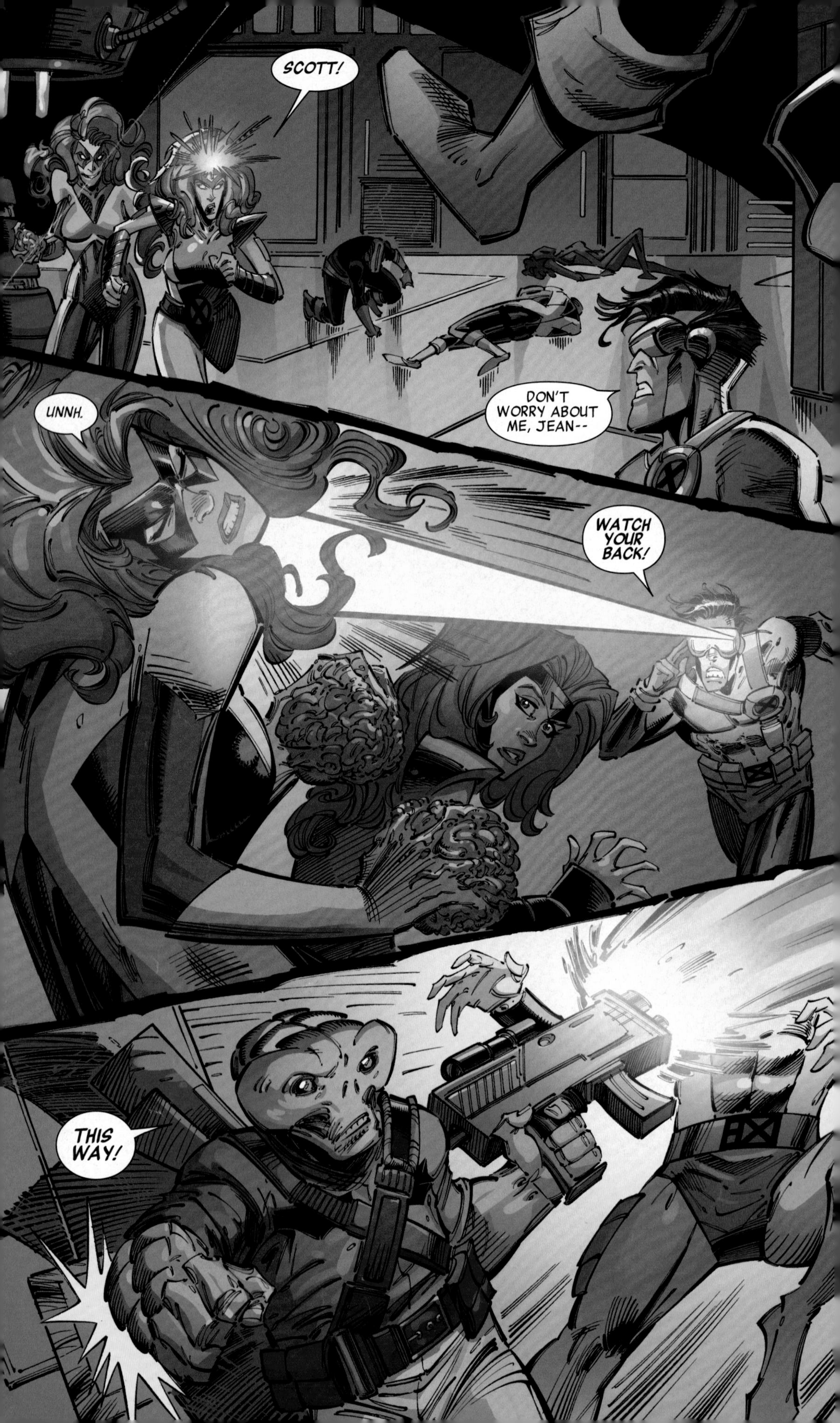
SCOTT!
DON'T WORRY ABOUT ME, JEAN--
UNNH.
WATCH YOUR BACK!
THIS WAY!

COME ON, SCOTT! I'LL CLEAR A PATH!

RIGHT BEHIND YOU!

=KAFF KAFF=

HANG IN THERE, RACHEL.

DOOR'S SEALED BEHIND US. WON'T HOLD FOREVER, BUT IT SHOULD BUY US SOME TIME.

HELP ME UNDERSTAND THIS. THOSE THINGS OUT THERE--

IMPERFECT CLONES OF YOU AND JEAN. GROWN FROM TAINTED GENETIC MATERIAL.

SINISTER'S ALWAYS BEEN FIXATED ON US, BUT WE'RE TWO THOUSAND YEARS IN THE FUTURE--WHY DOES HE STILL CARE? WHAT'S HE DOING HERE?

IT HAD TO BE YOU.

RACHEL? ARE YOU ALL RIGHT?

WE'RE NOT HERE TO DESTROY SINISTER, ARE WE, RACHEL?

NO.

OH, DON'T LOOK SO SHOCKED!

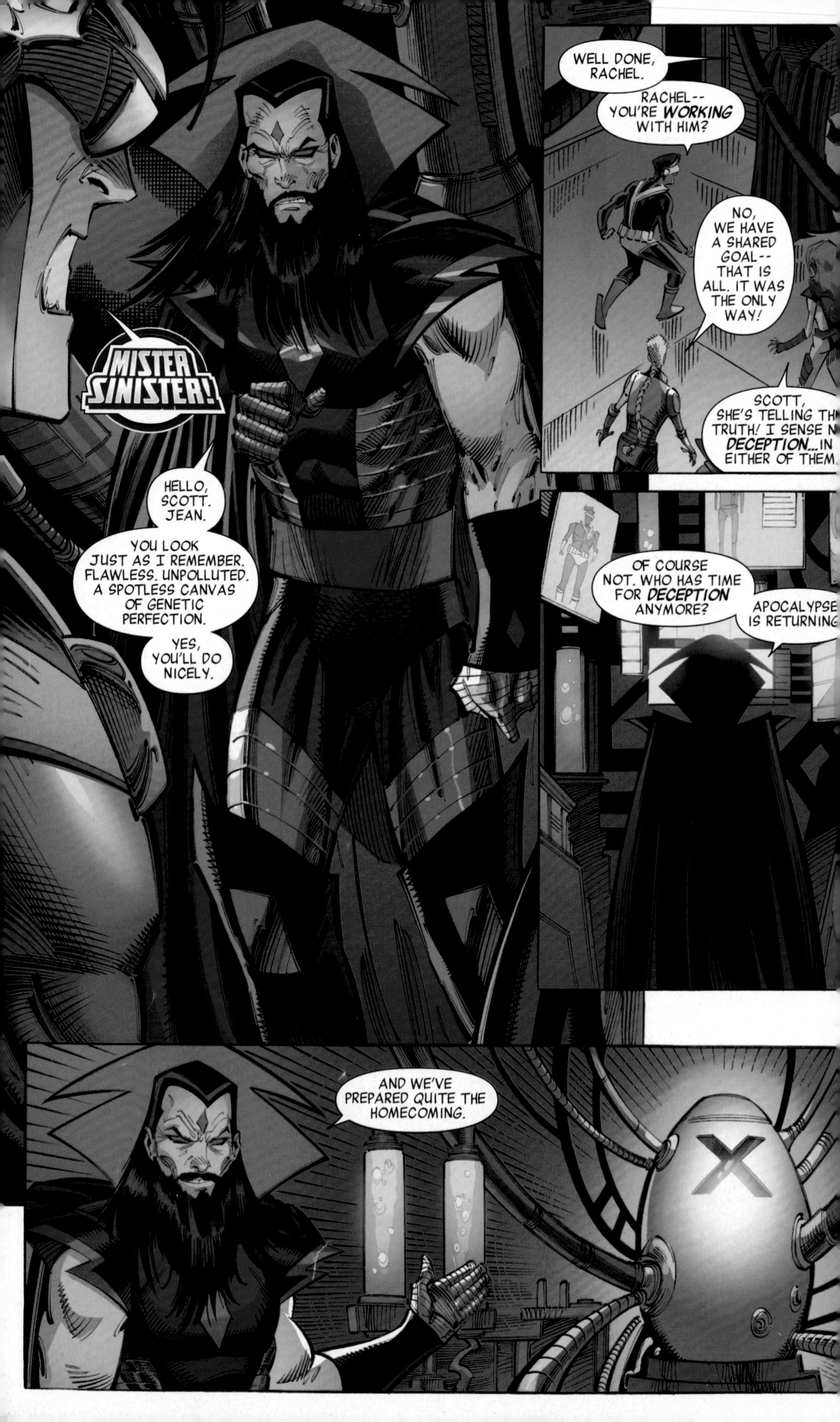
MISTER SINISTER!
HELLO, SCOTT. JEAN.
YOU LOOK JUST AS I REMEMBER. FLAWLESS. UNPOLLUTED. A SPOTLESS CANVAS OF GENETIC PERFECTION.
YES, YOU'LL DO NICELY.
WELL DONE, RACHEL.
RACHEL-- YOU'RE **WORKING** WITH HIM?
NO, WE HAVE A SHARED GOAL-- THAT IS ALL. IT WAS THE ONLY WAY!
SCOTT, SHE'S TELLING TH TRUTH! I SENSE N **DECEPTION...** IN EITHER OF THEM.
OF COURSE NOT. WHO HAS TIME FOR **DECEPTION** ANYMORE?
APOCALYPSE IS RETURNING
AND WE'VE PREPARED QUITE THE HOMECOMING.

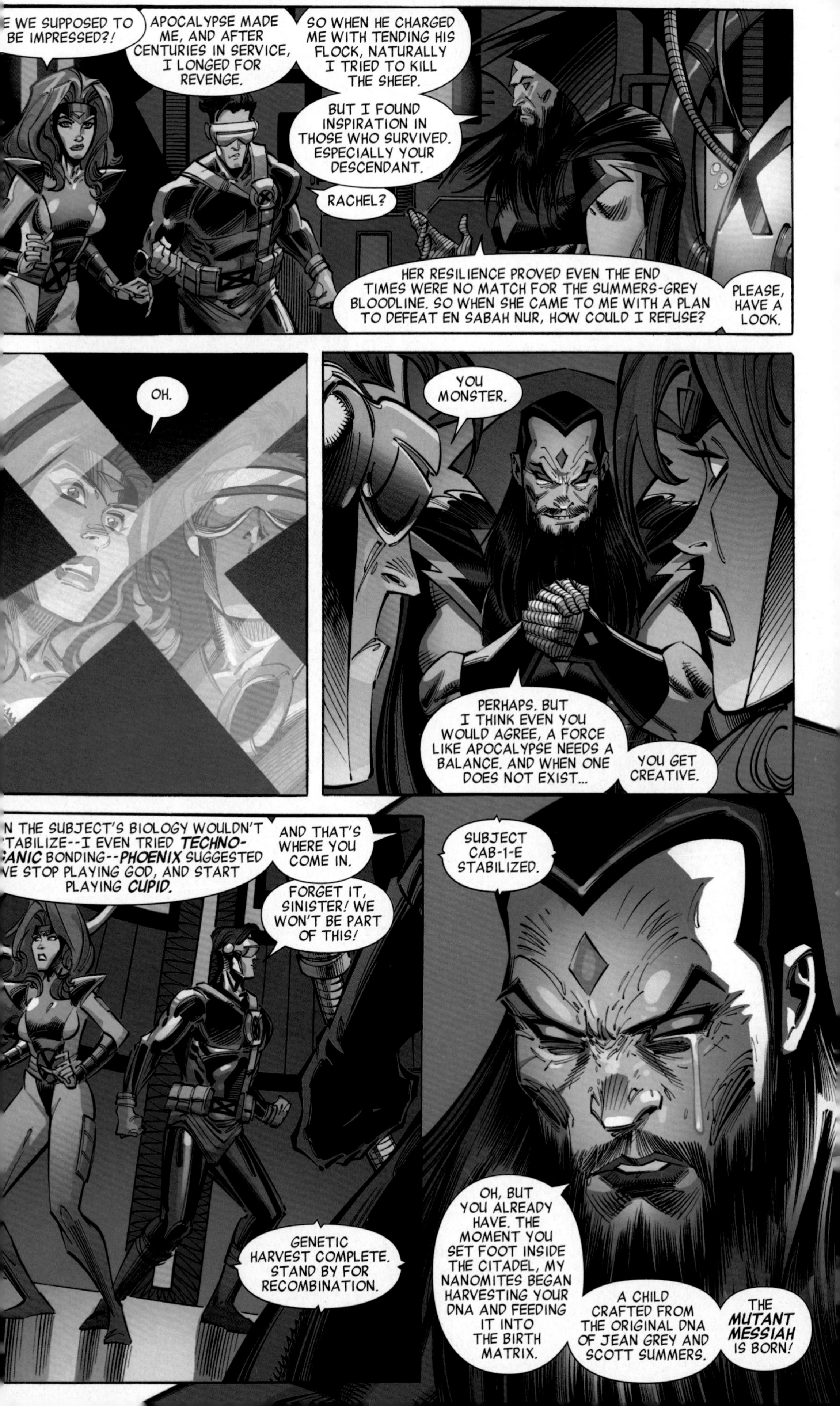

E WE SUPPOSED TO BE IMPRESSED?!
APOCALYPSE MADE ME, AND AFTER CENTURIES IN SERVICE, I LONGED FOR REVENGE.
SO WHEN HE CHARGED ME WITH TENDING HIS FLOCK, NATURALLY I TRIED TO KILL THE SHEEP.
BUT I FOUND INSPIRATION IN THOSE WHO SURVIVED. ESPECIALLY YOUR DESCENDANT.
RACHEL?
HER RESILIENCE PROVED EVEN THE END TIMES WERE NO MATCH FOR THE SUMMERS-GREY BLOODLINE. SO WHEN SHE CAME TO ME WITH A PLAN TO DEFEAT EN SABAH NUR, HOW COULD I REFUSE?
PLEASE, HAVE A LOOK.
OH.
YOU MONSTER.
PERHAPS. BUT I THINK EVEN YOU WOULD AGREE, A FORCE LIKE APOCALYPSE NEEDS A BALANCE. AND WHEN ONE DOES NOT EXIST...
YOU GET CREATIVE.
N THE SUBJECT'S BIOLOGY WOULDN'T TABILIZE--I EVEN TRIED TECHNO-GANIC BONDING--PHOENIX SUGGESTED VE STOP PLAYING GOD, AND START PLAYING CUPID.
AND THAT'S WHERE YOU COME IN.
FORGET IT, SINISTER! WE WON'T BE PART OF THIS!
SUBJECT CAB-1-E STABILIZED.
GENETIC HARVEST COMPLETE. STAND BY FOR RECOMBINATION.
OH, BUT YOU ALREADY HAVE. THE MOMENT YOU SET FOOT INSIDE THE CITADEL, MY NANOMITES BEGAN HARVESTING YOUR DNA AND FEEDING IT INTO THE BIRTH MATRIX.
A CHILD CRAFTED FROM THE ORIGINAL DNA OF JEAN GREY AND SCOTT SUMMERS.
THE MUTANT MESSIAH IS BORN!

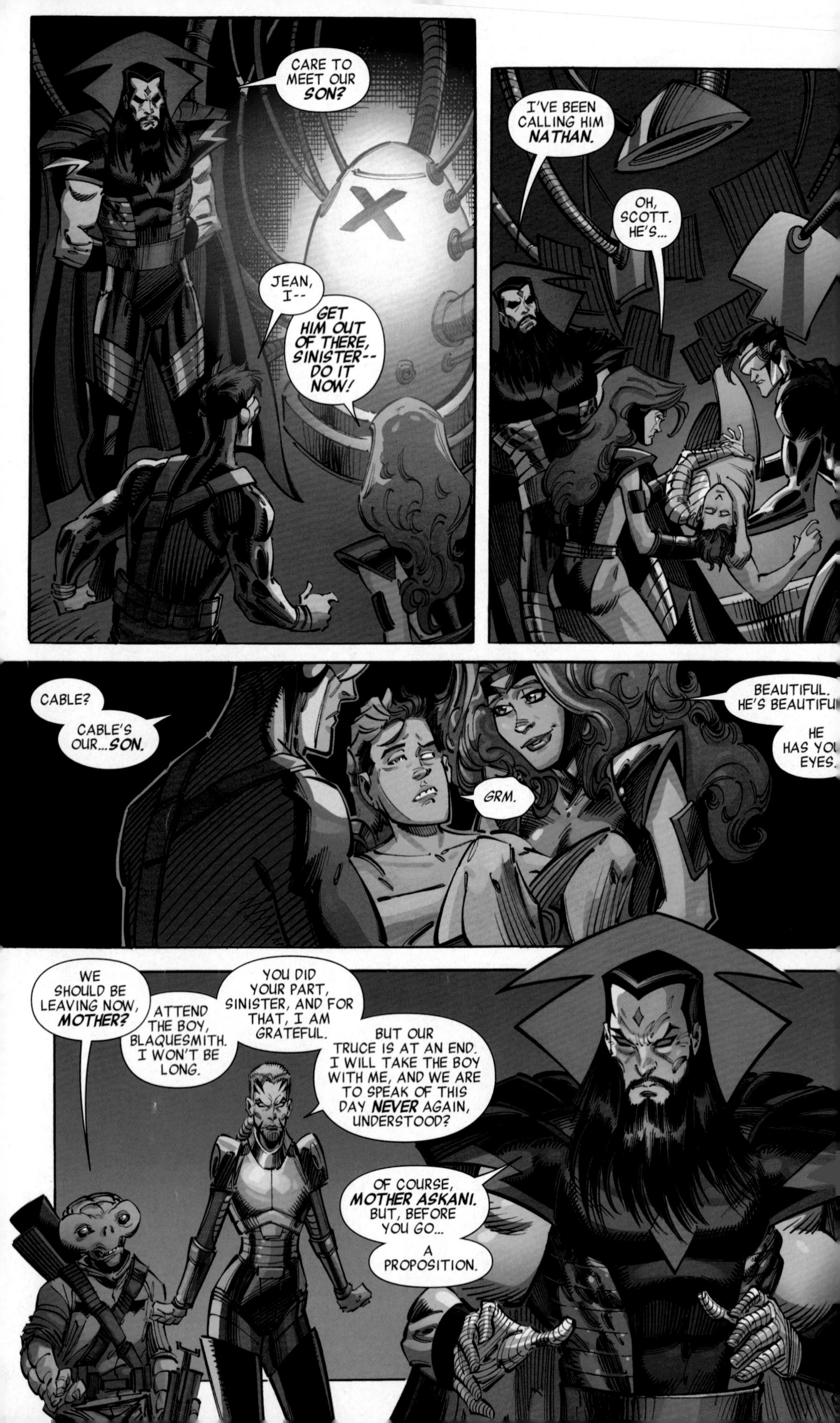
CARE TO MEET OUR SON?
JEAN, I--
GET HIM OUT OF THERE, SINISTER-- DO IT NOW!
I'VE BEEN CALLING HIM NATHAN.
OH, SCOTT. HE'S...
CABLE?
CABLE'S OUR...SON.
BEAUTIFUL. HE'S BEAUTIFU
HE HAS YO EYES.
GRM.
WE SHOULD BE LEAVING NOW, MOTHER?
ATTEND THE BOY, BLAQUESMITH. I WON'T BE LONG.
YOU DID YOUR PART, SINISTER, AND FOR THAT, I AM GRATEFUL.
BUT OUR TRUCE IS AT AN END. I WILL TAKE THE BOY WITH ME, AND WE ARE TO SPEAK OF THIS DAY NEVER AGAIN, UNDERSTOOD?
OF COURSE, MOTHER ASKANI. BUT, BEFORE YOU GO...
A PROPOSITION.

LOOK AROUND YOU.

WOULD THE BOY NOT BE BETTER SUITED FOR HIS FUTURE WITH ME?

WHAT'S HE SAYING? RACHEL--

NO. THIS IS BETWEEN THEM.

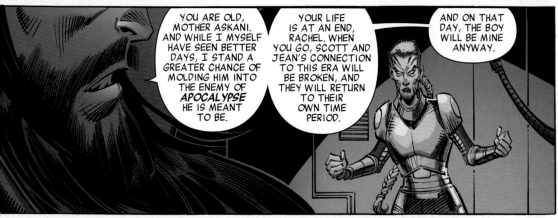

YOU ARE OLD, MOTHER ASKANI. AND WHILE I MYSELF HAVE SEEN BETTER DAYS, I STAND A GREATER CHANCE OF MOLDING HIM INTO THE ENEMY OF *APOCALYPSE* HE IS MEANT TO BE.

YOUR LIFE IS AT AN END, RACHEL. WHEN YOU GO, SCOTT AND JEAN'S CONNECTION TO THIS ERA WILL BE BROKEN, AND THEY WILL RETURN TO THEIR OWN TIME PERIOD.

AND ON THAT DAY, THE BOY WILL BE MINE ANYWAY.

THE PHOENIX HAS LONG OFFERED YOU GREAT WISDOM, RACHEL.

LET IT DO SO AGAIN. LISTEN TO WHAT IT'S TELLING YOU... IT KNOWS I'M RIGHT.

YES.

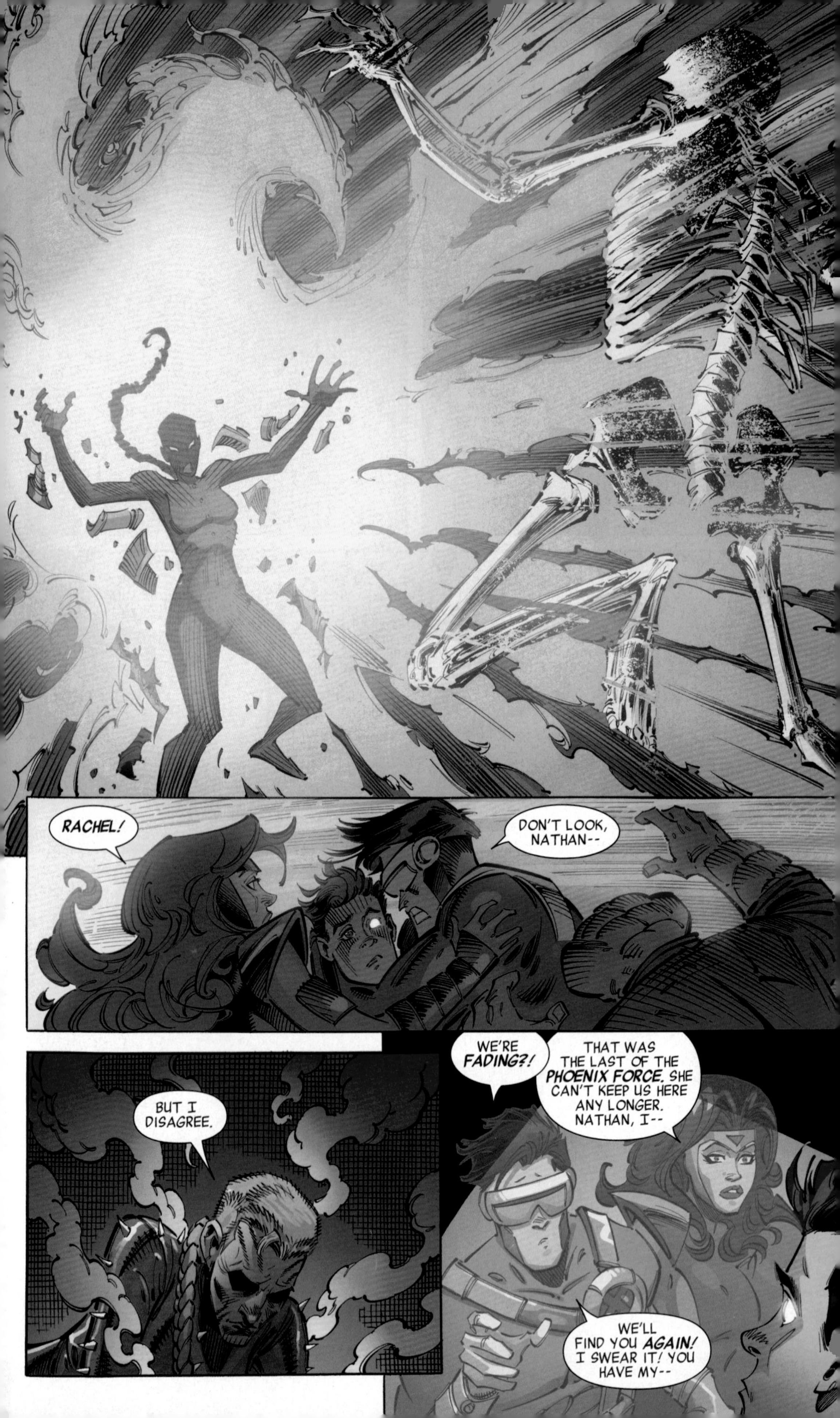
RACHEL!
DON'T LOOK, NATHAN--
BUT I DISAGREE.
WE'RE FADING?!
THAT WAS THE LAST OF THE PHOENIX FORCE. SHE CAN'T KEEP US HERE ANY LONGER. NATHAN, I--
WE'LL FIND YOU AGAIN! I SWEAR IT! YOU HAVE MY--

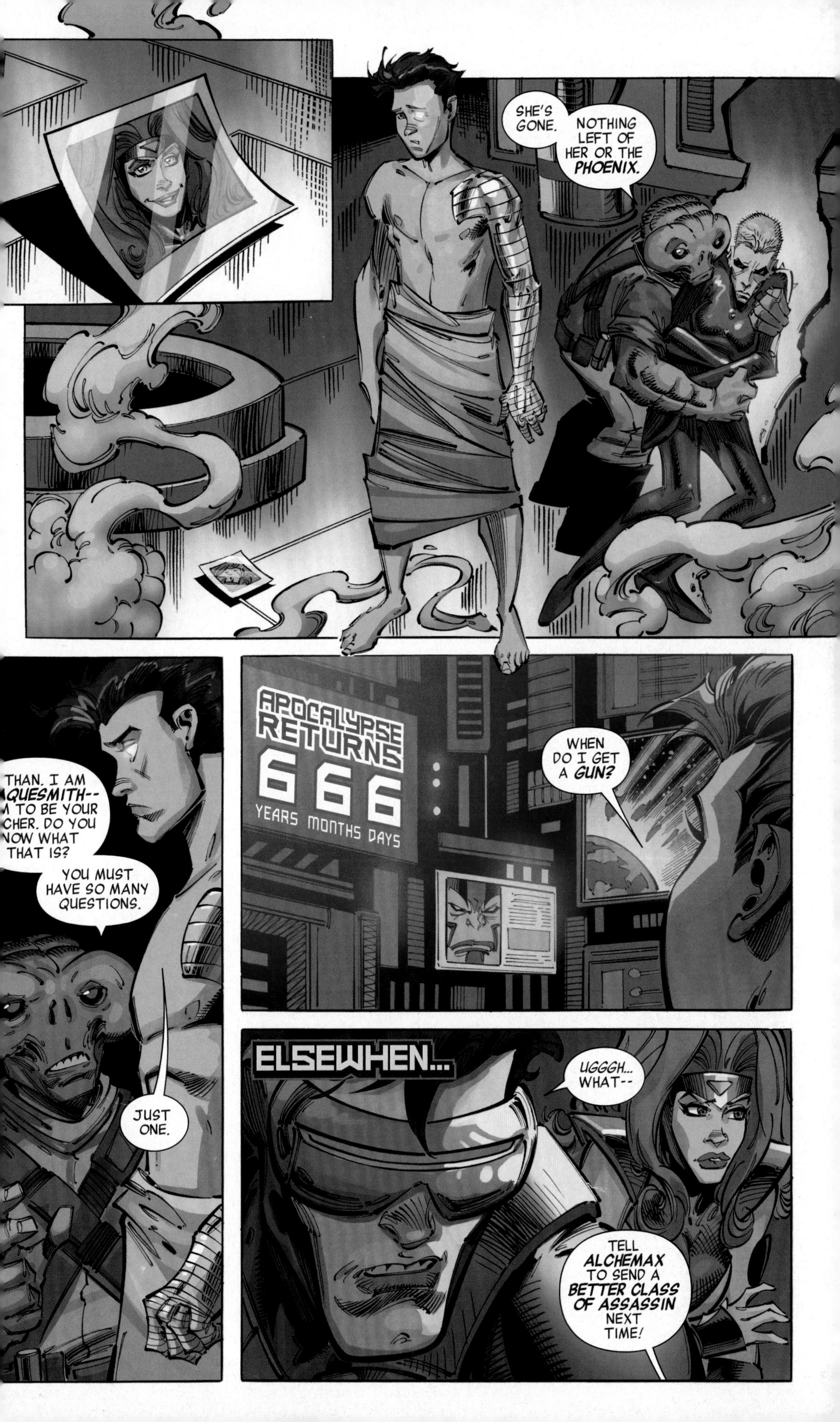
SHE'S GONE.
NOTHING LEFT OF HER OR THE PHOENIX.
APOCALYPSE RETURNS
6 6 6
YEARS MONTHS DAYS
WHEN DO I GET A GUN?
THAN. I AM
QUESMITH--
M TO BE YOUR
CHER. DO YOU
NOW WHAT
THAT IS?
YOU MUST HAVE SO MANY QUESTIONS.
JUST ONE.
ELSEWHEN...
UGGGH... WHAT--
TELL ALCHEMAX TO SEND A BETTER CLASS OF ASSASSIN NEXT TIME!

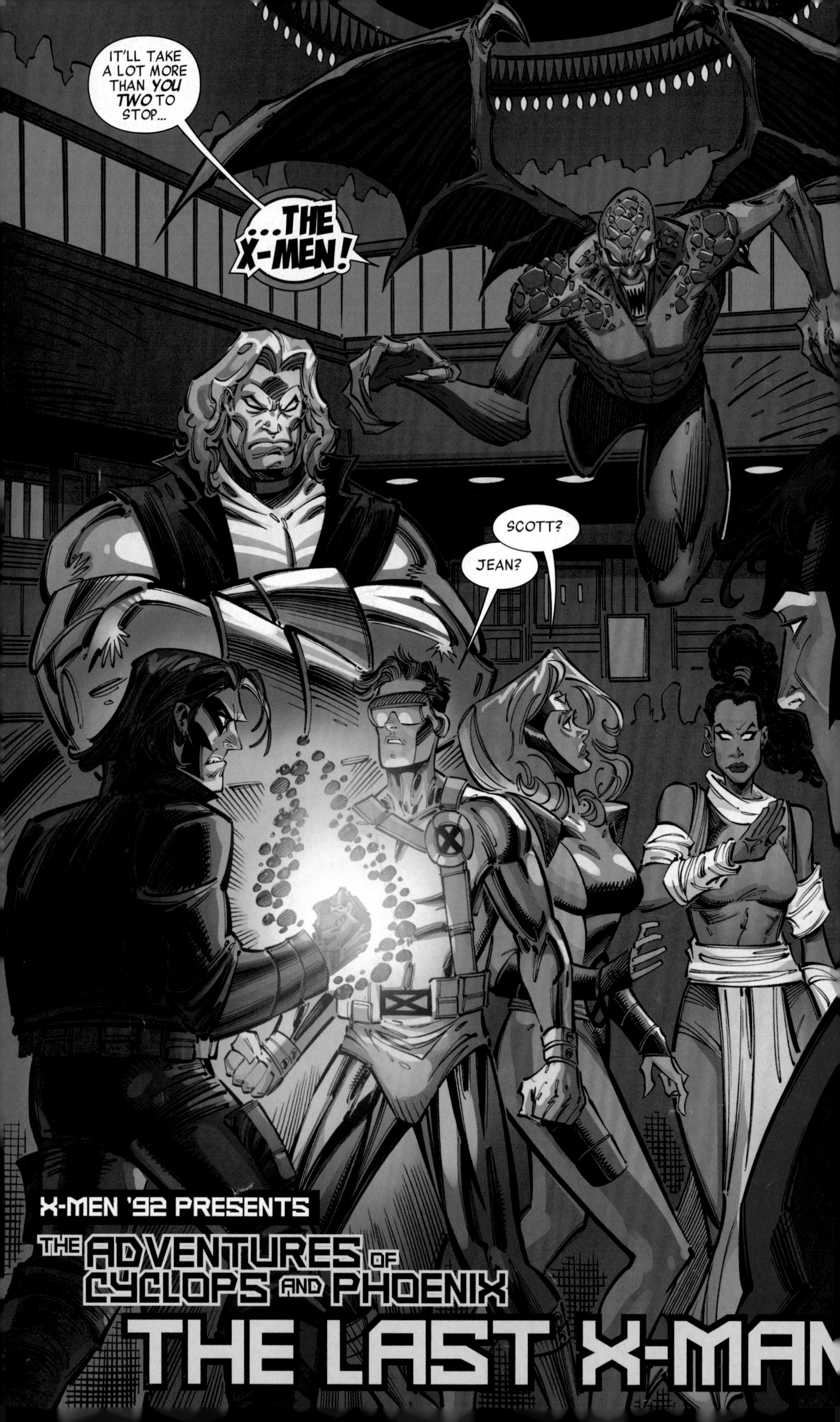
IT'LL TAKE A LOT MORE THAN YOU TWO TO STOP...
...THE X-MEN!
SCOTT?
JEAN?
X-MEN '92 PRESENTS
THE ADVENTURES OF CYCLOPS AND PHOENIX
THE LAST X-MAN

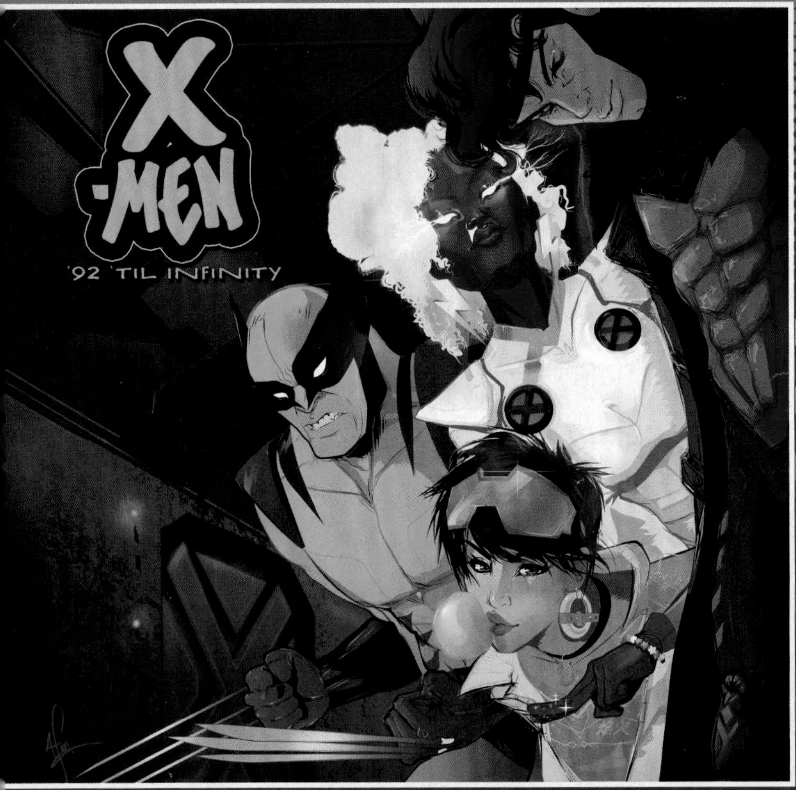
X-MEN
'92 'TIL INFINITY

#1 HIP-HOP VARIANT BY
AFUA RICHARDSON

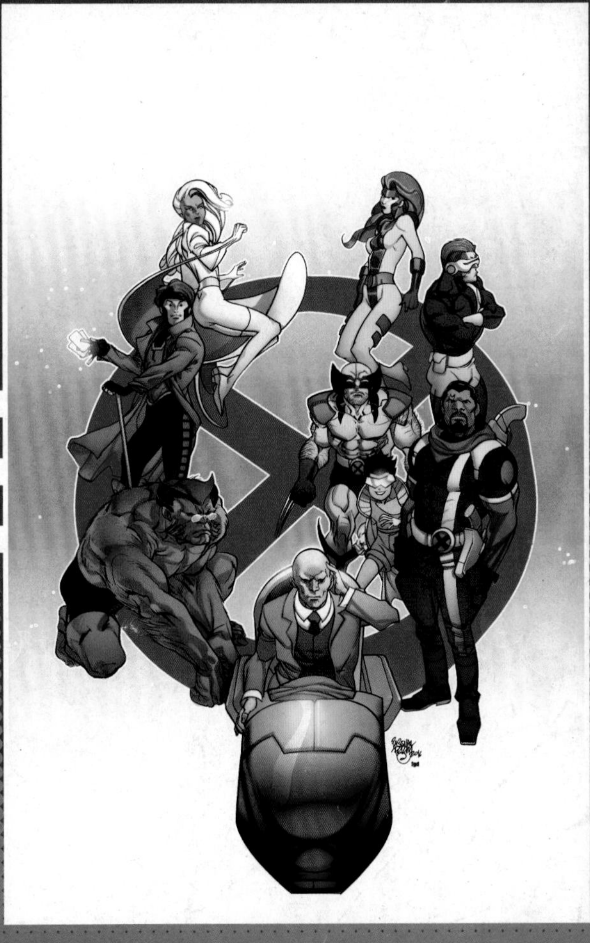

#1 VARIANT BY
PASQUAL FERRY & FRANK MARTIN

#2 VARIANT BY
JOYCE CHIN & CHRIS SOTOMAYOR

#3 VARIANT BY
PASCAL CAMPION